The Ben Hecht Show

For Ted Yates

THE Ben Hecht SHOW

*Impolitic Observations
from the Freest Thinker
of 1950s Television*

Adapted and Edited by
Bret Primack

WITH A FOREWORD BY
Mike Wallace

McFarland & Company, Inc., Publishers
Jefferson, North Carolina, and London

British Library Cataloguing-in-Publication data are available

Library of Congress Cataloguing-in-Publication Data

Hecht, Ben, 1893-1964.
  The Ben Hecht show / edited and adapted by Bret Primack.
     p. cm.
  Ben Hecht's "bedtime stories," which closed each television
program, several interviews, and his assorted comments transcribed
and edited from the Ben Hecht show, broadcast Sept. 1958-Jan. 1959,
along with annotations.
  Includes index.
  ISBN 0-89950-857-X (lib. bdg. : 50# alk. paper) ∞
  1. Ben Hecht show (Television program) 2. Hecht, Ben, 1893-1964.
I. Primack, Bret, 1949-   . II. Title.
PN1992.77.B447H4 1993
791.45′72 — dc20   92-56682
                                                             CIP

©1993 Anchovy Productions and ©1959 Mike Wallace. All rights reserved

Manufactured in the United States of America

McFarland & Company, Inc., Publishers
  Box 611, Jefferson, North Carolina 28640

Acknowledgments

The author wishes to thank the following individuals for their gracious assistance:

Stella Adler; Charles Bell of the University of Texas at Austin Film Collection; Yitshaq Ben-Ami; Walter Bishop, Jr.; Carolyn Davis of the George Arents Research Library, Syracuse University; Jose Ferrer; Diana Haskell and the staff of The Newberry Library; Mark Kaplan; Marty Khan; Hillel Kook; Jerry Johnson; Will MacAdams; Karen Mason of the Bentley Historical Library; The University of Michigan; Samuel Merlin; Lee Morgan; Paul O'Dwyer; Al Ramrus; Eric Rosenberg; Joseph Matthew Santi; Harry Louis Selden; Rex Stewart; Mary Wallace; Mike Wallace; Paul Zegler; and Sidney Zion.

Table of Contents

Acknowledgments   v

Foreword (by Mike Wallace)   xi

Introduction   1

Ben Hecht, Television Performer   5

Preamble: How to Survive These Frightening Times   19

A Reporter's Testimony
    A Valentine to Some Early Journalists   21
    How I Became a Newspaperman   22
    The Picture Chaser   23
    My First Newspaper Story   24
    The Wired Woman   25
    Roost in a Brothel   26
    Carnation Dan's Epitaph   27
    Hearst's Sex Life   28
    The Marathon Drinker   30
    The Pole Climber   30
    Further Thoughts on Newspapers   32

Birds of the Gallows
    Society and the Criminal   35
    Hand Me My Sword   36
    The Wedding Band   37
    A Mannequin Who Grew Hair   38
    One Cure for Juvenile Delinquency   39
    Leanin' Willie   40

Hangings	41
The Singing Murderer	42
Dr. Kirsh's Final Scream	44
Not at This Time	45
Free to Go	46
A Murderer from the Other World	47
On the Lam	48
The Perfect Murder	50
Weegee and Ben Hecht: *The Crime Beat*	51

Faces in the Crowd

The Sculptor's Father	59
A Silent Poet	60
The Artist's Enemies	61
Capote's Barking Raven	63
I Want to Go Home	63
The Deadly Chocolates	65
Mrs. Rodjeske's Haunted Hat	66
Concerning a Red Velvet Dress	67
Joe Feeny's Soul	68
Is There Life After Death?	69
Lincoln's Ghost	70
Sandberg's Lost Copy	72
Purple Dancing Shoes	74
Belle of the Ball	75
An Unsuccessful Execution	76
Kid Hogan's Sacrifice	77
The Search for Gold	78

Politicians Past and Present

My First Meeting with Teddy Roosevelt	81
Voting	82
Hinky Dink and Bathhouse John	83
A Great Land Runs Amok	85
Drew Pearson and Ben Hecht: *The Collapse of America*	87
The Devil's Song	92
Westbrook Pegler and Ben Hecht: *They Call It Justice*	93
Why the Troops Froze	98

Goose Steps in the Night
- The Last of Quinn Lusk — 101
- Who Really Won the War — 103
- Dusseldorf's Dictator — 104
- Rudy Hise's Demise — 105
- The Dictator of Art — 106
- Docility and Mass Murder — 107

Lotus Land Gold Miners
- My First Oscar — 111
- S.J. Perelman and Ben Hecht: *The Hollywood System* — 113
- Harry Cohn's Boat — 118
- The Soul of a Hollywood Producer — 120
- Screenwriters' Victories — 122
- The Blue Couch — 123
- A Goldwyn Conference — 125
- The Lederer Wars — 127
- Barrymore's Hamlet — 128
- A Forgotten Speech — 129
- Tryst at the Chicken Farm — 130
- Barrymore's Death Scene — 132
- The Ladies' Man — 132
- Chaplin's Vocabulary — 134
- A Christmas Gift — 135
- The Music Lesson — 136
- Yes Man Says No — 137
- Jessel and Ratoff Live! — 138
- Memories of C.B. DeMille — 140
- The Collapse of Hollywood — 141

The Writer's Craft
- Advice to Young Writers — 143
- What Influences a Writer — 144
- Writing for Hollywood — 145
- Budd Schulberg and Ben Hecht: *The Writer's Dilemma* — 147
- Art and Literature — 153
- Nietzsche in Plano — 155
- The Writer's Antagonists — 156
- Flavius Is a Dirty Dog — 158
- Let the Critics Live — 159

My Semitic Brothers
    The Broken Vase   161
    Jews for Sale   162
    Fifty Rabbis Can't Say No   163
    They Will Not Be Forgotten   165
    A Frenchman's Gallantry   166
    What the Allies Did   167
    The Irgun   169

From Where I Sit
    The State of Our Country   173
    Censorship   174
    Individualism   175
    Prostitution   177
    Audiences   178
    Television Commercials   179
    A Toast to Television   180

My Favorite Quotations   183

The Mail
    Viewer Letters   195
    The Lost Type   211

My Epitaph
    Mankind, Today and Tomorrow   213
    My Attitude Towards Life   214
    The Only Way to Apologize   215

Index   217

Foreword
(by Mike Wallace)

Ben Hecht was a man of words. They were his weapons and few men in his time wielded them with such carefree courage. Wherever words and wit mattered, Ben Hecht made his mark.

As a sixteen-year-old, he ran away from his home in Racine, Wisconsin, to make his way in the world, and make it he did. Tough and rebellious, Ben Hecht became one of the top crime reporters in America. He also wrote poetry, plays and novels, and as a Hollywood writer, he earned the equivalent of $100,000 per week. A flamboyant iconoclast, Hecht became a legendary figure for his attacks on American politics, American education and assorted sacred cows.

He ran from platitudes, abhorred conventional wisdom. Defiant and frequently alone, he strode through life with his banner flying and a plume in his hat. In print or in person, armed with a wicked grin and a ruthless wit, Ben was at his best when he wore the hat of social critic. He delighted in sticking pins in stuffed shirts and letting the air out of inflated egos.

I first interviewed Ben in 1958 on *The Mike Wallace Interview* for the ABC network, and he lived up to his billing as one of America's most caustic and entertaining critics. With a twinkle in his eye and an unlit cigar rolling around his mouth, Hecht unleashed a stream of pungent barbs calculated to either shock or amuse.

When I asked if he got any consolation from religion, he told me: "I regard religion as part of a rather odd mythomania which has persisted in the world, and anybody that gets consolation from it is much the same as scientists who might have gotten consolation from the delusion that the world was flat." Later in the broadcast, he opined that then–President Eisenhower was "as perhaps as inaudible and invisible an executive as this country has ever had."

Not surprisingly, Ben's remarks irked ABC's executives, who at that time tried to tailor their programming to be as inoffensive as possible. Critical reaction, however, was most favorable. A full ten years after the broadcast, television critic John Crosby wrote that the Hecht interview was "one of the most wickedly entertaining" he'd ever seen on television.

Following that interview, my producer Ted Yates and I agreed that Hecht's opinions and remarkable stories were amusing and provocative enough to be the basis for an interesting show. Conversant on any topic and an enthusiastic jouster to boot, Ben seemed a likely candidate for talk show host. Perhaps a regular dose of Ben Hecht, we thought, would awaken the viewing public from what he called "the optical opiate" that television has become.

And so we came to produce *The Ben Hecht Show*, which ran on WABC-TV in New York for only five months starting in September of 1958. I was on a fact-finding mission in the Soviet Union at the beginning of the show's run, but when I returned a few weeks later, Ben's sarcastic repartee already had the station management in an uproar. Television of that era, particularly local television, shied from controversy, and Ben's nightly disputations had quickly sent the television executives scurrying.

A series of incidents, including the forced cancellation of guests Norman Mailer, Alger Hiss, and a panel of Bowery bums, found Hecht and our Newsmaker Productions staff at loggerheads with the management. By today's standard, this type of talk show and guest list seems rather tame, but in late 1958, penetrating programs with frank discussions of religion, sex, and politics were practically nonexistent.

The conflict climaxed the night Ben interviewed Surrealist painter Salvador Dalí, who revealed his discovery of a new type of orgasm. Orgasms of whatever stripe were hardly grist for the WABC mill. So the next morning, *The Ben Hecht Show* was canceled. But in less than six months, the program had garnered a dedicated following that included discerning viewers and critics in the local and national media.

Ben's "Bedtime Stories," several interviews from the program, and his assorted comments are included in this volume, along with annotations to assist contemporary readers in better understanding Hecht, and the era. More than thirty years have passed since *The Ben Hecht Show*, but his tall tales and biting commentary remain entertaining and provocative. Take a look.

Introduction
(by Bret Primack)

Ben Hecht, 1893–1964, was a very prolific writer. For sixty years he produced a torrent of crafted prose that cut like a rapier through streams of newspaper articles, novels, plays, films and propaganda. From accolades that included three Academy Awards to the scorn of the British Empire for his work on behalf of the Jews, Ben Hecht capped his prolific career at the age of sixty-four with a television program, *The Ben Hecht Show*.

A talk show seemed the ideal forum for Hecht's flamboyant criticism and outspoken ideas, but the management of the local New York television station that broadcast his program found Hecht too outrageous for the rather narrow standards of the time. Ben Hecht was taken off their air after only twenty-two weeks, an early victim of television censorship.

All that remains of the broadcasts are audio transcriptions featuring Ben Hecht and his guests. The audio tapes, recorded by Ron Johnson, were sequestered in a closet for thirty years until the present author's research for a Ben Hecht play led to their discovery.

Every story and essay in this book was spoken by Ben Hecht on his television program. The material has been transcribed and edited to present the spoken word entertainingly. Hecht recycled his material throughout his life, and some of the stories have appeared in previous Hecht books (only his autobiography, *Child of the Century*, remains in print).

Comparisons of the same basic story reveal Hecht's fondness for embellishment, of both fact and fiction. Hecht's affection for realism and iconoclasm, his love of radiant phrases and word combinations that arrest the eye and ear, and his examination of the bizarre and sometimes amusing lives of such people as criminals and prostitutes as well as luminaries from show business and politics, reveal the work of a master craftsman.

Edited transcripts of four interviews from *The Ben Hecht Show* have also been included as part of this collection: famed photographer Weegee, muckraking journalist Drew Pearson, and fellow scribes S.J. Perelman and Budd Schulberg. These gentlemen generated the most spirited dialogue from Hecht. The topics they discussed—criminals, politics, writing and Hollywood—were particularly close to his heart.

There was no shortage of viewer mail during the twenty-two weeks the program was broadcast, but it was the Weegee and Drew Pearson interviews that elicited the strongest rejoinders. Every Wednesday night, Hecht took particular delight in answering his mail. A sampling of these letters and Ben's fiery rebuttals have also been included. Most of the correspondence the station received was favorable. After he spent one entire program discussing his fifty favorite books, the station received nearly ten thousand requests for copies of the list.

Hecht closed each program with a "Bedtime Story." These picturesque tales recounted some of his favorite episodes and characters. Hecht developed his storytelling acumen as a reporter in pre-World War I Chicago, which he labeled the "Athens of the New World."

Without radio or the movies for diversion, Ben and his journalistic compatriots were compelled to entertain themselves with the fine art of conversation. Within a few years of his arrival in the Windy City, Ben Hecht gained a reputation as one of the most spellbinding storytellers in town.

Hecht became an ace reporter while still in his teens. His Chicago, 1910–25, was a throbbing metropolis replete with colorful criminals, crooked politicians and obliging prostitutes; "a hooligan center of prose, poetry and intellectual freebooting." And, as Hecht related, it was "the greatest newspaper town in the land." After fifteen years of Chicago gun battles, hangings, and city hall skulduggeries, and a stint in post–World War I Europe, Hecht was fired from *The Chicago Daily News* because of a 1923 obscenity conviction. He used the word "pissing" in the introduction to a book and was indicted for the transport of lewd, obscene and lascivious literature through the U.S. mails (Hecht was defended by Clarence Darrow, with his hero H.L. Mencken serving as his character witness). Undaunted, he began publishing his own newspaper, *The Chicago Literary Times*, and kept writing short stories and novels.

As a distinguished reporter, prolific short story writer and novelist, Ben Hecht was a prime mover in Chicago's literary renaissance, which included associates Carl Sandberg, Sherwood Anderson and Maxwell Bodenheim. A significant fixture on the Chicago scene, his departure inspired a farewell of sorts on the front page of a rival newspaper, the *Herald Examiner*. Its drama critic, Ashton Stevens, called on Chicago to fly its flags at half-mast because Ben Hecht was leaving town.

While both were on the trail of culprits and con men, Ben Hecht first encountered fellow reporter Charles MacArthur. From their initial collaboration, a real murderer's last words, they graduated to screenplays, and the stage classic *The Front Page*, based on their newspaper exploits.

Ben Hecht's first film, *Underworld*, invented the crime genre and was an immediate hit. During the 1930s Hecht quickly became the highest paid screenwriter in the movie business, taking home as much as $100,000 a week. He contributed to some seventy screenplays, sometimes writing solo but preferring to work with collaborators MacArthur, Charles Lederer and Gene Fowler. Hecht and MacArthur were also among the first writers to produce and direct their own films. They created six motion pictures at a studio in Astoria in the mid-thirties, including *The Scoundrel* and *Crime Without Passion*. Hecht wrote and directed several independently produced films after the studio's demise: *Actors and Sin, Angels Over Broadway* and *Specter of the Rose*.

Although it offered princely paydays, Ben Hecht found Hollywood an intellectual wasteland. Commanding large sums of money for his prized scenarios, he would labor only until he squirreled away enough cash to last the year, then retire to his oceanfront house in Oceanside, California; a home overlooking the Hudson in Nyack, New York; or his apartment in Manhattan. But if Hecht eschewed Hollywood, he found the movie colony ripe with congeniality, and its characters juicy provender for his growing repertoire of legendary tales.

In the early forties Hecht returned to newspapers with a column for the New York afternoon daily *PM*. His concern with the growing threat to Jews in Europe caught the attention of a small group of extraordinarily dedicated men whose mission was the rescue of their brethren. Hecht immediately enlisted in the campaign to sway American public opinion and policy against the continuing massacre. Tragically, his dramatic newspaper advertisements and a pageant, *We Shall Never Die*, saved few Jews and incurred the wrath of the Jewish establishment, President Roosevelt, the FBI and the IRS.

After World War II, Hecht continued fighting for Jews. He worked with the Irgun in their attempts to wrestle Palestine from the British to establish a Jewish nation. Hecht's play *A Flag Is Born* (with a cast that included Marlon Brando and Sidney Lumet) raised nearly one million dollars and financed a boat, the S.S. Ben Hecht, which transported refugees to Palestine. One of his sensational newspaper advertisements, "Letter to the Terrorists of Palestine," so enraged the keepers of the crown that his films were banned throughout the British Empire.

The British blacklist may have eroded his movie career but Hecht, true to form, kept writing, most notably a dazzling autobiography published in 1954, *Child of the Century*. In the final decade of Hecht's life, his most successful creations were based on recollections of Chicago and Hollywood: *Gaily, Gaily*, featured charming early Chicago stories; *Charlie*, written for Charles MacArthur; and a play, *Winkelberg*, based on the life of poet Maxwell Bodenheim. Hecht's movie work was limited to script doctoring and collaborations for old friends, or an occasional script he tried to peddle independently.

In 1958, Hecht appeared as a guest on the ABC television program *The Mike Wallace Interview*. Never one to shy from controversy, Hecht intrigued Wallace and his producer, Ted Yates, with his outspoken views on selling out, religion, and politics. Seven months later, *The Ben Hecht Show* made its debut on WABC-TV in New York, produced by Wallace and Yates. Besides friends Billy Rose, Otto Preminger, S.J. Perelman and Jimmy Durante and cultural icons Salvador Dalí, Jack Kerouac and Drew Pearson, Hecht's guests included an executioner, revolutionists, a photographer who specialized in the corpses of mobsters, a stripper, a medium and a former heavyweight boxing champion. This eclectic brew was far removed from the rather pristine bill of fare television served at the time.

Ben Hecht, Television Performer
(by Bret Primack)

When Ben Hecht was first invited to appear on *The Mike Wallace Interview* in 1957, he demanded ten thousand dollars. Producer Ted Yates believed the outspoken Hecht would be a striking subject, as did the show's ace writer Al Ramrus, but guests were not paid for their services and so Hecht was politely rebuffed. At the time, several guests turned down the invitation to go one-on-one with Wallace because of his Torquemada-like reputation. For Hecht it was strictly a matter of money. He savored a verbal joust in any setting but had long become accustomed to receiving substantial compensation for his work. Although no longer the highest paid screenwriter in Hollywood, Hecht still commanded princely sums for his occasional cinematic contributions. With nothing to promote and no burning desire to air his notions before a national audience, Ben Hecht wasn't about to cut his price for a television interview.

A year later Hecht's play *Winkelberg*, a collection of theatricalized anecdotes on the life of friend and poet Maxwell Bodenheim, was marooned in a snowstorm Off Broadway. With winter's wrath and a taxi strike conspiring to keep theatergoers at home, Hecht's agent of the moment, Jacques Chambrun, contacted Newsmaker Productions to offer Hecht as a guest, gratis. The Wallace team, always in search of suitable quarry, readily accepted Hecht's offer. After network approval of Hecht, a pre-interview was arranged. The pre-interview was an important tool for Mike Wallace. To capitalize on his skills as an interviewer and his theatrical presence, the show utilized considerable research to arm him with provocative details.

Al Ramrus was dispatched to meet with Hecht. A Hecht devotee,

Ramrus was a lean, curly-haired twenty-seven-year-old who relished Hecht's screenplays and, as a young reporter, had been inspired by reading Hecht's autobiography, *Child of the Century*. Working with Wallace, Ramrus quickly learned that, one-on-one, celebrities rarely lived up to their image. Hecht, however, did not disappoint. Physically, he was an imposing man, chubby but nonetheless dashing in a blue suit, slanted hat and bowtie. Just about to turn sixty-five, Hecht was rather vain about his body, dying his hair and occasionally working with a trainer in the gymnasium of his Nyack home. "He was as interesting and eloquent as his autobiography," Ramrus remembered, more than thirty years after the initial meeting. "Ben was the Wyatt Earp of conversation. He could blow someone away with a phrase."

Hecht's February 15, 1958, appearance on *The Mike Wallace Interview* disturbed ABC management, who found his comments on religion somewhat distressing. Already plagued by lawsuits and network meddling, by then the program had an attorney present to warn Wallace if anyone ran amok. Their problems had begun when Hecht's gangster friend Mickey Cohen opened a Pandora's box of libel and innuendo by calling the Los Angeles chief of police "a sadistic degenerate" on Wallace's third network broadcast.

Wallace's interview with architect Frank Lloyd Wright also upset the network chieftains. Wright was building a dream house for Marilyn Monroe and Wallace asked him, "What do you think of Marilyn Monroe as architecture?" That nettled the network brass, who were concerned that viewers might interpret the question as a reference to Miss Monroe's vital statistics. Such were the concerns of the news division of the ABC television network in the late 1950s.

Wallace's chief antagonist at the network was the man who oversaw the news operation, John Charles Daly. In addition to his management duties, Daly served as anchorman for the ABC evening news broadcast, and once a week as moderator for the popular CBS entertainment show *What's My Line?* (Daly's acting portfolio included a brief run playing Walter Burns, the newspaper editor, on a television version of *The Front Page* in 1949.) From the start, Daly was wary of Wallace. The Cohen incident only served to fuel his contempt for Wallace, whose patented brand of direct and unequivocal questioning has continued on *60 Minutes*. Fearing a threat to his stronghold at ABC news, Daly restricted Wallace's activities to the interview program.

As he flew to Hollywood for the Hecht interview, Wallace reread *Child of the Century*. Equipped with the facts that Ramrus had gathered, and his own impressions of Hecht's work, Mike Wallace grilled Ben Hecht about squandering his talent, about selling-out. The curmudgeon from Chicago was prepared. He told Wallace, "Everybody who works sells out. Usually they sell out more than their minds—they sell out their souls, their character, their point of view.... They usually throw in the sponge when they're twenty-two or twenty-three and they quit, they become echoes, they echo each other—they're terrified of making any odd remark, even at the dinner table. The American has become in my time one of the most ironed out human beings I've ever seen. Sort of an imitation Russian today."

Hecht was fearless, an outspoken iconoclast, and he provided one of Wallace's more memorable tête-à-têtes. A decade later the Hecht interview was remembered by television critic John Crosby, who wrote that the Wallace-Hecht colloquy was one of the most wickedly entertaining things he'd ever seen. Hecht also struck a responsive chord with the production staff.

Producer Ted Yates, a sardonically witty fellow, was eager to work on other projects besides the Interview. It was Yates who had conceived the Wallace-as-Inquisitor format that worked so successfully on *Night Beat*, a late night local New York interview show. The sparks Wallace and his guests generated quickly drew a sizable audience, and before long ABC wanted Wallace for prime time. Concerned about compromise, Wallace and Yates were repeatedly assured of free rein by network management and promised other opportunities at the American Broadcasting Company, then a bargain basement operation that usually ran a distant third in the ratings. If Wallace produced controversy, perhaps the network could benefit from the publicity.

But by the time of the Hecht interview, after the Wallace show had aired for ten months, it had become apparent that the network had no further plans to utilize Wallace's talent and charisma. His production team, however, decided to pitch the idea of a Ben Hecht program to the executives at the local New York network-owned outlet, WABC-TV. And because it was a local show, Wallace and Yates would not have to contend with John Daly. If the program should happen to capture viewers, perhaps a network slot would be possible.

Hecht was enthusiastic about the opportunity. In his mid-sixties, he was writing sporadically at best. Thanks to the British boycott on his films, the result of his propaganda on behalf of the Irgun in the 1940s, Ben Hecht's Hollywood assignments were mostly from friends. With pal Charles Lederer, he rewrote portions of Marlon Brando's version of *Mutiny on the Bounty*. For Otto Preminger, he doctored *Man with the Golden Arm* and *Walk on the Wild Side*, both based on novels by fellow Chicagoan Nelson Algren. For longtime compatriot David Selznick he co-wrote, with John Huston, the screenplay for *A Farewell to Arms*. Hecht had also continued writing books in his later life. The year 1957 saw the publication of *Charlie: The Improbable Life and Times of Charles MacArthur*, a moving biography of his friend and sometime collaborator. In January of 1958, a month before the Wallace interview, Hecht received an advance for a biography of Mickey Cohen entitled, *The Soul of a Gunman*. By June, Hecht and Cohen had traveled to Mexico to work in peace. Days before *The Ben Hecht Show* first aired, Hecht learned that Cohen had given a lengthy interview to the *Saturday Review*, ending Hecht's exclusive. Hecht abandoned the project but, not surprisingly, the Cohen friendship endured.

So when offered a thousand dollars a week to host a nightly television talk show, Hecht immediately accepted. He had earned and squandered millions, bankrolling homes in Oceanside, California, and Nyack, New York, in addition to a Manhattan apartment. There was also a domestic staff as well as a precocious teenage daughter to maintain. *The Ben Hecht Show* was his first steady work in years. Although he had earned as much as $100,000 a week during his Hollywood salad days, Hecht's price and desirability were irreparably tarnished by the British boycott.

There was some initial concern from station management that Hecht would offend some viewers and thereby limit his audience, but miraculously the program received approval for a thirteen-week run. For the most part, television talk shows in the late fifties were pretty bland affairs. Aside from Mike Wallace, who was the only interviewer asking pointed, outrageous questions, television interview or talk programs were largely show-biz patter. The Hecht program promised to continue the course set by Wallace—incisive, thought-provoking dialogues. Largely advertiser controlled, television had an overriding programming philosophy: the ideal program was one that pleased everyone and was as inoffensive as possible. Nonetheless, WABC-TV decided to take a chance on Ben Hecht.

The Ben Hecht Show made its debut at 10:50 PM September 15, 1958, after the local news. The program ran for twenty-five minutes. It was followed by *Shock Theater*, a series of horror films hosted by a gentleman named Zacherle who dressed as a ghoul. Competition for the Hecht program included the later portions of *Masquerade Party, Racket Squad, Suspicion* and *Studio One*, as well as news and movies. After his theme music, "Mack the Knife," Ben was introduced by his assistant, an attractive blonde he christened "Missy." In the opening segment, Missy would solicit Ben's opinion on the evening's topic or on current events. After a commercial break, Ben would interview his guest. The interviews were more like discussions than the probing exchanges of producer Wallace. He may have been a top reporter in Chicago in his heyday, but Hecht seemed awkward at times during his television interviews. Frequently working with questions prepared by Yates and Ramrus, he rarely followed up his guests' responses with penetrating questions. The program mainly became a springboard for Hecht's ideas, with his guests usually serving as a backboard for his comments. Following another commercial break, Hecht would close the program with a Bedtime Story. These oft repeated tales, taken from his remarkable career as a journalist, playwright, screenwriter and propagandist, served as a sort of icing on the cake for the evening's festivities. On Wednesdays, he appeared without a guest and spent the program answering his mail.

Lynn Merrill, a delicate woman in her late thirties, was Missy, Ben's sidekick. When the program was conceived, Ted Yates felt that an attractive woman would make a suitable foil for Hecht and the chemistry worked from the start, although much of Hecht's outrageousness seemed to sail right over Ms. Merrill's head. She had difficulty keeping up and, given the program's extemporaneous format, had to use the written questions that were prepared for her. But on the air, she came across quite well, although the production staff sometimes doubted she understood the full import of what was being said.

The Ben Hecht Show had a difficult time attracting sponsors. Ramrus and Yates could never understand why Schiffly, an embroidery and lace company, signed on as a sponsor. Their commercials were delivered by the late Jacqueline Susann. Ms. Susann came to the studio for her live pitch and the production staff found her presence rather comical. She tried especially hard to project the image of an

Ava Gardner–like femme fatale. Who could have ever imagined that the husky-breathing vamp would go on to become one of the best selling novelists in the Western world? But since Schiffly helped pay the freight, all involved kept their comments to themselves. California Sherry also ran some advertisements on the program and they seemed a more likely sponsor, though it was Jack Daniels that Hecht drank regularly on the air.

Press reaction to the show was largely positive. *The Nation*: "Stormy Ben Hecht makes waves nightly on Channel 7 with his commentary and interviews." *TV Guide*: "A daring, new show; offering a fearless and probing look at people and issues." *Time*: "Hecht has always been a fast man with the spoken word. He is so fast, in fact, that ever since he took over a TV week-night interview show on Manhattan's WABC-TV this fall, his guests have been hopelessly outclassed in the fight for mike time. Mixing it up with experts in varied fields ranging from erotica to execution by hanging, Hecht has been calculatedly outrageous and often funny."

Hecht's champion in the New York press was John Crosby, who told his readers, "Unexpected is the word for the conversation you encounter on the Hecht show and much of it comes from Mr. Hecht.... While Hecht is foursquare in favor of heterosexuality, it is probably the only orthodoxy you'll hear espoused on that show. At various times, he has expressed his distaste or downright loathing for—let's see now—general education, Roosevelt, Eisenhower, Churchill, Stalin, politicians, lawyers, judges, Louella Parsons, and, oh, lots of other things. When he isn't making with the iconoclasm bit, his guests are." Crosby reported that when Hecht was asked if he was an atheist, "Hecht's reply was 'I'm a Jew. How can you be atheist if you're a Jew?' said Hecht and plunged into his nightly Bedtime Story, a pleasant tale about the massacre of 45,000 Jews in the Warsaw ghetto by the Germans. But then, if you don't like strong meat, you shouldn't be listening to this Jewish leprechaun in the first place."

Not everyone in the fourth estate was a Hecht sympathizer. *Variety* led the naysayers: "Considering Hecht's poor delivery and negative, ill-tempered approach and the clumsy planning, it's easy to see why the series has such a small audience."

As the format of the Hecht show coalesced, station management became increasingly anxious. What kind of monster had they let loose? Here was an opinionated old man talking about anything he pleased, including religion, politics and orgasms. An aging Jew who was in their minds a social subversive, a fearless rebel who might say or do anything on their air. Suddenly, as with the Wallace interview program, every potential guest for the Hecht show needed station approval.

Hecht's coworkers worshipped their male Scheherazade. Almost every day, the staff of Newsmaker Productions, including Yates, Ramrus, their assistant Rita Quinn and attorney Jerry Johnson, gathered on the floor of the office to listen to Hecht's stories. Ramrus fondly recalled, "You could throw any subject at Ben Hecht, be it prostitution or capital punishment, and he could spin true or semi-true stories on that subject for as long as he wanted. That's why Ted and I were having such a good time on the show." Hecht had a hypnotic, rhythmic way of telling a story, enhanced by his phenomenal memory for aphorisms and *bon mots*.

The Ben Hecht Show quickly garnered a small but dedicated group of viewers. Within a week many letters began to arrive each day, and most were positive. It was the angry letters, however, that served to heighten the management's paranoia. When political dirt digger Drew Pearson guested, Hecht and Pearson ruffled quite a few feathers with their comments on President Eisenhower. A raft of angry phone calls occurred following the appearance of photographer Weegee, who detailed his passion for photographing dead mobsters. *The New York Post* reported that Weegee and Hecht's lurid recollections of criminals inspired "some fifty viewers to call the ABC switchboard to protest the relish of it." Several callers demanded Hecht's ouster.

As the weeks progressed, the management continued to oversee the show's production, approving guests and carefully monitoring Hecht's comments. The first real firestorm erupted with the booking of Alger Hiss. Mr. Hiss had become Richard Nixon's scapegoat when the young congressman from California charged that the government was infested with Communist agents. After three trials, Hiss was convicted of perjury although he repeatedly declared his innocence. On the air, Hiss and Hecht were slated to discuss his authorship of the U.N. charter. Station management initially approved the Hiss booking, and it was announced to the press. Then Hiss was abruptly canceled, ostensibly because he was an ex-convict and anyone who had served time was not allowed on WABC-TV. A surprised Ted Yates told the press, "The station has the final say on who goes on and who doesn't."

Al Hollander, program director of WABC-TV, claimed Hiss was never actually booked. He told a reporter, "I wouldn't want to get involved in a statement of policy on it . . . Ted is guilty of revealing information before it's in final form. Hiss was never a confirmed guest. It isn't a question of a guy being canceled because he wasn't booked — that is, not formally booked."

While co-producer Mike Wallace was off to the Soviet Union for a state-sponsored visit to scrutinize Russian television, relations between WABC-TV and the Newsmaker Productions team further deteriorated in early November when Hecht decided to interview a group of Bowery bums. Instead of the usual syrupy Norman Rockwell–type portrait, Hecht sought to present a unique outlook on American life for the upcoming holiday season. Ramrus and Yates drove down to the Bowery early one evening and rounded up eight bums, offering them twenty-five dollars apiece to appear on television. Then Hecht, Yates and Ramrus pre-interviewed the derelicts for several hours, outlining television's language restrictions. Everyone involved felt they were ready to offer an unusual and perhaps moving program. Then, only minutes before the program was scheduled to go on the air, the station pulled the plug. *The Ben Hecht Show* did not appear on television that night. At 10:50 *Shock Theater* was broadcast in its place.

Writer Al Ramrus was so incensed by the sudden decision that he considered taking a poke at program director Hollander, but when Ted Yates, an ex-cowboy and ex–Marine, remained a gentlemen, he figured a nice Jewish boy from the Bronx should follow his example. According to press reports, the station's supposed reason for canceling the broadcast was the fear that someone might, despite the precautions that had been taken, utter a "hell" or "damn," or something even more shocking. In a series of interviews the next day, Mr. Hollander confirmed these suspicions, charging that station manager Bob Stone suspected the bums were loaded with Hecht's booze, or their own.

Hecht disputed this. "We were saving the booze until after the show. When they found out that they couldn't go on, the bums took their defeat with a minimum of pain. We gave them their booze and they left for the Bowery. I've never felt so sorry for a cast of performers in my life."

Ted Yates felt it was all in the interest of sociology:

> We had eight unbelievably eloquent, touching, fascinating, conscience-striking stories. We went down to the Bowery to get these men. We screened them carefully and I had clearance for the show from the program manager, Al Hollander. I explained to him that the show, which we were going to call "An Obit to a Nobody," was to describe the plight of these sad people who are alone in the world with no beginning and no end. Then, ten minutes before we were to go on the air, I got a call from Hollander saying we'd been preempted. Nobody bothered to talk with them the way we did or to even say "boo." The best I've been told is that somebody got the idea that these people could not be trusted.

A guard at the station reportedly phoned Stone a few minutes before air time to report the bums were intoxicated and out of control. He was in the minority, however. The program's director, Roger Shope, and sponsor spokeswoman Jackie Susann, who arrived at the station nearly ninety minutes before air time, thought the characters in question were model gentlemen. On his next broadcast, an interview with Mike Todd, Jr., Hecht told his viewers about the sudden cancellation. "The show that we were going to do involved the participation of eight Bowery bums, and when the officials got a look at these eight Bowery bums, they saw eight very wild and desperate fellows and concluded they were terribly drunk and out of control. They noticed correctly they were wild and desperate looking, but it was because they were sober. There's nothing as desperate looking as a sober bum. This is a fact not generally known. And being good showmen, they put on a movie in my place called *Son of Dracula*, hoping that the change wouldn't be too noticed."

Hecht was obviously upset by the reaction. After a lifetime of dealing with the insipid idiosyncrasies of Hollywood studio moguls who repeatedly manhandled his scripts, this was his first brush with the television "bosses." In a newspaper article, Hecht announced, "This is the first time they've stepped in and annoyed me. The station has been nice and invisible up to now. I thought I'd been hearing lies about television, but I guess it's true what they say. I felt like I was back in preschool again."

The discord between the Hecht show and the ABC bosses escalated with the booking of writer Norman Mailer. Mailer and Hecht were scheduled to discuss Mailer's essay "The White Negro," which dealt with the then semicontroversial Beat Generation and contained a frank discussion of interracial sex. Again the station did an about-face. Al Hollander told Yates to de-book Mailer, citing a decision to try to broaden Hecht's sphere of guests beyond the literary and theatrical worlds. The press reported that the station felt Hecht's ratings were low because the program catered to a "limited intellectual group." Guests were invariably "specialists in fields of narrow interest" and because the time had arrived for a decision on Hecht's video future, the station did not want to waste even one episode when air time could be otherwise devoted to raising audience levels.

Yates was livid. In a memo that was written in an attempt to change Hollander's mind, Yates wrote:

> Mailer's essay cannot, and has not been, construed as anything but the most stirring tribute to the Negro, and one of the most penetrating analyses of men ranging from Kerouac to Walt Whitman.... Besides, the NAACP (if it's group acceptance that is needed to assure you that this is a well-received article), praised Mailer's work highly, as did Dr. Ralph Bunche. Incidentally, Mailer is considered one of America's most promising and outstanding literary figures. Besides, he can be a provocative speaker, talker and expresser of ideas, which from the chalk talks we had once, was the kind of man that you wanted for the program.
>
> The thing, Al, that baffles me most at this point is the reason for revoking your approval for Mailer as a guest. The network even approved Mailer for Mike's show.

Hollander refused to budge. He suggested that Yates write another memo, this time to the station manager.

Yates' anger was further fueled when the Fund for the Republic, a Ford Foundation–funded think-tank, called Newsmaker Productions attorney Jerry Johnson to reveal that *The Ben Hecht Show* was under consideration for the prestigious Robert E. Sherwood award. Yates wrote a second memo to station manager Robert Stone. He had tried unsuccessfully for several days to reach Stone, persisting because he wanted to try and reverse the Mailer de-booking.

> It is, of course, disastrous and embarrassing to call the Sherwood Committee and report that Norman Mailer has been arbitrarily rejected by the station.

Ben Hecht, Television Performer 15

Bob, one thing I am sure of is that you are fair-minded, completely reasonable, and quick to resolve problems without red tape or double talk.

I implore you to consider reinstating Norman Mailer, or at least to discuss the matter with me briefly on the telephone.

The exhaustive campaign Yates waged did not persuade the management. Mailer remained de-booked, replaced by the considerably less threatening Henry Morgan.

Later that month, another war of words was waged over Hecht's remarks concerning Germans. Hecht's dislike of Germans was no secret; he discussed his feelings on the show repeatedly, most notably in response to letter-writers. The German language press in New York condemned Hecht in its editorials, calling for his removal from the airwaves. Hecht continued his attacks until the program's sole sponsor, Schiffly, demanded that he read an on-air statement on behalf of the company and their policy against discrimination. A prepared statement was read, in which Hecht tip-toed around an apology and announced that he would continue to "hate these garbage makers of Europe as long as I live."

The appearance of Archbishop Makarios of Cyprus on *The Ben Hecht Show* also caused a stir. Makarios was battling the British in Cyprus the same way Hecht and his Irgun comrades had done in Palestine, and although the cleric shied from television interviews, he was anxious to appear with Hecht. Their anti–British comments drew publicity because Makarios was in the headlines at the time, perceived as a Yasir Arafat of sorts.

A few weeks after the interview, *Variety* reported that a new attempt to ban the films of Ben Hecht had failed. The attempt had been made at the general council of the Cinematographers Exhibitors Association in England, and it was flatly turned down. The Notts and Derby branch of the CEA had complained that a statement attributed to Hecht in a London newspaper was "anti–British."

The final nail in the coffin was driven on January 30, 1959, in what proved to be Hecht's last broadcast. Hecht's guest was Salvador Dalí and it was their discussion of a unique form of sex that so offended the management at WABC-TV that they felt they had no other choice than to remove the Hecht show from the airwaves.

Hecht and Dalí began by discussing art, but a worldly figure like

Dalí easily made the transition to other subjects. Dalí proudly revealed to Hecht that he had discovered a unique new form of love-making (he called it Cladelism) and had found that lovers could achieve orgasm without even touching each other. Hecht seemed rather disappointed at the lack of bodily contact, but hardly shocked by Dalí's revelation. He continued the interview, unaware that it would be his last.

When word of the cancellation came down, Yates, Wallace and Ramrus were hardly surprised. After almost five years of conflict, they were well aware that most television executives ran from controversy. They were, however, elated to have spent a few satisfying months producing a program that gave them as much joy as *The Ben Hecht Show*.

Hecht was unfazed by the program's demise. He told the *Journal American* that he was "about to resume the life of a normal human being. The station felt our sponsors just didn't think the show was pulling enough viewers." The newspaper also revealed that Hecht had received fifty to two hundred letters daily and that the mail was "eighty to eighty-five percent favorable, and more mail than I ever received in my life." About being bounced, Hecht said he "had a feeling more or less it'd be soon," so he wasn't very bothered. In fact, he was more worried about his staff's being resituated than about his own immediate need for regular work.

"I do not like being considered a hatchet man," Hecht proclaimed. "When I come back to TV, it will not be an interview show but something more amusing. It will unveil more of my gentle side." Commenting on what he had tried to accomplish with the program, Hecht said, "As George Bernard Shaw said, audiences are not to be pandered to, but experimented with."

Ted Yates' friendship with Hecht continued to blossom following *The Ben Hecht Show*'s demise. Following the ABC episode, Wallace and Yates did an interview program for Channel 13 in New York, on which Hecht appeared as a guest. When Wallace left Channel 13, Yates and his family moved to Hecht's Oceanside, California, home to collaborate on a number of projects that never came to fruition. Yates' spirit had significantly animated Hecht's television venture and in return, working with a man only half his age, Hecht found in Yates a reincarnation of his beloved Charles MacArthur. "Ben Hecht and I were hired by Selznick to write the life of Mary Magdalene," Yates told an interviewer in 1963. "But we had a problem. Neither of us could understand why she reformed." After his Hecht fling, Yates returned to television news and quickly earned a reputation as one of television's brightest news producers and correspondents. The *New York Times* reported that "his programs remain equally distinct from each other. If removed from television, they could pass the test of survival as short subjects in movie theaters." Ted Yates was killed in 1967 while serving as an NBC correspondent in the early hours of the Six Day War in East Jerusalem. He was thirty-six.

Hecht kept on writing: *The Sensualists*, a novel that was widely panned by the critics; *Gaily, Gaily*, a charming collection of stories from his Chicago days; and *Letters from Bohemia*, a posthumous volume of Hecht correspondence from Gene Fowler, Charles MacArthur, Maxwell Bodenheim, Sherwood Anderson, H.L. Mencken, George Grosz and George Antheil.

Two years after the cancellation of his program, Hecht's final creative tempest was the publication of *Perfidy*, a polemic on the ruling clique of Israel. Focusing on the trial of an accused Nazi collaborator, Hecht contended that the men who populated Ben-Gurion's government essentially did nothing to stop the Holocaust. A firestorm quickly developed and the book was suppressed, both in the United States and abroad. Ben-Gurion was so angry that he denied Hecht permission to be buried in holy Israeli ground. Hecht died in 1964.

Preamble: How to Survive These Frightening Times

September 15, 1958: Ben Hecht's premier broadcast began with a statement of his intentions.

All the big and little thinkers are moaning low. The word optimism has almost gone out of our language. They say we are the fearful fifties waiting for the sinister sixties. There's hardly a man, woman or child able to turn a television dial who isn't convinced that our planet will wind up shortly as a lifeless cinder spinning emptily in space.

Most of the thinking going on today is trying to figure out who is to blame for our impending extinction as a species. The way it looks now the last two humans left on Earth, presumably an American and a Russian, will point a righteous finger at each other and with a triumphant cry of you did it, drop dead. End of world. Invective and despair have taken over an era that waits for this distinction.

I can think of no cure for this mood of panic. The best I can do as one man is not to add to it. Voltaire's hero young Candide cried out after each disaster that smote him, "It's the best of all possible worlds." Voltaire meant this cry to sound bitter, and ironic. It never has to me. I've found the grin of life, however ironic, more important and persuasive than all its defeats.

The inanities of our politicians, the poppycock produced by our fear of Communism and our fear of ourselves, in fact the whole climate of invective and despair which covers us with its smog, is no more than that. An unsunny day. An individualist doesn't have to strike his colors in bad weather. That in a fashion is my theme. I'll try to stick to it and keep Candide's slogan sounding: it's the best of all possible worlds.

A Reporter's Testimony

A Valentine to
Some Early Journalists

September 23, 1958: Lou Carroll, an editor at The Daily News *was Ben's guest. Hecht used the occasion to reply to those skeptics who questioned the veracity of his journalistic recollections.*

Among the foolish things I sometimes hear said today is that together with Charlie MacArthur and *The Front Page*, I helped to invent a type of newspaper man who never existed. This truly sad as well as foolish disbelief shows how square the world has grown.

We all existed once as MacArthur and I put it down, the Chicago newspapermen a little before and after the twenties. We were a tribe of assorted drunkards, poets, burglars, philosophers and boastful ragamuffins. Supermen with soiled collars and holes in our pants, stony broke and sneering at our betters in limousines and unmortgaged houses. Cynical of all things on earth including the tyrannical journal that underpaid and overworked us and for which, after a round of cursing, we were ready to die. We were unable to imagine any other vocation as worthy of manhood.

We despised the advertising department for using up the paper's valuable space and cutting down on our Dostoyevsky reports of killings and hangings. We had contempt for a growing group of highfalutin fellows who called themselves foreign correspondents and who also used up valuable space in the paper with gabble about foreign affairs. We looked down upon our own Washington correspondents as semi-broken-down newsmen who had been retired from the hotter chores of local reporting to spew double talk masquerading as political writing.

When we were done with stealing photographs, climbing into mansions through bathroom windows, impersonating bill collectors and gas inspectors in our quest for statements from abandoned wives or dentist-slaying paramours; when we had shaken the ashes of lumberyard and stockyard fires out of our hair, earned our bottle of rye from our favorite barrister by informing the public that his final pleas had reduced the jury to tears; when the fourteen hour workday was done, we looked for play.

We assembled in a half dozen saloons to brag and cadge drinks and fight with each other. We came to blows over topics that ran from *Vers Libre* and car debts to women's duplicity and whose city editor was the bigger dunce. We slept little and spent nights caroming through brothels and sitting around in dives denouncing the mayor, the chief of police, women, literature, politics and morality. We were the least angry of men on earth but we found endless glee in destroying the world.

We devoured books as if they were popcorn. There was hardly a panhandler or fire chaser among us who didn't know Proust, Gide, Pushkin, Tolstoy, Nietzsche and all the rest of the great scribblers in good standing.

On the whole we were a somewhat pathetic crew of paupers and ignoramuses, but with an arrogant wind in our sails. We were red eyed with lack of sleep, but in the first ten years of penal servitude under the city desk, there wasn't one of us who would have refused an authentic pass to heaven. That's what we were like. And I have an idea that it wasn't only newspapermen, that all the young of the world were much the same until the idealists and the cause leaders took it over and fixed it up fine as it is today. When even newspapermen often doubt we existed.

How I Became a Newspaperman

December 30, 1958: As the year was drawing to a close, Hecht devoted a broadcast to his own life. Ben Hecht was born in New York City on February 28, 1893. By the age of ten, his family had relocated to Racine, Wisconsin, via Chicago. An early violin prodigy, Ben also excelled as an acrobat and sailor. Although he fancied himself a poet, he had little interest in academic pursuits.

I found it terribly difficult to graduate from high school. Miss Wheeler, my French teacher, to whom I was devoted, faked a diploma so my mother wouldn't be too disheartened by my failures. I went to Madison, Wisconsin, and enrolled in the university where I pledged to the Delta Tau Delta fraternity. At lunch the first day of school, I offended the fraternity members by some derogatory remark about the school. Asked to apologize, I left the university and came to Chicago to try and get a job as an acrobat, because I'd been in the circus several summers during high school, touring the country. If that failed, to get a job on a sailing boat somewhere, because I loved sailing.

Instead, an uncle ran into me while I was buying a ticket to a vaudeville theatre. I had three hundred dollars in my pocket, my year's allowance for the school. He was a funny looking uncle with a big red nose, bright red eyes, grey hair. A liquor salesman, he sensed something was wrong. So he grabbed me and said it was stupid to try and be an acrobat. He thought acrobats were very low people and so were sailors.

He took me to one of his customers, John C. Eastman, the publisher of the *Chicago Journal*. Mr. Eastman had a whisky nose, white hair and bright red eyes. I was introduced to Mr. Eastman as a genius because my uncle had heard some of these doting rumors from Wisconsin. Mr. Eastman asked me if I could write poetry and I said yes, I was rather good at that. He asked me if I could write a dirty poem because he was giving a stag party and wanted a poem to be printed and distributed to his guests. I was sixteen and a half but very proficient.

While I sat at his desk, he went out to lunch with my Uncle Leon. I wrote a dirty poem about a bull. He came back and was enchanted. So he took me down to the local room and introduced me as the newest member of the *Journal* staff.

The Picture Chaser

October 2, 1958: Photographer Weegee was Ben's guest for a spirited discussion of crime. Ben told a Bedtime Story concerning his own humble origins as a crime reporter.
After working for several months as a messenger and errand

boy at the Journal, *Hecht graduated to a now extinct journalistic calling, the Picture Chaser.*

We used to have picture chasers on the papers in the early days, when the cameras were big and hard to lug around and people wouldn't pose for pictures in the paper. A chap called the picture chaser would go out and try to steal a picture off some bureau or the wall. I was one of the picture chasers and very good at it. We would go in, pretend we were census takers or gas bill collectors and try to grab a picture.

But there was a fellow in Chicago who was forty times better. He used to drive me crazy. I never met such a man. This fellow's name was Leroy T. Benzinger. He'd wait until we'd all be thrown out and then he would appear and say, "I am Leroy T. Benzinger from the *Chicago American*." The woman would say, "Get out of here I don't want to talk to any newspapermen." He would say "Madam, I'd like to see a picture of your daughter." And as he was talking, he would put his finger up and remove his glass eye. The woman would look at him, faint and fall down. Then he would step over her and go into the closet or the bedroom, cop the picture, put his eye back in, and scoot.

My First Newspaper Story

December 30, 1958: On a program devoted to his own career, Ben remembered his first reportorial opportunity.

I swiftly fetched cans of tobacco and cigars for the journalists for some time. Dick Finnegan, who was the assistant city editor, and Sherman Duffy, who was the sporting editor, then got a little sorry for me and decided to try me out on a story. I was sent to interview and get a picture from a woman who was being divorced, a Mrs. Campbell.

I was about seventeen when I arrived at Mrs. Campbell's home. Her husband had charged that she'd been unfaithful with a number of men. She greeted me, fed me coffee and cake, sewed a few buttons on my blouse, and began to sob and weep that she'd been terribly maligned. The lovely lady told me that she'd never done a wrong thing in her life, that she'd been true blue to this man who was an elderly maniac, suffering from delusions of persecution and so forth.

She cried and held me in her arms and sobbed and begged for my white sword.

I rushed back to the paper and sat down at the typewriter and wrote a story that began, "We think that Mrs. Campbell is a victim of the foulest injustice that has ever been visited on a woman and we think her husband is a cruel and monstrous fellow." I went on this way and sent the copy in. As I kept writing I noticed it was being terribly well received. Not only the assistant to the editor, but the city editor, the managing editor, the head of the composing room, fifteen men were reading my copy, waiting eagerly for each new page.

On the sixteenth page Sherman Duffy came over, tapped me and said, "That'll be enough kid. Get out of here." Mr. Boyer, the editor had the story printed and distributed among saloons as a joke. This was my first story.

The Wired Woman

September 22, 1958: Ben's guest was Hy Stierman, publisher of Confidential, *a 1950s exploitation tabloid, for a discussion of the seamier side of journalism. After turning down Stierman's offer to write for the magazine, Ben told a Bedtime Story about the first nude he encountered as a newspaperman.*

It was a wild, rainy, thundering afternoon and I was covering a murder. I was sixteen going on seventeen. As a young reporter, I used to carry sort of a burglar kit consisting of a jimmy, a screwdriver, flashlight and other accoutrements so I'd be prepared for anything. The staff photographer, a fellow named Gene Cour, was with me.

Gene and I entered a basement on North Dearborn Street where we were told we would find the body of a woman who had been killed brutally by some ax murderer. We came down the stairs and at the end of the basement two cops were standing. Sitting in an abandoned rocking chair was a red haired young lady of twenty, nude and dead. Gene asked, "Have you got your flashlight?" I said, "Yes." "Well, put it on her face so I can focus my camera."

I lit her face and as I was holding my flashlight, there was a clap of thunder. The face vanished and the head rolled off. Then an arm rolled off and a leg dropped away and what was left of the beauty slid out of the rocking chair. One of the officers said, "I told you there was no use trying to wire her up, Schmitty." And Schmitty said "Well wait a minute boys, we'll wire her up again, the ax murderer did a pretty thorough job."

At that moment Gene Coor took his photograph. He photographed Officer Schmitty holding the head in his hands and Gene made a joke. He said, "I got a good caption for this. Nude loses head to handsome cop."

It was at least a week before I could recover any interest in nudes.

Roost in a Brothel

December 23, 1958: Ben's guest, Judge John Murtagh, discussed prostitution in New York. For his Bedtime Story, Hecht recounted an amusing incident from his teenage years.

Women of easy virtue were no strangers to young Hecht. Chicago was bubbling with brothels at the time, where journalists and the general public found both entertainment and fulfillment. But Hecht's first encounter with one of the city's finer houses took him somewhat by surprise.

I was seventeen, a veteran journalist in Chicago and not too popular in the local room because I was too young, a little too nutty, and a little too unprofessional. The only person who spoke to me was a fellow of eighteen, a very handsome chap named Edward H. Griffiths, who became the big movie director. Ned and I finally, being more or less exiles from the merriment of the local room, decided we would live together. I was living with an aunt, so was Ed. One November day we walked down North Dearborn Street, looking for a room.

Most of the rooming houses looked pretty bad. We came to one with a large marble exterior and balustrades outside. It looked very swanky so Ned suggested we try it. We rang the bell and what looked to be a society leader opened the door with a white pompadour and an elegant gown. Faltering, we asked her if she had a room to let. After looking at us for a moment she said, yes, if we didn't mind the fourth floor. We got a room on the fourth floor and she charged us four dollars a week.

Ned and I moved in with our books. We bought one bottle of booze and waited to entertain. Our guests were chiefly my mother, his aunt, my aunt, his sister, and other members of the family. We lived there for six weeks and not one of the newspaper boys visited us despite our prepared bottle of booze.

Towards Christmas time the phone rang and we were called down to the third floor to answer it. It was my mentor, the sporting editor, Mr. Sherman Duffy, who was calling to invite me to join him in some pre-Christmas holiday drinking at the Virginia Hotel. I asked Mr. Duffy, "Why don't you come and visit Ned and I, we have a room. We live very near the hotel." "Where do you live?" "838 North Dearborn." He asked if the place had a marble balustrade in front of it. I told him it did. There was a pause, he chuckled and said, "We'll be there very shortly."

About twenty minutes later we heard an awful noise on the floor below. It was Mr. Duffy and some eight other journalists, screaming, yelling, laughing and dancing, whacking ladies on the rear and carrying on no end. Ned and I yelled down that he was on the wrong floor, that we lived upstairs. Duffy said, "No, this is the right floor!" It turned out that we were on the fourth floor of the most famous brothel in Chicago, Madame Francis'. The boys left about three in the morning.

At nine o'clock, it was a Sunday morning, Ned and I had packed our books and started down the stairs, departing our premises. We couldn't bear living there any longer. As we passed the door where the society queen lived, it opened. She came out and asked, "Are you leaving boys?" We answered, "Yes ma'am." She handed us the twenty four dollars in room rent that we'd paid her in the six weeks. We paused and we took it and then she wished us a Merry Christmas. We walked on, and found other diggings.

Carnation Dan's Epitaph

November 19, 1958: Ben answered his mail and discussed newspapermen, past and present. The evening's Bedtime Story featured one of his favorite yarns, concerning a Chicago news gatherer who had some difficulty finding steady employment.

One of my favorite old time newspapermen functioned in Chicago. His name was Carnation Dan Thethoroe. His face was pink, his language matched the ever present flower in his faded label, and he was a very bad newspaperman. In fact, he wasn't really a newspaperman, he was a journalist. That means he had no employment and couldn't get a job. That's what it used to mean in Chicago, anyway.

Carnation Dan was an elderly boy and he had certain handicaps as a news coverer. He couldn't stand bad news, murders, any trouble at all in the human race so he was always writing sweetness and light stories. He supported himself on two to five dollars a week. Jack Lait, who was city editor on one of the Hearst papers in Chicago, used to pay him that; space rates for little feature stories about things that happened in Lincoln Park. What was going on at the zoo and things like that. Poor Carnation Dan tried for fifteen years to get a job. He had known many famous people in San Francisco, Ambrose Bierce, Jack London, many people but he couldn't make the Chicago press.

Finally, one day he arrived at Jack Lait's office and said he needed twenty-five dollars. That he was marrying a very fine waitress, much younger than himself but eager to become his wife. "Well," Jack said, "I don't know what you can write for twenty-five dollars." Carnation Dan said, "I'll write you my obituary." And he sat down and wrote for several hours and gave it to Jack. Jack read it and gave him twenty-five dollars and filed it away.

About three months later the news came that Carnation Dan was dead. Jack remembered the obituary, got it out of the morgue and slapped it into the front page of the *Herald Examiner*. It happened that Mr. William Randolph Hearst, the publisher of the *Examiner*, was in Chicago at the time. He picked up the paper and read the obituary and came charging into the local room, very excited, and said to Mr. Lait, "This is the most marvelous story I've ever read. We must hire the man who wrote it. Get him at once, hire him and put him on the staff."

That was Carnation Dan's epitaph.

Hearst's Sex Life

November 28, 1958: With cartoonist Al Capp as his guest, Ben fondly remembered newspaper baron William Randolph Hearst. Hecht's memories were a departure from the usual anti-Hearst recitals.

It was a wild and happy time that first saw the birth of comic strips in this country. William Randolph Hearst was the first young publisher who whistled most of the cartoonists into his papers. Mr. Hearst is a man who never received his correct stature in this country. He was one of the great journalists. I remember a story about him that illustrates the wildness of the time, and of the comic strip's birth.

My friend Gene Fowler, who came from Colorado, was named the first managing editor of the *New York Mirror* before the newspaper was yet printed. Mr. Hearst called him up and said, "Gene, before we print our first issue, I'd like you to do a dummy run of the paper to see how the presses are going, to see if there's any smudges, any ink troubles. To see if everything clicks right. Get up a paper and print it and see how it works and then we'll put the regular edition in."

So Gene sat down and, with the aid of only one bottle or two of whisky, wrote an entire newspaper. All the headlines and all the copy. What he wrote were fifty different stories about the sexual activities of Mr. William Randolph Hearst. His triumphs, his defeats, his oddities. Each story topped the other in its Rabelaisian charm. Gene finished his stories, put this paper to bed and brought it to the pressman. They ran it off, and everything worked fine.

Gene then called up Mr. Hearst in San Simeon and said, "Mr. Hearst, chief, the presses work absolutely perfectly, nothing to worry about." Mr. Hearst thanked him and Gene went to a saloon to have a drink. While he was gone Mr. Hearst called back and told one of the pressmen, "I'd like to have a copy of that test edition, I'd like to see for myself. Maybe Gene's eyes aren't too good. I need to be sure. Mail one right away." So they mailed a copy.

When Gene came back from the saloon, he discovered this incredible thing he'd written about Hearst's sexual gooniness had gone out to San Simeon. So he returned to the saloon and there he sat for three days, without budging. Giving up journalism forever, drinking as much as any man had ever drunk. The fourth day he was discovered and the telegram from Mr. Hearst was handed to him. And as I remember the telegram it read: "Dear Gene Fowler. Found your first issue of *Mirror* very lively, very entertaining. Hope succeeding issues will be a little more careful about libel. Good luck, William Randolph Hearst."

The Marathon Drinker

December 31, 1958: Ben was joined by his producer, Ted Yates, for a New Year's Eve broadcast of toasts and whimsical stories.

An avalanche of copy has been devoted to the synergistic relationship of alcohol and the newspaperman. Ben Hecht and Charles MacArthur certainly helped propagate this illusion with the fast talking, hard drinking newspapermen that populated their plays and films. Never an alcoholic, Hecht could certainly hold his own in the company of his intoxicated peers. On this New Year's Eve broadcast, he recalled one particularly memorable journalistic imbiber.

I knew a fellow who stayed drunk for eighteen years, a journalist named Larry Malm.

When I came on the paper as a kid, I noticed he was always wandering in and out of the office with his coat open. It was summer but he wore an overcoat. Mr. Malm was always grinning, never able to talk, never able to write. He was always lushed and always admired by the city editor.

Finally I found out his story. It seems that about fifteen years before my arrival on the paper Larry Malm had been sent to cover a great fire. The Iroquois Theatre had burned down with a thousand or more people burned to death in it. Larry had arrived shortly after the fire started. He spent about eight hours counting and identifying corpses, and when he got to the four hundredth, he quit. He needed a little rest. So he retired to the back room of a saloon and stretched out on a large table to take a nap. Larry Malm snoozed for about an hour. When he woke up he found that they had piled some two hundred corpses on top of him. He woke up in a black hole of burned, charred corpses. He pushed them off, fought his way to the bar, ordered a bottle of liquor and kept drinking for eighteen years until he died. An unhappy tale I'm afraid.

The Pole Climber

December 10, 1958: Ben replied to his letter writers and discussed the newspaper strike. His Bedtime Story recalled another of his early idols, Christian Dane Haggerty, an Associated

Press correspondent. Hecht's first mentor on the Journal, *Sherman Duffy, had introduced young Ben to Haggerty and a number of other journalistic legends.*

Within months of his first byline, Ben Hecht had become one of Chicago's premier reporters, covering important trials, political conventions and such major events as the Dayton, Ohio flood of 1913.

This story is about a notable newspaper deed. The hero, Christian Dane Haggerty, was an ace correspondent for the AP. I was on my first out of town assignment, the Dayton flood. The city was well under water. It was March, very cold, full of snow in Ohio. I got to Indianapolis and I was the youngest one there. We sat in the barroom and I had only one objective: to sneak away from all my fellow correspondents and be the first one to get into Dayton, Ohio.

I left my overcoat and hat in the barroom and walked nonchalantly out, without being noticed. I was terribly happy. After stealing a lantern, I realized there was one high bridge standing over the Eagle River so I decided to cross that. I was all alone. Finally, my first real scoop. As I started crossing the bridge I turned around and saw all the reporters following me. All the reporters were called Christian Dane Haggerty of the AP. Mr. Haggerty was about fifty-five years old and had a potbelly, having consumed hundreds of gallons of liquor. He had a whiskey flask in his hand at the moment, had asthma, could barely walk, and he started to cross this high bridge with me.

I kept telling him it was very dangerous. He not only crossed the bridge but he kept talking all the time, reciting anecdotes, as newspapermen will. He told me about the Boxer rebellion, he told me about the Boar War. We crossed the bridge finally and I thought, Haggerty can't keep going, he's too old. I was very young, I could still do a hundred yards in ten seconds.

We finally found a handcar on a railroad track. Mr. Haggerty took his place at one end of the pumping apparatus and pumped away and didn't stop telling anecdotes. He was now in Port Arthur, telling me about the Russo-Jap war. I thought I'd never lose this man but I was sure he'd have to give out before we got to Miami junction, which was just outside of Dayton. We got off the handcar and waded through snow for a couple of miles. Haggerty still talking, still drinking his whiskey, still moving his potbelly right along side of me.

There were a few people who took shots at us, mistaking us for looters. Haggerty dived into the snow with me. I couldn't get rid of him. And he represented all the papers. Finally as we neared Miami junction, we were about a mile away, and Mr. Haggerty stopped and said, "Wait a minute kid." I looked at him with great hope in my heart. "I want to catch my breath," he said. He stood still for about three or four minutes and said, "Just wait here two minutes for me."

And then suddenly he did an odd thing. I hadn't known this but Mr. Haggerty had been a linesman, a telegraph linesman, before he became a correspondent. He started climbing an icy telegraph pole. He mysteriously got to the top. He removed a pair of pliers from his back pocket and performed some mysterious gestures on top of the pole. I found out later that what he did was to tap out a message to his home office in Chicago. The message read: "Dayton, Ohio, AP everywhere, Haggerty." The message tapped out, he slid down the pole and lay in a coma in the snow.

I left him there and went on to the Miami junction, a little station. I notified them that a newspaperman in a coma was lying at the foot of a telegraph pole and to rescue and hide him somewhere for day. And they did.

That was the spirit of the press in my time and I believe that's the spirit of the press today.

Further Thoughts on Newspapers

December 11, 1958: A newspaper strike in New York was beginning its second week. The Ben Hecht Show had received mostly favorable notices in the press but certain critics, such as Jack O'Brian in the Journal American, served as regular antagonists. No matter what the daily columnists had written, Hecht quickly mourned the deprivation of one of his most treasured daily rituals.

A town without a newspaper is a dead town. Without newspapers, without their daffy headlines, their pontificators and buzzing columnists and pictures to look at, a town loses its identity. You don't realize how important the papers are when they're rolling off the presses, but when the presses stop you feel Scheherazade has left town. One can't help but yearn for the fellow who writes the daily mad-hatter drama of the town, Mr. Journalism.

I miss most, first those little black electric headlines about the raided love nest, the defiant bigamist, those old songs of life and travail, they haven't changed since I was a boy. Humanity at grips with itself, fighting its moral codes. Rioting, killing, shooting, loving. These are the stories in the *Daily News* and the *World Telegram* I look at quickly. After that, I plunge into the trouble that the *Times* offers me, in the crossword puzzle. The greatest thing that journalism has invented is the *Times* crossword puzzle.

After I solve the crossword puzzle I get busy with the columnists. First there's Walter Winchell who invented the fife-and-drum-corps school of journalism that is so popular now. I like Ed Sullivan whose Irish heart keeps finding the world more and more charming as it gets worse. And Louis Zobel who neatly informs me every day where Marlene Dietrich spent the evening and about Prince Rainer and other visiting fireman. And Leonard Lyons who keeps alive the illusion that our cafes are full of wits and wags. And Bugs Bayer who to me is the most acrobatic, comical writer we have in our time.

Yes, a city without a newspaper is a like a city that has been captured by some enemy and reduced to silence. Its poets, all its philosophers are mum. It's a very sad town.

The newspapers are sort of an art, they've really degenerated into that. They used to be a thriving business, but now they've become an art form and they should be supported somehow. The church you know, went along for twenty centuries, only kept going because it was allowed to pass the hat all the time. Some similar trick should be figured out for the press to keep it alive.

Birds of the Gallows

Society and the Criminal

December 9, 1958: Ben's guest was recently paroled murderer John Resko. Ben Hecht's fascination with criminals had its roots in Chicago and extended to his later years, when he befriended mobster Mickey Cohen. From the time he spent in their company, Hecht developed an understanding and appreciation for society's outcasts. Before his interview with Resko, he delivered this essay on criminals.

Crime is an old hobby of mine. Not as a contributor, but as an observer. Crime itself is always interesting, not from the point of view of crime but from the point of view of where I sit, society. Our country is probably the most hypocritical in the world towards crime. It professes to be sneering, righteous and contemptuous towards criminals, very stuffy about them, and at the same time spends billions of dollars watching their antics on television, and on the movie screen. At the same time crime is the backbone of our journalism.

The general hypocrisy that our society has towards criminals has always interested me. It's as if criminals were really different than we are. Society preaches such a double standard. On one hand they preach, let he who is without sin cast the first stone. With the other hand they cast all the stones that they can at a sinner and try to stone him to death. This hypocrisy doesn't confuse the sinner, it confuses our society. It makes us kind of crazy. We're a schizophrenic civilization.

I noticed when I used to be among them, three different kinds of criminals. One was the spontaneous, natural throwback. Born sometimes to a good, pious or low family, he was man who wasn't hatched into our society. He might have been born ten thousand years ago. He wasn't meaner or more vicious, he just didn't believe in society. He looked on it as a fat pigeon to pluck. He had no awe or kowtowing sense.

The second type of criminal is a psycho and he is the dangerous one. He's a mad, crazy man who should be put away. I've always felt that if there was any reason for capital punishment, it should be for the sake of these people, as well as society.

And the third criminal I've noticed is myself or rather you and I. We're criminals. We're exactly like two-thirds of the people who are in the penitentiary. We're born with a fine social sense. We have all the nice decent attitudes human beings should have. A little extra pressure, a little extra hunger, a girl or an odd companion suddenly makes us commit a deed and then we are judged by the deed. This is where society is wrong. A doer should never be judged by a deed. Blackening a man's whole life because of one thing he did is as wrong as condemning a kid to solitary for smoking a cigarette because the crime is only a very small part of that human being.

Hand Me My Sword

December 9, 1958: Ben discussed the criminal mind and prison life with murderer John Resko. Hecht's Bedtime Story concerned a legendary lawbreaker.

One of my favorite criminals was Charlie Gagin, who later became known as Blackie Gagin. Blackie Gagin was possibly the most inept crook who ever lived. He was a holdup man who operated in small Illinois towns. It was his oddity that whenever he entered a shoe store to hold it up, there would usually be two policemen there buying shoes. He was always caught and sent to some small town jail.

His genius began in jail. Blackie Gagin was a man who thirsted for freedom and no jail could hold him. He managed to achieve something like seven jail breaks. He became quite a character around town. Everyone knew him as a stumble-bum crook but a man for whom iron bars did not a prison make.

Blackie made the big time when he did a job in Chicago that involved a little shooting. He was sent to Joliet but this was not a jail that was easy to break out of. Charlie knew one way to get out, though. He always entered jail fully equipped, carrying a yard of emery thread hidden in his mouth, ready to use.

The only way to get out of Joliet in those days was to get into the hospital ward, which was easy to break out of. The only way to get into the hospital ward was to pretend he was crazy. So he'd sit in his cell all day staring blankly. And when the guard came and said, "Whata ya want, Gagin?" Gagin would always have the same answer, "Hand me my sword." This went on for four months, day and night. It wasn't Gagin that went crazy, it was the guard.

One night around midnight, the guard, who'd been very upset by four months of harassment from this idiot prisoner, appeared outside of Gagin's cell and said, "Gagin, whata ya want?" And Charlie Gagin, sticking to his guns answered, "Hand me my sword." The guard had heated a four-inch iron pipe and it was white hot. He held it up with a big pair of pincers and shoved it through the bars and said, "Here's your sword Gagin." Charlie reached his hand up and took the white hot iron. His hand was burnt off and he went into the hospital and they fitted him with a black hand. That's how he got the name Blackie Gagin.

Two months after he was in the hospital he used the emery thread and got out. Nobody ever found him. The man became a legend in Illinois.

One day my editor looked at a little item that had come in that said Blackie Gagin, the notorious crook and convict, had died and was being buried in the local potter's field, outside of Chicago. My editor told me to go cover the story and he said, "Make sure that's Gagin in the coffin."

The Wedding Band

January 2, 1959: Voluptuous ecdysiast Tempest Storm was Ben's guest. As he eyed her with a sense of awe, they discussed temptation and infidelity. For his Bedtime Story, Ben told a tale about the consequences of jealousy.

This story has to do with a lovely lady that was once in past newspaper headlines. It reveals that you can sometimes do a little too much teasing. The girl's name was Clara and she was married to Fred Metzger, who was sort of a small, on the rise meat packer in Chicago.

Mr. Metzger married this glorious, voluptuous girl and they were very, very happy for some time. Fred, however, became very jealous because Clara insisted on wearing the most abbreviated bathing costumes when she went on the beach for a swim. She even went around the park in shorts, which was unusual in those days.

Fred kept getting more and more jealous and there were terrible rows. So loud that even the neighbors got worried. Suddenly the rows stopped and Clara was no longer in evidence. The police came around after a few weeks and there was no sign of Clara anywhere. Fred Metzger, the rising young meat packer, went on with his business.

Everything would have gone very well except that one of Mr. Metzger's customers cut into a sausage one evening and out popped a gold wedding ring, reading: "To Clara 'til death do us part." Mr. Metzger was arrested and charged with the murder and conversion of his wife into sausages. I remember the lead I wrote: If Fred Metzger is hanged for the murder of his beautiful wife it will be because of the little gold wedding band he gave her on their marriage day.

Mr. Metzger was hanged, Clara was avenged, and people in Chicago didn't eat sausages for a long time.

A Mannequin Who Grew Hair

January 9, 1959: Actress Zsa Zsa Gabor was Ben Hecht's guest. Hecht followed a rather lightweight interview with Miss Gabor by gallantly apologizing for his Bedtime Story, which would describe a woman even more beautiful than his guest.

This story is about the hazards that sometimes beset the way of great feminine beauty. The girl's name was Maxine Martan, she was married to Felix Martan and I think she was the most beautiful girl I ever saw.

Maxine had been married to Martan for some time, and he was getting very angry at her. He'd married her because he was a blossoming couturier. After opening a little store and exhibiting his latest creation in the window every other week, he'd wanted Maxine to model. With such a beautiful model he could not help but succeed. Maxine refused anything that had to do with his store, his business, or his dreams. She was off to cocktail parties and enchanting the world. Finally, she left him and went back to her people in South America.

However, a policeman walking down the little street where Felix Martan had his couturier shop finally got to wondering about something that was in the window. He passed the window everyday on his way to cover his beat and he'd always seen the same mannequin in the window. But the first time he'd seen her she'd had a short Italian bob. During the summer after about four or five weeks, he began to notice that the hair was changing. This bothered him a great deal.

Finally went in, made an inquiry and discovered that Maxine had finally been put to work by her husband, the inspired couturier. Felix had murdered Maxine, embalmed her and put her in the window where she could demonstrate his creations the way he'd originally intended when he'd first married her. Hair sometimes grows on embalmed people and this time it had grown a good six inches. It resulted in Felix ceasing to be a couturier.

One Cure for Juvenile Delinquency

November 25, 1958: Ben interviewed New York Times correspondent Harrison Salisbury, who had just written a book on juvenile delinquency, The Shook-Up Generation. *After a very serious discussion of the horrors of the problem, which seemed to be on everyone's agenda at the time, Hecht told a rather wry Bedtime Story on child care.*

This story takes place on a wonderful sunny spring day in middle Illinois, in the farm country around Plano. I was sent there as a reporter to interview a woman called Mrs. Vermilla. She was a charming, motherly looking woman of about sixty with a wonderful white pompadour, red cheeks and a wide smile. Mrs. Vermilla was running a sort of baby farm. People from Moline, Peoria, and even Chicago, used to send her their children. She would house, feed, educate and take care of them, and would receive so much per month per child for her activities.

The reason that I was interviewing her was that one of these parents had found it necessary to inquire into the welfare of the child and received some ambiguous answers. Out of the sixty or seventy parents who had given their children to Mrs. Vermilla, only one had inquired as to their welfare for six to eight months.

On this day, there were about fifty policemen on the premises digging everywhere. After three or four days of talking to this benign, smiling woman, the police finally dug up thirty-eight bodies of children ranging in age from two to seven. It developed that Mrs. Vermilla was running a remarkable institution. No sooner would she get one of her little charges then she would strangle it, bury the child, and keep the money without having to spend any on the upkeep or feeding of the child.

This was one of the early cures for juvenile delinquency which I ran into as a newspaperman, long ago.

Leanin' Willie

January 1, 1959: Ben Hecht interviewed Hazel Wells, a representative from the Woman's Christian Temperance Union. Although Hecht treated his guest with the utmost respect during the interview, he frequently drank from a glass filled with Jack Daniels. As was often the case, he used the evening's Bedtime Story to make a rather capricious comment on the subject under discussion.

This story is about the havoc Prohibition worked on one fellow that I knew. His name was Willie Sams. He worked the carnivals as a leaning man. Willie used to appear on a platform and stand at an angle of thirty degrees. He would sometimes get himself off to forty degrees and people used to look at him and applaud.

Willie Sams was playing up in Minneapolis one time and a professor came to see him, a medical professor who was terribly interested in the phenomena of his leaning. He told Willie that if anything happened to him, he would like the privilege of examining his head. In case he died, he would like to dissect it. He believed that there might be something odd in this man's head. So Willie Sams agreed. His father was with him. And the professor gave his father $200 and promised $300 more if, in the event of death, the body of Willie Sams was sent to him.

Well about four months later the professor received the body of a leaning man who looked like Willie Sams. He dissected the head and found nothing unusual about it. Then all over the country, six or eight other professors received the bodies of Willie Sams. Willie Sams had turned into a mass murderer. He was killing people and sending them off to various professors around the country for their examination and getting $300 per head.

The police quickly became interested in where Willie Sams could be. They started combing the country for him. Well, there was a policeman in Kansas City, which was in a dry state in those days, forbidding alcohol. This policeman was walking down the street and he saw a man standing against a building, leaning, and he arrested him as a drunk. And this non-drunk but terrible murderer was Willie Sams. It was the dry law in Kansas City that put him on the gallows.

Hangings

September 18, 1958: Ben Hecht's preoccupation with hangings led producer Ted Yates to book an actual executioner as a guest on the program, Donal MacNamara. Hecht relished the opportunity to discuss his fixation with this now outmoded form of punishment. Before the interview, he delivered an essay on the ancient art of execution.

I was once an expert on hangings. As a reporter I covered dozens of them. Among the men I saw through the trap was a fellow named Teddy Webb. He was a small, fierce young man who stepped a bit too far out of line, even for Chicago. He killed a policeman. His capture was an odd story.

An aggrieved girlfriend had notified the police that Teddy could be found on the fourth floor of a certain address in the embrace of a blond, if they hurried. The police hurried. Teddy Webb jumped out of bed stark naked as the first policeman entered the room. He yelled fiercely at the officer to get out. The officer stared and dropped dead of heart failure. Twenty minutes later after Teddy had been apprehended on the roof, Chief of Police Herman Shutler arrived on the scene. We used to call him wooden shoes. Chief Shutler put a bullet into the side of the officer whose heart had failed at the sight of the terrible Teddy. He was shot in the performance of his duties the chief told reporters. We knew better but that's the way we wrote it because he was a good cop.

After each of the hangings I reported, my newspaper always received scores of letters protesting against capital punishment. This debate is still going on. Through the wars and massacres of our era, people have kept worrying about the ethics of executing a man guilty of murder. It shows how we cling to a theory of civilized behavior, while violating it up and down the earth. How can we help ourselves by sparing the lives of one or two or a dozen guilty murderers at the same time go in for wars and mass killings? How can we turn our eyes and backs on the massacres that happened in Europe?

The only distaste I feel towards capital punishment is towards the alleged progress in the methods of execution — the use of the electric chair and the gas chamber for the disposal of criminals. A rope or a gun are ancient, even poetic associations of death. Electricity and gas seem miscast as judicious killers. The introduction of the electric chair and gas chamber seems to me part of the gadget mania that has gripped the U.S.A. since Thomas Alva Edison. There's no extra sadism in substituting the hot seat and the cyanide smog for the gallows of song and story. It's more likely part of the American drive to remove all evidences of the past from its eyes and ears. The gallows were discontinued in most states for no other reason than that they were old hat. I'm not raising any voice against any modernizing of anything. Even a mutter against the modernizing of life sounds like treason in these times. However, there's no onus attached to remembering the softer outlines and quainter face the world once wore. The old gallows chamber I submit nostalgically was one of them.

During my years as a reporter, I only witnessed hangings, I've never seen an electrocution. Witnessing a hanging, you feel a deep compassion. Whoever is being hanged, you feel its your own brother. And you also feel a great dramatic sense. You feel yourself or your very dearest brother is being killed and you close your eyes to the whole business of laws, society and criminal courts. You think they're all wrong during the five minutes you watch an execution.

The Singing Murderer

December 29, 1958: Comic Orson Bean was Ben's guest. Bean came on the program to discuss the inequities of cabaret cards, which were then issued to performers in New York clubs by the police department. Artists such as vocalist Billie Holliday were denied cards because of minor infractions. The mention of crime sparked another Bedtime Story from Hecht's Chicago days, this time concerning a close friend.

> Ben Hecht and Charles MacArthur began a lifelong friendship when they first met as Chicago crime reporters. Their escapades included plays, films, and wild adventures. In Hecht's paean to MacArthur, Charlie, written in 1957 after MacArthur's death, he wrote, "In our twenty years of off and on collaboration there was never any debate between us. We worked without ego as if we were playing a game, the rule of which was, 'who-ever objects, wins.'" In addition to The Front Page, they co-wrote such classic films as Twentieth Century, Gunga Din and Wuthering Heights. Hecht and MacArthur's initial effort was conceived on the eve of an execution.

My first collaboration with Charles MacArthur took place when we met the most amiable murderer I ever knew. His name was Lieutenant Carl Wanderer and he was a war hero. One night he was coming home from the movies with his wife and was confronted by a man demanding money or his life. Trained for combat, the Lieutenant whipped out his gun and shot and killed the robber, but not before the criminal had shot and killed Mrs. Wanderer.

The next day Carl Wanderer was acclaimed in the morning papers as a hero for having at least put up a fight. Because of his veterans credentials, he was of course backed by the police and the American legion. When I went to interview him, I went up the back stairs of his Chicago apartment building, as was the custom of Chicago reporters in those days, to come in the back way. I looked through the screen door and there was Lieut. Carl Wanderer in his shorts, pressing his trousers and whistling, "there are smiles that make you happy, there are smiles that make you sad." I quickly concluded that he was a murderer.

And so I went to see Captain Norton of homicide. I met MacArthur at the police station. Charlie, who was covering the story for another paper in Chicago, was also convinced that Wanderer had killed his wife and that the whole thing was a frameup. Charlie had a hunch that the ragged stranger, that's what he called him in print, that this pathetically puny fellow could never have fired the murder weapon. After that MacArthur traced the gun to Carl's cousin Fred who revealed that it was on loan to cousin Carl. Wanderer finally confessed. He killed his young wife, who was pregnant, and hired the Ragged Stranger to pull a little gag.

Carl was tried and convicted and as he awaited hanging, MacArthur and I became his buddies. We played rummy with him, for money. He thought we were the brightest people he ever met because we helped land him in this death cell.

On the eve of his walk to gallows, Charlie asked if he had anything in mind for his last words. Carl had nothing. Charlie told him that he'd written a short speech for him to recite. It was an attack on the *Examiner*'s city editor. Wanderer liked that. I added a few lines to attack my city editors. From the gallows, Carl Wanderer would say that he owed his present predicament to the fact that he was a constant reader of the *Chicago Daily News* and the *Chicago Herald and Examiner* and they had both driven him to purgatory.

When Wanderer got to the gallows we realized that in the excitement of collaboration, we'd forgotten that a man on the gallows has his arms strapped to his sides. When the warden asked for his last words, Carl tried to read the paper but couldn't. He looked at us apologetically, threw back his head and began singing, "Dear Old Pal of Mine." The drop banged and the song ended. Our first collaboration died in the hands of the most amiable and helpful of murderers I have ever known.

Dr. Kirsch's Final Scream

September 18, 1958: Executioner Donal MacNamara was Ben's guest. He welcomed Hecht's genuine curiosity concerning his calling and answered his host's inquiries eagerly. For his Bedtime Story, Ben told a favorite hanging story.

As a reporter, he had spent many hours in jail cells with doomed criminals about to "meet their maker." On his program, he regularly recounted these relationships with particular enthusiasm.

This story is one of my favorite hanging memories. It was a wild and stormy night in Chicago, below zero and the snow coming down in carloads. I was sitting in the death cell in Cook County Jail where a man named Dr. Emil Kirsch was waiting to be hanged at six AM. Warden Jacoby was in the death cell and the three of us — the warden, the doomed man and I — were playing gin. Dr. Kirsch was losing.

At around two-thirty he threw the cards down and said, "Enough of this, I want to talk to the sheriff. If you'll do me a favor," said the doomed doctor, "I'll make a confession."

In those days we used to hang people whether they made a confession or not but it was always a nice thing to have a confession in the sheriff's files. So we sent for the sheriff. He arrived around three o'clock in the morning.

The sheriff asked Dr. Kirsch what he wanted, what sort of favor. The doctor said, "If you'll get me a woman's vanity case, I'll confess." I was sent out in the storm to fulfill Dr. Kirsch's request.

Around four-thirty I came back with a fully equipped woman's vanity case borrowed from one of the girls at Queen Lil's. The doctor opened it and started confessing. Telling how, when and why he had killed his wife. And as he confessed, he started making himself up. He rouged his lips, his cheeks, mascaraed his eyes, powdered his ears, and turned himself into a very pretty, pretty fellow. The sheriff was horrified by all this but a promise was a promise and let the fellow go ahead with his makeup.

Finally, the death march began. The death warrant was read and Doctor Kirsch ended up on the gallows looking very blooming. When they put the white robe on him and the white hood over his head, he went to the trap and started spinning and winding up. When the body strangles in this fashion they usually make a grunt. A roar of pain comes out. Well, out of the bundled figure of Dr. Kirsch came a falsetto scream.

Not at This Time

November 11, 1958: Ben devoted the program to a list of his fifty favorite books. He felt that reading these classics would be a suitable substitute for a college education.

For his Bedtime Story, he remembered an avid reader he met in a jail cell.

This story is about a great reader. I met this reader shortly after he got into a bit of trouble. He was a black man and a dentist by the name of Dr. Johnson.

Dr. Johnson was leading a parade riding on a horse and a policeman tried to stop the parade because they had no permit. Dr. Johnson, who was leading the parade on behalf of freedom in Liberia, drew a gun and killed the cop. He was arrested, tried and convicted. When he was waiting to be hanged, I got to know him. In his jail cell, the doctor became a mighty reader. He used to shag me out to get him books on Africa. I brought him back almost one a day and he poured over these books without any other thought in his mind until the day of his hanging came.

The big reader, my friend, walked out to the scaffold and they put the rope around his neck. He stood there lost in thought. And when the sheriff, as was customary, said "Doctor, do you have any last words, anything to say?" The doctor paused, looked at the sheriff and said, "Not at this time." And he went through the trap with all his books.

Free to Go

October 21, 1958: Former Senator William Benton of Connecticut was Hecht's guest. After leaving the Senate, Mr. Benton became Chairman of the Encyclopedia Britannica. *They discussed the state of education in America, and the effect of our great institutions on individuals. To end the broadcast, Hecht chose a Bedtime Story he felt best illustrated his concerns.*

The Frenchman Elie Faure, a great art critic, wrote a book called *The History of Art*. The theme of his book was that when a nation begins to think alike, paint alike, and dream alike, that nation dies. And he proves it through history beginning with the Saites epic of the Egyptians. Institutions are usually a substitute word for nations. When institutions become more powerful than a human being, they become very weak and they vanish.

When I was a reporter I once went down to see a man who was being let out of Joliet, the state penitentiary in Illinois. He'd been there forty years. He'd been in an institution just as we are under institutions, mentally, physically and spiritually. He'd been in one physically. When he got out of the institution, Joliet, I took him to Chicago.

The man had been in a cell for forty years. When we walked down Michigan Avenue, he kept his eyes on the sidewalk. I took him to a room on Halstead Street that he'd rented. He bought three newspapers, went to his room, sat down on chair in the corner and started to read.

I used to come and call on him every three months. For the two years that I wrote stories about him, this fellow never went out of his room. And that's the effect that institutions have on people. Mentally, physically and spiritually.

A Murderer from the Other World

October 24, 1958: Ben Hecht's guest was the Rev. Helen Thuri, a medium who conducted a seance in the studio. During this rather unusual occurrence, probably the first and last seance to occur on live television, she claimed to be in contact with one of Hecht's departed relatives. After she returned to the real world, Hecht told a Bedtime Story about his first experience with the spirit world.

This story is about my experience with the other world. When I was a newspaperman, I came home one wintery night and found the family very busy with a ouija board. That's a little contrivance that's heart shaped, has a pencil, a point, and two little wheels. If you put your hand on it and ask a question, a spirit will reply.

I discovered to my amazement that I could run this thing all by myself. I put my hand on it and asked it a question. What I asked if anybody was there, it wrote yes, very violently. I asked who and it drew a picture of a coffin with a man's head sticking out. I asked, what's your name and it said William Wilson. I asked what his problem was. He said he was unburied. That he'd been murdered by his wife in a rowboat in Lake Michigan. She killed him with what he called a susovy. We couldn't untangle this word but we discovered that Mr. Wilson was in great trouble because he was floating between the land and the water. He said, at that particular moment, he was being washed up on Jackson Park Beach.

It was about midnight and I went to the Englewood Police Station and got two confused Irish policemen with searchlights. We dashed down in the storm to look for Mr. William Wilson. We searched the whole beach for about an hour or two. Got soaking wet and frozen to death. I came back and chided Mr. Wilson. I said, we didn't find you. Under pier, he wrote. He said he was stuck under the pier.

I didn't get the cops this time. I went alone. I looked all over the piers and no Mr. Wilson. After looking, I went to my editor and told him I wanted a few days off because I was on a big murder story. I wouldn't tell him what. And I sat with that ouija board for seven days and nights, consulting Mr. Wilson as to his whereabouts. He led me on quite a chase and I never found the body. I never found out anything about Mr. Wilson except that I was able to talk and argue with him very excitedly. He argued back.

After the seventh day, I came in and confessed to my editor that I was after a ghost who was a little bit more evasive than a live murderer. The editor forgave me and docked me a week's salary. Since then, I have not had too much faith in ghosts through ouija boards. But they may exist in other mediums.

On the Lam

December 18, 1958: Vaudeville legends Smith and Dale were Ben's guests. Shortly after their interview began, Ben lost control of the program and the aged comedians rambled on uncontrollably.

When he returned after a commercial break, Ben told a Bedtime Story that he heard from Mickey Cohen. Cohen, a man whose underworld activities rather amused Hecht, first contacted Ben in the early 1940s when Hecht was busy raising money for the dying Jews of Europe. Once Cohen ascertained the importance of Hecht's mission, he regularly contributed funding to Hecht's propaganda activities. After they became friends, Hecht started writing Cohen's autobiography. When Cohen granted a lengthy interview to another writer, the project was abandoned. Their friendship, however, remained intact.

Although the lion's share of Hecht's stories came from his own experiences, he nevertheless was always on the lookout for new material, no matter what its source. Anything a bit askew, with the right twist or unique point of view that he could add to his vast story arsenal.

This is a rather comical story. There's been a newspaper strike in New York recently and much of the news is unknown to New Yorkers.

A reporter from the West Coast came in. He's not actually a reporter, he's known in other circles. His name is Mickey Cohen and he told my producer Ted Yates and myself a story the other day at the lunch table. It's been printed all over but I haven't seen it in New York. I think its one of the funniest jokes with a morbid macabre overtone that I've ever heard.

It seems there were a couple of fellows in San Francisco, one called Bill Carr, a nice boy who'd been in the gambling business, and another fellow called Ralph Laskum, who owns a bar. They were great pals and Ralph was always playing jokes on Bill, which was discouraging to Bill because he couldn't think of a joke to play back. So after several years of brooding on the matter, Mr. Carr finally got an idea.

One day he went to sort of a horse pound, a place where they dispose of horses that have gotten too old that are going to drop dead anyway. And he bought one of the mares there. At around midnight when his friend was tending bar he took the horse to Ralph's apartment. It was up about four flights up in one of those hillside apartments in San Francisco. He walked the old mare up the four flights carefully, walked her into Ralph's parlor, closed the door, took out a gun, shot the mare and left her dead on the floor.

Ralph came home at three in the morning, and found a horse with rigor mortis, in his parlor. The horses leg stuck out straight, and its head had also stiffened. He couldn't get it out of a door, couldn't get it out of a window, he couldn't do anything with this dead horse in his room. So he called up the ASPCA. They called the police, and the police called the fire department, they roped off the place.

For almost twenty-four hours they tried to figure how to get the horse out of Ralph's place. Bill was beside himself with laughter, as was the rest of San Francisco. Finally they had to turn Ralph's home into an amateur abattoir. They took out the horse piecemeal. This excited the city no end. The police, however, got quite angry and got to looking for Bill, the man who shot the horse. Bill had to take it on the lam. He rushed off and landed in Pennsylvania. Mickey Cohen told me that when he saw Bill, Bill was laughing. He said the indictment had been quashed but it was the first time he had ever been on the lam for doing anything to a horse.

The Perfect Murder

> *December 3, 1958: Hecht spent the show reminiscing about Hollywood friends. For his Bedtime Story, he remembered an incident he claimed to have happened in Hollywood back in the early 1930s. In truth, this tale is a retelling of his classic short story, "The Great Gabbo." In the 1929 movie version, director Erich von Stroheim was cast as the ventriloquist.*

Some years ago in the old Friars Club, I was sitting with Groucho Marx and some other comedians. Groucho said to me, "See that fellow in the corner sitting by himself at the table?" I saw a furtive looking fellow in an orange wig sitting at the table and glancing nervously to the left and the right. Groucho said, "That fellow is a perfect murderer. He's called Gabbo the Great. He used to be a tremendously popular ventriloquist. But he was a little odd, always very close to his dummy, who was called Jimmy."

It seems that Gabbo used to talk to Jimmy as if Jimmy the wooden dummy were a human being. He would either scold or praise him after every show. Gabbo would also go to the booking agent and demand more money for Jimmy, or less money if Jimmy had misbehaved. Gabbo would even demand more billing for Jimmy. He was very fond of Jimmy. He fed him milk after the show. He had a tube through which the milk ran and disappeared.

Finally Gabbo the Great hired a girl, an ornamental young lady to decorate his act. She used to appear in tights and hand him a handkerchief or glass of water or any of the things he needed. Gabbo fell in love with this girl. She didn't like Gabbo at all. He was too crazy talking to this dummy all the time after the show. She began to kid Gabbo a little and would wink at Jimmy as she passed. Sometimes she would tickle Jimmy under the chin.

After a month of this Gabbo couldn't stand it any longer. From the start, he'd been yelling at Jimmy for stealing his girl. One night he took Jimmy in the dressing room after the act and he began to scream and shriek and tell Jimmy what an ingrate he was. That he had made him. That he'd been nothing more than a piece of wood and Gabbo had given him a soul and a brain and now he'd betrayed him by stealing his girl's love. While he was talking, he opened his suitcase and took out an axe and began to chop Jimmy into splinters. After about thirty minutes Jimmy was just a mass of toothpicks. After the murder, Gabbo opened the window of his dressing room sneaked out into the alley and disappeared. No one saw him for about six months. Groucho said, "He'd come back about two weeks ago. On the run. He thinks nobody knows him. He sits there, having committed his perfect crime with his orange wig, a murderer who nobody will apprehend."

Weegee and Ben Hecht: *The Crime Beat*

October 2, 1958: Arthur Fellig, aka Weegee, was Ben Hecht's guest. Weegee achieved considerable notoriety as a news photographer from the 1930s until his death in 1958. Working from the back of a beat-up Chevy equipped with a police radio, Weegee combed the streets of New York in search of salable snapshots. His photographs of fires, murdered mobsters' corpses and other frazzled denizens of the night captured a candid, dramatic slice of the big city. Although he claimed to be disgusted by the sight of blood, he once revealed that he was "spellbound by the mystery of murder." One picture editor reportedly welcomed the paunchy, cigar-smoking cameraman by asking, "Have you got any new corpses?"

Hecht approached the interview with uncommon gusto, sensing they were fellow travelers of sorts. He began the program with a sermon on society's hypocritical attitude toward the modern-day outlaw.

I always feel I have to put in a good word for crime because it seems to me terribly unfair for a country like ours to adore crime, to spend billions of dollars a year looking at pictures of criminals on television, at the movies, and always sneer at it when they talk about it.

The professional criminal was actually invented in Chicago. Chicago was their Plymouth Rock, back in the Capone era. Before that the criminals were known as outlaws. After Chicago they were sort of in-laws. They had behind them the power of the country, the state, the governor, the mayor, the police officials. The only people they disturbed were each other. During the Capone era about four hundred people were killed in the streets of Chicago. Yet it was the happiest town I think I've ever seen. It was like a television preview of television. Instead of murders on the little screen they saw them in the streets. And nobody was hurt except hoods.

Capone was perhaps the most popular Chicagoan. He used to be cheered for twenty minutes at the race track. When he appeared at the theater he'd get a standing ovation from the audience. For this reason I think it's well to remind the public that they love criminals almost as much as they love Mickey Mouse.

I know it's been said that I like murderers better than people who don't commit murders. This is a romantic notion. They seem to me to be the last surviving individualists in the country who look on society with real love. Their only interest in society is not reforming it but robbing it. They adore society. In fact, the only contented people I know in this country are the criminals.

B: Weegee, what was it that endeared Murder Incorporated to your heart. After all, you liked them, didn't you?
W: I was a freelance photographer and if I had one stiff a night, I could live, with blintzes, coffee, hot tea with lemon.
B: It wasn't an emotional pull?
W: Not at all.
B: Purely business, eh?
W: Purely business.
B: Who did you admire most of the murderers you've known?
W: I think Dutch Schultz. The first time I became acquainted him was when he was arrested after a shooting in Central Park. He asked me for an aspirin, so I gave him two aspirins. And then he was bumped off in a gin mill in Newark one night. After that they had him in the hospital and they wouldn't allow photographers or reporters in. I fooled them. I went out to the back of my car and put on a doctor's uniform. I had more uniforms than Willie Sutton, the bank robber. I sneaked into the hospital room and made some beautiful candid shots of him, paying special attention to the bullet holes in his chest. He looked like an awful dope, dead or alive.
B: Did you like your work?
W: Oh sure.
B: They liked to pose didn't they, dead or alive.
W: There was no appointment necessary with me. They got locked

B: up, I would arrive at the station house and make some sittings. However, when they bumped off, then I gave them all my love and care. Made them look like they were just taking a little rest. Then I would send flowers to the funeral home. Yeah, I had a special fund for flowers.
B: You must have liked them more than financially, because you went beyond the call of duty, didn't you?
W: Well, a gangster like Dutch Schultz, Jack Legs Diamond, they're arrested, they'll pose for a picture. Never any trouble. It's these young punks that see too many movies that cover up. They think they're Greta Garbo or somebody.
B: I knew one gangster, I wonder if you knew him. He was a gunman. The gunmen I knew, the killers, were a kind of sweatshop labor. They were the most underpaid people.
W: Not in New York. We have a high standard for killers here.
B: In Chicago a killer got about a hundred to a hundred and fifty dollars a week.
W: How could they live on that?
B: Well, they had to do a little heisting on the side. There was one fellow who broke all records, he got six hundred dollars a week from Al Capone. He was his head machine gun boy. His name was Neddy Herbert. And he was a wonderful fellow. He read a lot. He also kept a gorilla in his apartment, he called it his alter ego. He was a very educated fellow. Mickey Cohen hired him much later to be one of his gunmen. Neddy was shot in one of those Sunset Strip battles. He had a big record. But when he was shot he was ashamed of one thing, he didn't want to tell the doctor he'd been an alcoholic and had one kidney removed. He was embarrassed by having been a drinker once, so by not telling the doctor that, they gave him a medicine that knocked him off. If he'd have had two kidneys, he would have lived. You never heard of Neddy?
W: No. Of course, I think they have better murderers in New York.
B: Oh no, no. In Chicago, remember Hymie Weiss the fellow who used to lie and wait in the window and eat pastrami for three days.
W: Chicago for my money only had one gangster, Capone and he died a natural death.
B: He wasn't a gangster, he was just a boss.

W: No, New York had a little class.
B: Remember, "Nails Norton," the equestrian, who used to ride horseback?
W: Whata you a name dropper? Soon you'll start with Shakespeare and so forth.
B: Nails went riding in Lincoln Park every day, he wore pants just like a horseback rider. Once the horse threw him and he shot the horse.

Weegee stood up with his camera and started to take a picture.
B: Wait, I'm still alive, Weegee. Why don't you wait awhile. Wait two weeks.
W: I took a picture of Maxwell Bodenheim and he was bumped off the next night.
B: I'm not afraid, go ahead.

Weegee took a flash photograph of Ben Hecht.
W: This is a very special camera. It's a single lens reflex so I can see exactly what I'm doing. That way, I don't cut off your head. This was all right in the French Revolution. As a matter of fact I'd like to see them revive the gentle art of the, how do you pronounce it?
B: Murder.
W: The gillotit [sp].
B: Guillotine.
W: That's it. I'd like to see them in the streets.
B: More photographs, eh.
W: It'd be good for business.
B: Were the Murder Incorporated killers you knew, outside their working hours, nice guys?
W: Oh yes, they were very nice guys. Dressed nice.
B: Polite?
W: Yes.
B: Loved their mothers?
W: Always. Let me tell you one incident. I was at police headquarters and they brought in a young jewel thief. You know when there's no crimes happening, the cops don't like it. They don't get their pictures in the paper. So they set the guy up with the jewels, and the guy looks at me, he says, please don't take my picture. It will break my poor dear mother's heart. So here's what I did. First, I let a big flash go off in his face to blind

Birds of the Gallows

him, and then I said you should have thought of your poor dear mother before you went into the thieving business.
B: That's a very moving statement.
W: Talk about Murder Incorporated. They used to have a garage in Brooklyn where they used to practice on targets. They used to go around looking for nice, clean cut junior executive types to break in. You know what a junior executive type is?
B: What?
W: He eats in Chock Full of Nuts.
B: We used to have that practice in Chicago, but not in garages. The boys would have target practice on street corners against lamp posts, knocking off insulator things on telegraph poles. I've seen boys go out on Lexington Avenue in Chicago, sit down on the curb and pop away with their machine guns. During our four hundred murders we had in about four years, I don't think there was a single arrest.
W: Listen, that's a very low rate of murders. I used to get one a night and it had to be a good high class stuff.
B: But they were amateur murders here. Most close relatives, shooting incidents.
W: Not necessarily, you know what amateur murder is Ben?
B: What?
W: When a woman commits a murder, it's not premeditated. I used to study women. My favorite subject, women, especially after they commit a murder. Then they become human.
B: You specialize in murdering women?
W: No, no. Photographing women who have committed murders. That shows a lot of spirit. They don't take no nonsense from a guy.
B: Did you find out that if a woman once kills a man, if she's let go, she'll kill another man?
W: No. After she's let go, she'll usually wind up on a quiz program on Sunday nights.
B: Or here. If we could find a good murderess, we'd welcome her. If you know one, shoo her over here, will you?
W: I've got first call.
B: Weegee, what do you think is the basic quality necessary to be a good murderer?
W: A good murderer?

B: An efficient one.
W: Not to get caught. As a matter of fact, listen, I don't know how it is in Chicago, of all the murders I've covered, there is not one solved. Between me and you, I don't think the cops wanted to solve them. Why go to all the trouble?
B: Why should they? Because if they wait, the fellow that did the killing gets killed.
W: That's right. Its like a chain reaction. There used to be one murder and I'd wait all week. I'd cancel all my social engagements on the Bowery, of course, and concentrate on the follow-up murders.
B: Weegee, do you think there's any hope that the gentle and gallant art of "professional murder" will come back?
W: No. As a matter of fact, I don't want to see it come back.
B: You're a rich man now, eh?
W: No, I've changed my act. No more murders now. There's no more murders now. What I do now is movies. I spend all summer in Brussels photographing the World's Fair.
B: Is that a step up or a step down?
W: Always a step up.
B: The word "movies" always confuses me. Whether a man is boasting or confessing.
W: Listen can I make my own announcement? I know you don't mind, you look like a regular guy.
B: Plug anything you want.
W: Oh good. Just what I was waiting for. I was going to do it anyway. Now I got your permission, so much better. Listen, I'm leaving for Paris Wednesday on the Sabina, and I'm looking for an assistant. I want a girl with a heathy body and sick mind. Fits into my mood.
B: Who has not committed a crime or has committed a crime?
W: It doesn't matter. I'll cover up. I'll be at the Olden Camera Exchange, Broadway and 32nd Street.
B: Waiting for the girl.
W: Saturday afternoon, that's at 1265 Broadway, take the elevator up one flight.
B: Wear a carnation?
W: I'll know her, don't worry. If any woman is interested in photography, there's something the matter with her. I can spot her.

Birds of the Gallows 57

Anyway, if a girl's interested in photography, I'll take her to Paris. Just meet me at the Olden Camera Exchange.
B: Weegee, interested in photography or photographers, let's make it clear to the girls who are listening.
W: I can't resist a girl with camera. I feel this way, if a girl's going to go out with a photographer, get the best one, and that's me. And I'm alive and available.
B: I've heard that you think that Hollywood gangsters are very low grade killers.
W: Oh absolutely. In 1946, I had my first book, *Naked City*, which was bought for the movies. I went out to Hollywood and, they don't know how to commit a murder. For instance, they usually commit a murder, stuff the body in a barrel, and take it out to the desert. Who wants to go four hundred miles to the desert. By the time you get there...
B: The body's decomposed. But they do a lot of murders out there. Remember that time Mickey Cohen had his battle with the world at large. Were you out there then?
W: Mickey Cohen? There you go name dropping again.
B: I can't help it.
W: I tell you Mickey Cohen is the future of the murder business. Gangsters and so forth.
B: Well, I think he's their past. He's a very good boy now. He sells flowers.
W: Flowers? For funerals?
B: No, for weddings.
W: All the gangster friends could get their flowers from him. They could open charge accounts. Hey, that's a new angle.
B: Do you think a perfect murder was one in which the murderer didn't get caught? The technique wasn't required?
W: Actually, there's no technique required. As I said before, I never seen a guy caught that committed a gangster murder.
B: I've seen them caught and hanged.
W: Well that's Chicago.
B: Did you know any of the Hollywood murderers when they were here? Did you know, what's his name, Bugsy?
W: As a matter of fact talking about Mickey Cohen, who's your favorite subject, one night I was in a restaurant on the strip and who comes in but Mickey Cohen with ten of his hoods. They

B: looked like a type B gangster movie. The reason I went into the restaurant was to try out the blintzes. That's the way I test a restaurant, their blintzes.
B: Where do you get the best blintzes in America?
W: At the Salvation Army on Christmas day and you don't have to pay for them.
B: Sounds good, I'll go there. Go ahead about Mickey.
W: You must have been in Hollywood police stations. You go in a Hollywood police station and they have machines where you can get cigarettes and candy, apples and juke-box. Then you go up to the detectives room and they all look like they're ready to, waiting to be cast in a picture.
B: All shaved. Pretty ties.
W: The whole thing looks like a setup. Mickey of course, I think he added a little prestige to Hollywood.
B: That wasn't very hard. It was any easy job. Let's get back to the killers, did you know Adonis when he was functioning here?
W: I had a shooting acquaintance that did.
B: Neddy Herbert got in trouble with Adonis here, the big boy here and he threatened to knock Neddy off. Neddy went up to him one day and instead of hitting him, he spat in his face. And this was called to the attention of the people where they have a table and give out verdicts. And the verdict of the syndicate was that either Neddy's two brothers beat him up into unconsciousness or they would shoot Neddy. That's how he happened to leave New York 'cause the two brothers elected to beat him up, they beat the pants off Neddy. Neddy got up, recovered consciousness, terribly depressed with New York and he left with his family for Chicago to make good, where he did. He got that six hundred dollars a week. Now Weegee, tell me, what was the most vicious murder that you ever ran into? Where they shot people in the face, the belly?
W: One of the early ones of Murder Incorporated, they took a guy in a lot in Brownsville, they tied him up with wires and poured kerosine over him and set him on fire. The guy was still alive, mind you. As he tried to free himself, he would just strangle himself more.
B: Why'd they do that? They must have been sore at him.

Faces in the Crowd

The Sculptor's Father

January 13, 1959: Hecht interviewed actor Keenan Wynn and discussed the acting profession and Wynn's beloved father, comic actor Ed Wynn. For his Bedtime Story, Ben remembered the father/son relationship of one of his favorite Chicago comrades, Stanislaus Szulkalski, an eccentric sculptor and painter. Many years before, Hecht called him "the most celebrated and renowned dark horse of the arts who ever starved in an attic." Szulkalski finally won recognition when he returned to his native Poland in 1939, at which time the government established the Szulkalski National Museum. Three years later Hitler's bombs destroyed all of his work.

This is story is about a father and son. The son was named Stanislaus Szulkalski. In my book, he was the greatest sculptor and painter in my time. He arrived in Chicago from Poland with his father, who was a blacksmith. Stanley as we called him, was about five feet ten, wore long hair, like a page bob, and had a long nose. He wore a velvet or corduroy suit, carried a big shillelagh and walked as if he were running to a fire. Stanley was a tremendously powerful boy and a tremendous sculptor.

He used to keep a date with his father whom he adored. They met every Sunday morning in Jackson Park and would walk all day, sometimes as much as ten miles. After several years, when Stanley was about eighteen, he came to the park to meet his father but saw a crowd around the bench where the father usually awaited him. Sadly, he discovered that his father and been run over and killed. The body was lying there in the road.

Stanley pushed his way through the crowd using his cane. He picked up his father and slung him over his shoulder and he walked with him for two hours, carrying him to a hospital. When he got to the hospital, he said that this man belonged to him. Stanley was very poor, he didn't have a dime, he'd never taken any lessons. They asked him what he wanted to do with the body. Did he want it buried by the county? He said no, he wanted to dissect it.

For a week Stanley dissected his father, bone by bone, muscle by muscle. In later years, when Stanley became very famous in Poland, people would say, "Heavens you know a lot about anatomy, who taught you?" He always answered, "My father did."

A Silent Poet

January 28, 1959: Ben went through the mail bag. One letter writer solicited Hecht's view on religion and the then new phenomena of television evangelists (see "Viewer Letters," p. 195). Ben used his Bedtime Story to further elucidate his feelings on altruism, remembering a poignant Chicago incident.

I don't like charity. Not because I'm adverse to people getting handouts. Everyone likes to get unexpected Christmas stockings full of goodies. But I've never met any charity workers who impressed me as being quite human. They're stuffy, cultish, vain oddballs, who are getting some kind of queer neurosis in peddling charity. I also think charity is a very false thing. It has more dishonesty connected with it, mentally, humanly and spiritually than any other human enterprise.

This story is about charity and is sort of an illustration of the fact that charity is a tiny little sop thrown to fate and never really changes any man's status.

Many years ago in Chicago we used to have a stamptish, that means a weekly luncheon place. It was called the Tip Top Inn, where at a great round table some fifteen or twenty people forgathered every Saturday to toast whatever celebrity was visiting Chicago. I don't remember who paid for the meal but it was freeloading and very charming.

I was on my way there from a newspaper office one Saturday, accompanied by Rose, not yet my wife, when we were stopped by a panhandler who said to me, "Mister, could you let me have a dime?" I looked at him carefully. The fellow looked a little bit gaunt, had piercing eyes, a dark shirt, no tie, thin, kind of interesting.

I said to him, "I don't have a dime." Since I was walking over to the Tip Top with Rose, I told him, "If you come along with me, I might get you a whole big meal." And he said, "I'd love to have a meal." He hadn't had one for some time.

I said that I would introduce him as Rene Dor, a Belgian poet, and that he was to just eat and sit there and say nothing. When I ordered something, he would just say, "The same." That way nobody would see through the fact that he wasn't a Belgian poet.

We arrived at the Tip Top Inn and I remember at the table were Sherwood Anderson, Carl Sandburg, all manner of literati, maybe twelve or fifteen of them. And I introduced the panhandler as Rene Dor the Belgian Poet. He sat down and said nothing. It didn't take long because in maybe twenty or thirty minutes all the conversation was being directed to him. He was being asked remarkable and very trenchant questions on Belgian poetry but he never got a chance to answer because the literati always answered their own questions so he was able to remain silent. He ate a full meal.

At the end of the meal he rose as we had agreed and said goodbye. Everybody congratulated him on being such a brilliant man. He had not spoken once. He was gone for about five minutes and suddenly I felt a tap on my shoulder and the panhandler was back and he said, "Mister, can you let me have a dime? I've got to get my hat out of hock." I had to borrow a dime to give to him.

The Artist's Enemies

October 31, 1958: Ben's guest was George Antheil, a composer Hecht believed never achieved the recognition his magnificent talent warranted. Antheil composed Ballet Mechanique *and musical scores for a number of the films Hecht directed.*

Ben used the occasion to tell a Bedtime Story about the survival obstacles artists sometimes encounter.

I love artists because they're so rare. One always loves rare things. Like children. All human beings are born artists. All infants, all children are artists. They're adventurers, explorers, finder-outers, defy-ers. They believe in nothing. They try to discover everything for themselves and keep going until life begins to get at them. Parents, governments, institutions, clichés begin to slap it out of them. Slowly as they get to be ten, eleven, fourteen years old, the explorer, the finder-outer, ninety-eight percent of this wondrous tribe disappears. What's left is the other two percent. Vague, crazy, still stumbling around, still trying to find out, still trying to express themselves and not echo what's around them. These are the artists and I love them.

The artist has always two enemies. One is his art and the other is the economic system. He is sometimes able to lick the first. He very very seldom licks the second.

I knew two remarkable artists when I was a kid. One was named Joe Davidson, he became a famous sculptor and painter later. The other was Max Kram who became head of the Ziegfeld's College of Music in Chicago. When I knew them they were a couple of awful looking bums living in a fourth floor garret over a saloon on the west side, the slum district of Chicago, in a room that had no doors or windows. It permitted them to sleep, to paint and to pound the piano. They had no money at all and they lived off a free lunch in the saloon run by Gus on the first floor. They would buy a schooner of beer and then eat their way through the ham or cheese, whatever was on the bar. Although they never paid for the schooner, they were always chalking up another five cents. Finally they got to owing Gus about ten dollars, and got to worrying about their credit. So they concocted a scheme to ensure their further credit at Gus's saloon.

The scheme was that Joe Davidson painted an amazing picture. He painted all night long, a four by five feet picture of a cow and a landscape. It was a very moving picture that they knew Gus would appreciate. Then the boys went out and raised some money from among their friends. Joe made a passionate plea to the reporters he knew. We all kicked in twenty-five or fifty cents and finally the boys had ten dollars with which they insured their picture for ten thousand dollars.

They brought the insurance papers and the painting to Gus the bartender and told him what a great work of art they had. It was a masterpiece that had been sent from the old country and they were going to sell it. Gus looked at this painting and was overcome. He said he would take care of it and guard it with his life. He put it in the back of his saloon.

About a month later, Joe Davidson and Max Kram were walking

home, a little tiredly, having sold nothing, having no jobs. Suddenly they saw a crowd, fire engines, smoke and flame. The saloon was on fire. When Max and Joe saw this, they grabbed each other and began to waltz. They began to spend the ten thousand dollars they acquired without any larcenous intent. They walked happily and dreamily up to the fire just in time to see bartender Gus snatch himself out of the hands of his wife and two firemen, dash into the burning saloon and three minutes later come out, his hair singed, his eyebrows gone, but with the masterpiece intact under his arm. So you see it's hard for an artist to beat the economic system even when larceny is on his side.

Capote's Barking Raven

January 8, 1959: Actress June Havoc was Ben's guest, and they discussed actors and writers. Ben told a Bedtime Story about one writer's rather eccentric pet.

This is about an author, a very bright author named Truman Capote. Mr. Capote was in Italy working on a movie and living in a hotel in Rome and he had three little pets with him. Two were little dogs. One was a raven. The raven used to sit on his shoulder while he was writing and say, "It stinks, it stinks." This pleased Mr. Capote no end because he was getting the full brunt of critical praise in advance.

Now it seems that the raven fell in love with the two little dogs. He jumped off Mr. Capote's shoulder and began running around with the dogs and started barking. And when the dogs would bark, the raven would go "woof woof," run up and down the carpet, and cease to be a raven entirely. Like some of us do when we change professions.

One day this raven, who thought he was a dog, was standing on the window sill at the hotel. Something jarred it and the raven fell off. It fell on top of a passing truck. Mr. Capote ran to the window and saw his raven standing on top of the truck barking, "woof woof" and being carted away.

Mr. Capote kept yelling "fly, fly," but to no avail. The raven kept barking and disappeared. It was never seen again.

I Want to Go Home

December 17, 1958: Ben devoted the entire program to

> *answering his mail. After three months on the air, he was receiving between eighty and two hundred letters a day. Hecht told a Bedtime Story from a trip he once took to South America.*
>
> *In 1935, Ben Hecht vacationed in Ecuador. While in the capital city, he began writing a play entitled* To Quito and Back *concerning a writer who leaves his wife and runs off to Quito with a young society girl. Whether or not the plot mirrored Hecht's own life is not entirely clear. He is reported to have had an affair with a young woman of means during this period. What is certain is that Hecht's south of the border excursion resulted in a number of interesting anecdotes.*

This story is about a near adventure I had in the South American country of Ecuador. Its a very tropical, very hot country. I was riding down the mountain from Quito, Ecuador, in a car one day driven by a fellow with bare feet wearing white pants who assured me he was the leading poet of Ecuador. He was taking me to a ranch at the foot of the mountain where an American lived.

He told me this American had come to Ecuador about twenty-five years ago and that he was an embezzler. That he'd stolen a lot of money from New York. He'd been hiding out in this hacienda of his, with a couple of servants and a parrot. He said if we went there and both talked to him, we might possibly persuade the expatriate to dig up this loot that he had buried in the ground for twenty-five years and put it to some good use.

We kept driving through this hot country, through semi-jungle and finally arrived at the embezzler's estate. When we got there one of the servants came out and told us that the señor had died the day before and that they buried him. It's a very hot country and they don't let corpses lie around.

We entered the courtyard of the hacienda where the embezzler had lived for twenty-five years as an exile and came upon the hammock on which he used to lie. The poet told me that the dead man would lie on his hammock every afternoon with a bottle of booze in his hand. His parrot would always sit above him, watching and listening. The hammock was empty but at the head of the hammock, the parrot perched. The parrot looked into the empty hammock and kept repeating, "I want to go home, I want to go home, I want to go home."

The Deadly Chocolates

November 3, 1958: On yet another evening of viewers' queries, Ben answered a number of letters on America's role in the continuing Cold War.

Ben Hecht's education bypassed college and throughout his life he remained somewhat skeptical of the necessity of mandatory higher education. His Bedtime Story was a vehicle for his thoughts on the role of education in the American/Russian confrontation.

As with any Hecht concoction, the tale is an amalgam of memory and imagination. Like great jazz musicians, Hecht embellishes, judiciously.

I think the only way we can possibly lose a war with the Russians is to shoo our young people into colleges where they don't belong. Our desire to match the Russians in the quantity of education is playing to the Russians hands. The Russians are interested in turning their people into robots. They're interested in stamping them, giving them identical coloration, identical mood and thought. We do the same thing by sending everybody to college. The Russians teach them Marxism, we teach them anti–Marxism. The result is flattened-out, ironed-out people.

I was forced to attend the university for two days, the University of Wisconsin. I was a pledge in the Delta Tau Delta fraternity and I seemed to have insulted the university on the second day at lunch. I was asked to apologize before being allowed to remain so I fled, happily. I've adored colleges ever since because I've never had to be in one.

My story is about an individualist, a non-college man who once reigned in Chicago. He was the leading oil tycoon of the town and his name was Leo Koretz. Mr. Koretz launched the sale of Bayano oil stock on Chicago. He sold two million dollars of it the first month. Two months thereafter he declared a dividend of twenty-five percent and managed to sell another two million dollars worth. The oddity of the transaction was that there was no place called Bayano and there was no oil whatsoever. Mr. Koretz was a swindler. A magnificent swindler.

After selling six million dollars of this stock and then returning four million of the investors money to them as dividends, he gave a dinner for all his investors at the Congress Hotel. Among the investors were William Randolph Hearst, Arthur Brisbane, John G. Shedd, head of Marshall Fields, John Hurtz, head of the Yellow Cab company. Some seventy or eighty people attended, all very happy to be given this dinner by the great tycoon.

Just after the main course, newsboys appeared at the back of the banquet hall, and rushed in screaming at the top of their voices, "Extra, Extra, read all about the great Leo Koretz swindle." They carried copies of the *Chicago Examiner* the front page of which bore a headline reading "Leo Koretz exposed in Oil Swindle." The poor investors who grabbed this paper, paled and trembled. A lynching party was being formed when Mr. Koretz rose and said he wanted silence. He wanted to explain, that it was entirely a joke. He just did that to divert his guests. They were very happy. They began to laugh and finally ended up singing, "for he's a jolly good fellow," all arms around Mr. Koretz. Leo Koretz then sold another four million dollars worth of stock as a result of this little joke he had played. And lit out for Canada.

He was caught, brought back and put in jail. His individuality was very upset by what happened and he didn't want to face trial. And so he tried to commit suicide. They watched him very carefully, preventing him from carrying anything he could kill himself with. Finally he asked the warden if he could have a box of chocolates before the trial started. The warden thought that was alright and went out personally and bought him a two pound box of Larney's chocolates. Leo Koretz sat smiling and ate the two pounds of chocolates and died. He was a diabetic. And thus ended the career of a very fine non-college tycoon in Chicago.

Mrs. Rodjezke's Haunted Hat

December 11, 1958: Ben's guest was Judge Anne Kross, of the New York Surrogate Court and they discussed the judicial system from her perspective.

For his Bedtime Story, Ben remembered a woman he'd encountered a number of times in Chicago.

This story has a slightly legal background. It's about a hat. A hat that's haunted me for decades. A woman's hat with beautiful lavender ribbons on it. With feathers and all kinds of charming gewgaws on it. It belonged to a woman called Mrs. Rodjezke. I first met Mrs. Rodjezke when she was arrested for streetwalking. She got up in front of Judge Neimayer in the Harrison Street Police Court in Chicago and was given two months in the bridewell.

I met her a second time. Then I ran into her again. It seems she'd reformed and gotten married. Then I ran into her again. This time she had two kids. Then I ran into her again. It turned out her husband had died and she'd taken to scrubbing floors and doing washing for people for a living. Her whole job was taking care of her two kids. The society that looks after such troublesome matters was very worried about Mrs. Rodjezke being able to take care of these two kids. She worked hard, from eight o'clock in the morning to midnight. She scrubbed the Barkley Building and washed it, all kinds of things.

Finally the society stepped in and said she was neglecting her children. They took the kids away and farmed them out. Mrs. Rodjezke continued to scrub floors but she had no kids. One day, one of the rich ladies she was washing clothes for gave her a hat. She said, "It's springtime. Here's a nice hat for you to wear." It was this hat with the ribbons and geegaws on it. Mrs. Rodjezke put it on.

She lived in a poor neighborhood and people began to sneer at her hat, poor people like herself. They said she was going back to her old trade of streetwalking. Mrs. Rodjezke kept wearing this hat when she went out to scrub floors and wash clothes. She kept wearing this very fancy bonnet. And people began to say, "Take Mrs. Rodjezke's hat off, it's a disgrace to the neighborhood."

Mrs. Rodjezke remembered her two kids who had been taken away from her and one day she came home with her hat on her head and she sat in her little kitchen. She took a ten penny nail and hammered the hat on her head. She was found dead with a nail in her skull. A humanitarian coroner, I think his name was Doc Springer, had her buried wearing her hat. And somewhere a band played, "in her Easter bonnet, with all the ribbons on it, she was the grandest lady in the Easter parade."

Concerning a Red Velvet Dress

January 27, 1959: Ben interviewed Charles James, a designer who spoke at length on the subject of women's fashions. Even though Ben Hecht was highly opinionated, fashion was not his bailiwick and he used prepared questions for the interview. But for his Bedtime Story, Ben was able to relate a story that was quite apropos for his guest.

This story is about a sort of a ball gown which rather illustrates the power of fashion. It happened some time ago and involved a couple that got married. The young bride was a very beautiful girl and she bought herself or had made for herself a lovely red velveteen gown. Her husband fell madly in love with this gown. He insisted she wear it for dinner at home, he insisted she put it on when he took her to the movies, when he took her to the theater or to a cafe.

After about five or six months the couple began to quarrel because the lady didn't like to wear this red gown. The gown had become sort of a fetish with the husband. And the quarreling led to much yelling, trouble, and recrimination. Finally the husband went to a psychoanalyst. He told the psychoanalyst his troubles from a couch for some time. Then the man abandoned the psychoanalyst.

After several months he ended up standing on the thirty-second story ledge of a building ready to jump off. And the usual contingent of policemen, priests and curbstone psychologists were on hand to coo him out of his suicide leap. Someone notified the man's wife and she knew just what to do. She immediately dolled herself up in this fetishistic red velvet gown and rushed to the scene where her estranged husband was preparing to leap off the thirty-second story ledge.

The police got her in a window across the street where the husband could see her. And she leaned out of a window, raised her red velveted arms to him and said, "Darling I love you. See, I'm wearing your dress, look." He looked, was overcome and jumped right at the dress and landed in the street, thirty-two floors below. And she never had to wear the dress again.

Joe Feeny's Soul

November 20, 1958: Ben interviewed a group of rocket scientists. In addition to space travel, they discussed the effects of nuclear war. For his Bedtime Story, Hecht returned to a favorite theme, the soul of man.

This story is a parable about the imprisonment of the human soul in materialism and industrialism. It's about Joe Feeny, a man who worked in the steel mills of Hagerstown, Indiana. He'd had too much beer the night before and while working there one morning, he was crossing over a great big spitting vat full of molten steel. He fell in and vanished completely. Not even a smell was left that could be identified as Joe Feeny.

Joe Feeny was being buried but there was no body of course. The coffin was empty and the people were singing around it. At this point, God happened to catch sight of the earth and he said, "I haven't seen one of my children for quite a while. There's one being buried in Hagerstown right now. Bring me the coffin and we'll have a look at him and see what his soul has been doing."

So God sent his two angels down and the angels brought the coffin to the feet of God. They opened it and it was empty. God was upset and he said, "Go find the soul of Joe Feeny."

The two angels, describing themselves as journalists, returned to Hagerstown, Indiana, pried around and discovered that Joe Feeny had been converted into a girder. That girder was in a pile being sent to New York. They were able to identify the Joe Feeny girder because it had a little silver shine under its red paint.

They followed the girder to New York City and they waited quite a while. Suddenly they saw the girder being lifted in the air on a great big chain and thought God had sent another messenger, another type of messenger down. But no, the girder was fitted into the top of a great, big, skyscraper. It was covered with stone and with glass, and paint.

The angels are still there. They hover above this great big skyscraper, waiting for Joe Feeny's soul to be released from the girder in which it was imprisoned.

Is There Life After Death?

November 8, 1958: Actress Monique van Vooren was Ben's guest. After commenting on her healthy contours, he queried the voluptuous actress on life after death, and reincarnation. Then he told a Bedtime Story in keeping with this theme.

Tonight is the anniversary of a dinner that took place fifteen years ago in a cafe on fifty-sixth street. There were four of us at the table. One was Franz Werfel, a very genteel and charming novelist. Another was Stefan Zweig who was a very strong and rather bitter novelist. The third was the enchanting Mr. Ferenc Molnar who was the author of *Lilliam* and some twenty other vivid and witty dramas. I was the fourth man at the table.

The war was on and our talk turned to death. We discussed whether or not there was life after death. Mr. Werfel, who had written "The Song of Bernadette" believed there was life after death. He didn't think that God would waste so wonderful a thing as humanity and destroy it utterly. Stefan Zweig said that he didn't think there was life after death because he didn't think God would waste such a thing as humanity because it was so delinquent and so stupid. And that God had probably become very irritated watching it sit around through the many eons giving its own bigotry and its own bad thinking in the name of "God." Mr. Zweig was sure that as soon as people had died, God was tired of them and disposed of them. Mr. Molnar said that he thought it was as hard for a child in the womb to think of being born as it was for a man at a cafe table to think of dying.

All being articulate people we agreed that if any of us died, he would make the greatest possible effort to communicate what was really going on in the great beyond. We would report in English so all of us could understand it. Around midnight we parted and walked off in the street. Three of us to die. Werfel died of a bad heart. Poor Molnar died from the flu. Zweig committed suicide in Brazil. I am the only survivor.

On the anniversary of the dinner, I want to report that I have not heard from my old friends yet. But being on television now and communication possibly being a little easier than it was before, I want to tell them that I'm expecting to hear from them. They're welcome to come on my program any night they wish.

Lincoln's Ghost

September 26, 1958: Ben Hecht's guest was poet John Ciardi and they shared their thoughts on poetry and poets, past and present. For his Bedtime Story, Hecht told one of his classics, about Carl Sandburg and the ghost of Lincoln. Sandburg repeat-

edly denied that the incident had transpired but Hecht loved the story, true or not.

One of the happy failures of civilization is that it has never been able to kill off the poets. It tries hard by ignoring and starving them. Luckily the poets have always been able to survive. It is the voice of the poets, more than the historians, that tells us who and what we are.

Poets haven't any better brains than other folk, it's even been argued that they haven't any brains at all. H.L. Mencken, a mighty thinker, held this position. He pronounced poets "An infantile lot." Possibly they are, but stacked beside the adult lot they look to me pretty impressive. Unfortunately, there aren't many of them. Nature in all its departments produces more chickens than nightingales.

The thing that distinguishes the poet as a member of the human family seems to me to be the fact that from the first pyramid boom, the poet has refused to participate in progress. He has small interest in our mountains of machinery and counting rooms of gold. In the poet's book, the adults busy with their powerful enterprises and lethal ideas are wasting their time in a depressing manner.

The function of the poet hasn't changed in the past five thousand years. It's almost the only thing on the planet that hasn't. This function is to keep alive the animal world of sense. The world of his own nerve endings. The real poet writes usually exactly as would the turtle, the ape and the eagle if they could manage a pen. People have always had little interest in the poet's news about the texture of their bodies and souls. They prefer gossip, plots and war communiques. Thus its always been hard to be a poet, as hard as it is to be a fan dancer in a gale. And with all this, there are still poets. Nicely dedicated to sunrises, female symmetries and to torturing new meanings out of kisses, lamp posts and silos. My friend Carl Sandburg was one of them.

My story is about one of our great American poets, Carl Sandburg. I used to work with him on a newspaper in Chicago, the *Daily News*. At one time, Carl suddenly stopped writing poetry and began writing a life of Abraham Lincoln. He became a very confusing figure to us. He was very moody, brooding and he lapsed into complete silence. He wouldn't talk or answer any questions. His friend Lloyd Lewis was disturbed about this and finally decided to play a joke on Carl to see if he couldn't shake him out of his "Lincoln obsession."

We used to go to Lloyd's place on the dunes at Lake Michigan on the south of Chicago over the weekend. He had a little shack there. Lloyd hired an actor called Frank McGlynn who was famous for his impersonations of Lincoln. And we told him to get a stovepipe hat and a shawl, he had his own warts, and to appear at a certain hour around the dunes when Carl took his usual stroll at sunset. We thought if Carl saw this sight of Lincoln and we told him what a joke we'd played on him, Carl would become a little more communicative.

Well, at seven o'clock Carl went out for his Sunday evening stroll. We waited in the shack for about forty-five minutes. Sandburg came back, sat down, took a drink and said nothing. He didn't talk about meeting Lincoln, or even seeing him. We thought that our actor McGlynn who we paid fifty dollars for this job, had fluked it.

The next morning we discovered from Mr. McGlynn that he had come around the dunes as agreed, dressed as Mr. Lincoln. That he'd shown himself to Mr. Sandburg who stared at him for five minutes, said nothing, turned and walked away. We finally figured out that Carl had been seeing Lincoln all the time and that a hallucination such as we had arranged and paid for was a commonplace thing to him. It proved to use that you don't have to buy and pay for hallucinations for poets.

Sandburg's Lost Copy

October 6, 1958: Ben fielded questions from Columbia University School of Journalism students. With writing against a deadline a topic of considerable interest to the students, Hecht chose another Bedtime Story featuring Carl Sandburg. Mr. Sandburg also disputed the accuracy of this story. He claimed he did provide the copy.

This story is about genius and how it's no good unless it is in its proper place. The genius in question is my old friend Carl Sandburg. Carl used to work on a paper called the *Daybook* which blew up and he was without a job. A fellow named Jack Malloy and I interceded for Carl with our prince of managing editors, Mr. Henry Justin Smith on the *Chicago Daily News*. We told Mr. Smith that Carl was a tremendous poet. We neglected to say that he didn't write rhyme poetry.

Mr. Smith was a marvelous editor, he hired the most incompetent newspapermen that ever set foot in a local room. We were all writing novels, sonnets, cantos, and everything else. In fact the readers of our paper must have been terribly confused. I remember covering one murder story involving three corpses with a lead that began: "Outside the pizzicato of the rain..." This was the sort of preacher story we used to write on the Daily News.

Well Carl got a job on the paper. The city editor, his name was Beitler, Brooks Beitler. He was a very bitter, cold fellow, but a charmer inside, didn't have the faintest notion of what Carl was all about. He'd see Carl walking around in a sort of a herring catcher's hat and wearing button shoes. Carl was the last man in Chicago to wear button shoes. He was a brooding, moody young man with hair falling over his eye like Will Rogers. Beitler couldn't think of an assignment to give Carl and was kind of baffled by the fact that Carl kept walking around and sitting down reading pamphlets to himself.

After three weeks, a labor convention was being held in Minneapolis, Minnesota. Jack Malloy and I rushed to Mr. Smith and said, here's the ideal job for Mr. Sandburg. If there's anything that Carl knows, it's labor. He's been in the labor reporting business longer than anybody we know. So, Smith dispatched the mysterious new reporter to Minneapolis. Herring catcher's cap, button shoes and all.

The next day we waited for news from Minneapolis but none came from Carl. So we used the AP report on the convention. The second day, we used the AP report. Smith was getting nervous, but we kept assuring him that Carl was warming up and that when the story came, it would be a terrific one. The third day, no word from Sandburg and the paper used the AP report again.

The fourth day, tremendous things happened in Minneapolis. The labor delegates who were attending the convention started shooting at each other. There were three of four shot. One, fatally. There was tremendous pandemonium in the labor convention hall, and Mr. Smith turned pale. No word from Mr. Sandburg. We used the AP story on that.

Finally Mr. Smith said he better call Carl back. He sent a telegram saying, "Dear Sandburg, please come back to Chicago." And we heard from Mr. Sandburg instantly. He wired: "Dear boss, can't leave now, everything too exciting."

Purple Dancing Shoes

October 17, 1958: Writer Jack Kerouac was Ben's guest. Familiar with Kerouac's reputation as spokesman for a new group of literary and social rebels, the Beats, Hecht queried Kerouac on a host of topics. Kerouac, promoting his latest novel The Dharma Bums, *seemed to enjoy Hecht's inquisitiveness.*

For his Bedtime Story, Ben remembered another old chum, poet Maxwell Bodenheim whom he once called "Chicago's cubistic nightingale." The subject of Hecht's play Winkelberg, *Bodenheim fell upon hard times in his later life. He was found murdered in the apartment of a female companion just off the Bowery in New York.*

Here's a story about an earlier member of the Beats, a fellow from the old days in Chicago, a pal of mine who was a poet named Maxwell Bodenheim. This story illustrates the fact that artists, beats, nearly everybody pays for life with the coin they received. Sometimes it's a rather false coin but as the old song says, "It's not a diamond but the thought is there."

Maxwell Bodenheim was a poet. He signed his letters, "Maxwell Bodenheim 376th ranking U.S.A. poet." He explained his title by the fact that he had competed in three hundred and seventy-six poetry contests and never won a single prize. Yet Yeats, Pound, Eliot, Sandburg and a hundred others had crowned him a bard. People were always writing about him.

In Chicago, Bodenheim, or Bogie as we called him, was remarkably in love with a kid who was a dancer, a girl out of work, very talented. Bogie adored her. And his sweetie told him all she wanted in the world was a pair of purple dancing shoes. This was quite an order for Mr. Bodenheim who made on the average eight dollars a year. He sat down and wrote about a hundred poems, peddled them furiously, and raised twenty bucks. And he was going out to buy the purple dancing shoes when he stopped in her boarding house and found out that his sweetheart was dead with pneumonia. He was inspired now, he knew he had to get her the dancing shoes and put them on her grave.

So as inspired as he was, he went out and began to drink. Bogie drank and drank and wound up with a tart in her room without a dime left. And when he woke up in the morning, not a penny left, snowing outside, he looked on the floor and there beside the bed was a pair of purple button shoes with rundown heels that the tart was wearing when she was walking.

Bogie picked them up, stole them, put them in his pocket and galloped out in the snow to the cemetery where his sweetie lay buried, and he put these tart's shoes on her grave. And this is the sort of coin we sometimes pay off in.

Belle of the Ball

> *January 16, 1959: A rather eccentric writer, Alexander King, was Ben's guest. The acid-tongued King was virtually unknown until the publication of his memoirs,* Mine Enemy Grows Older. *After appearing on* The Tonight Show, *then hosted by Jack Parr, King became an instant celebrity. His irreverent comments on life, art, sex and celebrities, as well as his recollections of a self-imposed stay in a mental institution amused Ben Hecht.*
>
> *For his Bedtime Story, Ben returned to Bodenheim, and an episode that mirrored King's quest for attention.*

After I was fired from the *Chicago Daily News* for my censorship conviction, I started a paper called *The Chicago Literary Times*. One day I received a letter, an amazingly long letter and amazingly brilliant. It came from the Great Lakes Naval Station and it was signed "John Armstrong." And I answered, "When you get off a day or so, why don't you come and see me at the office because I think you could write for this paper." Instead of a reply from John, I received a reply from a captain. I was told that John was a lunatic and was being held for further inquiry into his status but that if I would take the responsibility for him, they would release him to me. I wrote back and took the responsibility.

And so John Armstrong appeared at my house on the South Side of Chicago. A very fine, handsome fellow with suitcase containing a novel that was almost six thousand typewritten pages long. I don't think he had even read it through. I gave a party for him. At this party was Maxwell Bodenheim, who was our leading Bohemian, our leading everything that was on the other side of the tracks. Also the most eccentric man we knew in town. There were also some musicians at the party.

When it came time to sit down, John Armstrong didn't sit down. He went to the phonograph, put on a record, rolled up his trousers as if he were in sailor pants, turned on the record and played only one part of it. It was "The Fleece Song" from *Mephistopheles* and he played only the laugh part. John Armstrong kept changing the needle and repeating the laugh over and over and over.

Bodenheim kept listening with horrow because he realized he's run into a real Tartar, this fellow would be very hard to defeat. After about five minutes of standing by and playing this laugh constantly, "ha ha ha ha," Chaliapin laughing on the record, Bodenheim got very grim. He picked up a glass of wine at the table and he drank it. And when he finished drinking he started eating the glass. And when he ate the glass blood started pouring down his mouth. He kept eating the glass, he even swallowed some. The guests eyes were diverted from the new upstart lunatic John Armstrong, and back again to the belle of our ball, Maxwell Bodenheim, and he finished the evening bloody, but in triumph.

An Unsuccessful Execution

November 13, 1958: Ben's guest was Henry Morgan for some rather witty repartee on audiences, performers, television networks, and sponsors. In particular the difficulty some performers encounter in trying to please everyone. For his Bedtime Story, Ben told about an angry crowd that was somehow converted.

This story is about an unsuccessful execution that society once tried and missed. One night my wife Rosie and I went across the bridge to Queensboro to see a fight. A promising young lightweight named Al Singer, who later became lightweight champion, was on the bill. We were following his rise. His opponent was a fellow named Kid McGirk, a club fighter, a ham and egger, who'd fought about two or three hundred fights. A man with two cauliflower ears, a potato face and a foolish smile still left in his half-closed blue eyes.

In this fight Al Singer knocked him all over the ring. He hit him maybe a hundred, two hundred times a round, yet failed to drop him. For some reason Kid McGirk was mysteriously elated during the fight.

The crowd booed the kid, they yelled, they laughed. It was the funniest, stupidest fight they'd ever seen.

At the end of the fight the referee announced that Kid McGirk had a statement to make to the audience. The kid came shambling up and began to talk over the microphone and said, "Dear Ladies and Gentlemen..." and the crowd began to boo and roar. They were terribly amused.

He went on. "I wanna tell you that I got an announcement to make. That tonight was my last fight." The crowd screamed and roared and catcalls and derisive howls kept up but the kid kept smiling and talking over the microphone. "I'm glad you liked my fight tonight b'cuz it's my last fight, see? I've had a wonderful time fighting for you people and I've always appreciated it." The roars of derision drowned him out but the kid kept smiling and continued.

"So I wish t' take dis occasion to t'ank you for having been such a fine public and having been so good to me." And as he kept on, the derisive roars slowly stopped. There was silence for a moment and the kid said, "I have only the memories of the finest time to take back home with me and I want to thank the public for everything they done for me."

Suddenly a cheer went up from one end of the stadium, and in about half a minute the whole audience was cheering. They screamed and yelled their approval of this kid who kept smiling and whom they failed to execute that night.

Kid Hogan's Sacrifice

October 29, 1958: Ben replied to his mail and discussed institutions and their effect on individuals. For his Bedtime Story, he spoke of one man whose life was affected by his belief in our government.

This is a story about a soldier I knew in the First World War. He was a Chicago lad, a boxer and a dancer, a newspaperman, quite a fellow. His name was Kid Hogan and he rushed off to war because he was tremendously inspired by the slogans. The slogans in the first war read, *The War to End All Wars, The War to Put an End to Militarism, The War to Make the World Safe for Democracy* and *The War Against*

Power Politics. Well, being against all those things, Kid Hogan joined up, long ahead of anybody.

I was going to Europe at the end of 1918, a week after the armistice and I'd heard that Kid Hogan had returned to this country, he'd been wounded. I picked up his mother and went to call on him before getting on the boat for Europe.

Kid Hogan was lying in a Brooklyn hospital, he was quite wounded. He'd lost both of his legs, one of his arms was off entirely, the other was half gone. His face had been destroyed but they's patched him up. They'd put a new set of ears on him, a new nose, a new mouth. He had one eye they started working again, a new scalp and new skin. He laid there looking like a doll, all pink and stitched up. Like a doll in a store window.

His mother and I came into the room. His mother saw the empty place in the sheet where his legs weren't and where his arms weren't. She saw this doll with a strange unhuman face. Kid Hogan, the patriot said, "Hello Momma, we won."

The Search for Gold

> *September 30, 1958: Ben's guest was real estate developer William Zeckendorf who examined the real estate business in New York and his plans for a number of new skyscrapers to dot the Manhattan skyline.*
> *The evening's Bedtime Story featured Ben's real estate experiences with a mogul of a different sort.*

Many years ago, there was a land boom in Florida. In those days, the land boom was a sort of real estate con game. Kind of a fixed horse race and everyone in the fix, but it had a surprise finish because everyone lost. I arrived in Miami at the height of the boom and collided with my first zillionaire, a man named Charlie Ort. Mr. Ort was president of the Key Largo corporation, which was a ninety million dollar project. At the time, Key Largo was a snake, vermin, bug and alligator infested swamp which no one had penetrated since it was first discovered.

I was Key Largo's publicist. For five thousand dollars a week, I swam the ocean and produced a thing called the *Key Largo Breeze*, purporting to come from Key Largo where only monkeys and boa constrictors were residents. Finally, Mr. Ort said that I sould branch out and help him sell some of the real estate. I told Mr. Ort that I could sell the whole island for him in no time and explained my project to him.

Key Largo was right in the track of the Spanish Main. I was certain that all the pirates from Captain Kidd to Bluebeard had buried all the gold on Key Largo. I produced a map and a conch captain. Then I flew to Havana and talked to a terrific fellow who was called Machado, he was the president and despoiling the country no end. I found him rather charming. "El Presidente" loaned me two thousand dollars worth of old Spanish doubloons and an old Spanish crock. I came back to Key Largo and with the aid of my bride and Charles Samuels, we penetrated Key Largo and buried the two grand in doubloons.

Then I wired some one hundred papers asking them how much copy they wanted on the discovery of pirate gold in Key Largo. Fifty of them answered they would take a column. Twenty said they would be sending their own correspondents and staff photographers. I had one telegram that slightly disturbed me. It was from Herbert Swope of the *New York World* and it said, "If you assure me personally that this story is true, I will be down with my entire staff." I ignored that telegram.

In about two days the water around Key Largo was dotted with small craft of every kind: canoes, launches, sailboats, even some people with water wings. They all carried spades and picks and were ready to dig for gold. Only they had to buy a lot before they could dig. And in about a week we had sold several million dollars worth of real estate except we didn't get the money. We only got ten percent down on the purchase price. We even sold a place called Jewfish Creek which had not yet been discovered by anybody, it was too far inland.

After I got to know Mr. Ort, I asked him how he had made his first killing down there, how he had first become a millionaire. He told he he had first come to Miami about two months before Key Largo, with his bride on a honeymoon and three hundred dollars in his pocket. He headed hotfoot for a fortune-teller's place. There he struck up a bargain with a woman called Madame Zubedaya. The fortune-teller would tell all her customers that they could make a great fortune with a man wearing a black derby, smoking a fat cigar.

Mr. Ort lurked outside of Madame Zubedaya's until a limousine disgorged a fortune-telling customer. He shadowed the fellow to the beach, waited until he got into a bathing suit. The man got comfortable on the sand, looked up and saw a man in a black derby and a big cigar asking for a light and looking rather rueful. The man asked him what the problem was. Charlie told him he was having a lot of trouble unloading some real estate. The man bought it for fifty thousand dollars in cash and that's the way Charlie Ort got started.

Politicians Past and Present

My First Meeting with Teddy Roosevelt

October 27, 1958: Ben devoted an entire program to his only political hero, Theodore Roosevelt. One of Hecht's first responsibilities on The Journal *was to assist the newspaper's political correspondents at the 1912 convention of Roosevelt's Bull Moose Party.*

I was a tadpole journalist the first time I met Teddy, sort of a legman for our political editor. There was a Republican convention in Chicago in 1912, at the Colosseum, a great big rambling structure. That was the time Teddy bolted the Republicans and organized the Bull Moose party. The only journalistic champion of the Bull Moose party by the way was the *Chicago Tribune*, which was the most radical paper we had those days in the west.

The bolt was amazing. There were thousands of journalists and thousands of excited revolutionists there. They had all marched two miles on the streets, from the Colosseum to Orchestra Hall. H.L. Mencken was there, Irvin S. Cobb, many important journalists. They were led by Richard Harding Davis, I remember, who appeared in a pith helmet as if he were in darkest Africa.

I was assigned to go with my political reporter to interview Teddy at the Blackstone Hotel. We got up to Mr. Roosevelt's room about an hour after he arrived. My associate immediately passed out on the bed, dead drunk. And two of Mr. Roosevelt's cohorts, one was a cowboy from Montana, were sitting very glassy-eyed drunk. Mr. Roosevelt himself had finished a couple of bottles of booze and was pretending to write a speech. I stood wide-eyed watching Teddy drawing gorillas and elephants on pieces of paper pretending it was words. He looked at me and said he wanted some rye, a certain rye. I knew where I could get it and ran over to another hotel and bought him two bottles of rye.

Teddy continued to drink and pretend he was writing a speech. I got very worried because I adored him and thought he would possibly enter Orchestra Hall like Leon Errol on rubbery legs, fall down and have to be shoved out into the alley. I was terribly worried. Finally he ordered me out of the room, said he had to do some more thinking and he had to be alone.

I went to Orchestra Hall and waited for this terrible drunk to appear, shivering all the time. The people were very nervous because two and half hours had passed since he was supposed to be due. Senator Hiram Johnson, who was a mighty man in his day, a great orator and a great liberal from California, was on the stage. He'd been talking for an hour waiting for the rubber-legged Teddy.

Suddenly in the midst of his speech, there was a hush and a roar from the rear. Teddy came down the aisle like a customer looking for a seat. He walked as steady as a Baptist parson. Not only did he walk steady but he hopped up on the stage himself, jumping over the orchestra pit. Teddy stood there with the phony pad of gorillas and elephants he was holding. The cheer was the longest and loudest that had ever been heard in this country. It was clocked at fourteen minutes.

And when the cheering subsided, this great wonderful phony Teddy Roosevelt looked at his adorers and said, "I was going to make a prepared speech for you, but I won't." And he threw the elephants and the gorillas in the air and they fluttered all around him and with his squeaky voice, he started. That was my first charming memory of Teddy.

In my time, Teddy Roosevelt was probably the greatest American we ever had and let's hope his like appears again before it's too late.

Voting

November 5, 1958: Election night. Ben read his viewers political queries and fulminated on the current election. After revealing that he didn't cast a ballot that day, he offered an essay on going to the polls.

I've always wondered what there was positive or constructive about going in, pulling a lever and voting for somebody you don't know, don't like and have no interest in.

I don't vote because I have other ways of expressing my alleged Americanism. Voting is a tremendously overrated gesture. It's encouraged of course by politicians who want jobs more than by people who want freedom. I'm not ashamed of not voting.

Voting shouldn't be compulsory anymore than marriage should. If you fall in love with a lady, you marry her. If you fall in love with a politician, you can vote for him. This mere pompous nonsense of pulling a lever and voting for this Tweedledum as against that Tweedledee, it seems to be an utter waste of time. We really don't vote for anybody. These two faceless, mindless puppets are picked out for us and we're told to close our eyes and put the donkey's tail on them. That's our vote.

I've always thought that the whole process of democracy, particularly the business of voting was an archaic and dangerous thing these days. It was invented for a country of a few hundred thousand people and we use it like we use our narrow streets for our traffic. We use voting now as a thing which one hundred and eighty million people may do. Is voting responsible for the hypocrisy, the looniness, the blandness, the double talk we find in politics? Is there any other way of running a country besides voting people in?

I don't think its the people that are at fault. It is the system of presenting nothing to the people. Asking them always to choose between Tweedledum and Tweedledee and get immensely excited over this idiot choice. This is what corrupts the mind. It makes people seem stupid to me, which they really are not. Just like giving them two different kinds of chewing gum and asking them which ones they'd like to chew.

But I still have feelings of envy. I envy all those marvelous Americans who were able to figure out which Tweedledum and Tweedledee to vote for. They must have extrasensory perception.

Hinky Dink and Bathhouse John

January 29, 1959: Alexander King returned as a guest. Hecht and King spent the evening crucifying all politicians within shooting distance. Ben's Bedtime Story remembered old fashioned Chicago politics.

Politics in my Chicago days was wonderful rampant skullduggery. You could see every crooked bone of it, every rotten piece of its inner working was visible and very gay.

I remember the citizens of Chicago surrounding city hall, three thousand of them with ropes in their hands threatening to lynch the aldermen who had been bribed, if the aldermen passed the streetcar franchise to Mr. Yerkes, who was what they used to call a malefactor of great wealth.

I remember when Mr. William Hale Thompson, who was more or less a contemporary of Teddy Roosevelt, was running for mayor. His idea of getting votes was not to make speeches or annoy people with ideologies. He used to put on shows all over town and the shows consisted of one naked lady being chased by an imbecile who had been borrowed from the local loony bin. The audience would sit there, applaud and yell and Thompson always got elected.

There was a violent sort of expression that people had, everything was crooked. You took your life in your hands if you went into a voting booth and voted for the wrong man. You got a bust in the nose.

This story is about voting. The two politicians I most remember out of my youth were a couple of aldermen who ran the first ward in Chicago. This was the ward where all the brothels, all the gangsters, all the dives, all the bums were. The alderman were called Hinky Dink and Bathhouse John. And Hinky Dink was a little, wiry, nervous man and the Bathhouse was a portly fellow given to writing poetry.

They held their grip on the first ward in a very practical way. About a week before an election they would import from two to five thousand bums. They would put them up in rooms, twenty in a room. They would feed them a free lunch at the Workingman's Exchange, which was a saloon they ran. And when election time came these two to four thousand bums would go to the polls and vote. Not once. Each bum was supposed to vote five to ten times. Bathhouse John and Hinky Dink always came in by a great majority.

There was one election however, where something odd happened and the forces of law and order struck. The two aldermen took the count for a while. About two days before the election, the Workingman's Exchange opened. No sooner had it opened than somebody noticed there was a head sitting on the bar. It was the head of decapitated bum. Quite a story ensued. The papers all began to talk about someone who cut this bum's head off.

Around three o'clock in the afternoon, the door opened, a car passed and another bum's head was thrown into the bar. This caused a panic among the bums who started evacuating their crowded rooms and fleeing Chicago like it was a plague spot. As a result of the bums disappearing, the forces of law and order won. Bathhouse John and Hinky Dink were not aldermen for the next two years.

However, when the next election came around, they were prepared for law and order. They engaged the entire police department of the city of Chicago to protect their bums. Outside of every flop house stood five cops watching to see that no heads were cut off. Ever since this incident, I've been very careful not to lose my head over politics.

A Great Land Runs Amok

October 13, 1958: Muckraking political columnist Drew Pearson was Ben's guest. Before the interview, Hecht delivered this sermon on the current state of affairs in America.

There are a million reasons why we're going downhill. I think the chief of them is that we're a nation run by old men. We're sort of senescent. We were always run by old men, but there used to be youth around. Voices of youth used to catcall, throw dornicks at silk hats, carry on no end and sort of frighten the old boys from getting their bromides jelled around us. We haven't any youth anymore crying against the old boys. They have it their own way and they're kind of turning us into a semi-senile state.

Of course there are lots of advantages to elder statesmen but one terrible disadvantage. Old people are very dangerous. An old man with one foot in the grave is not the fellow to trust with the future of your country. He hasn't too much personal interest at stake. Power is the only immorality open to the aged. Once they lose their interest in sex, lose their looks, lose their friends, lose their earning capacities and friendships generally, they hang on to what they have and work it for all its worth. Power is about the only thing an old man can wield. If they're not checked by screams and yells from youth who are usually the ones who get injured by this power, they go right to the top with it.

Today, it isn't juvenile delinquency we're suffering from but elderly delinquency. The old men who use atom stockpiles instead of switchblades. They're much more dangerous to the country than the kids who stab each other on street corners. We have only those old men in charge now. If we have any young people, they pretend they're old and talk like old men. Nixon is pretty young, but he's one of the worst of the bromide slingers and one of the worst of the old men talkers.

This country was once run by politicians who had no power. Who were looked on with more or less contempt by the country at large. Politicians who were treated as freeloaders or semi-crooks, people who were a necessary evil. In the days when I was young, this country was a very wild, exciting, freewheeling nation. The politicians were a necessary nuisance in the backyard who kept things going and made speeches that nobody read.

You don't need politicians to run a country by dominating, you need them to run it only by taking care of its business like your servants do in a house. They're supposed to be political servants but they're not. Now they're our bosses. They tell us what to think, how to breathe and chiefly what to be frightened of.

Our politicians today would make first rate floorwalkers. There might even be a good Sunday school superintendent in the lot. What seems to be the matter with them, as far as I can make out by listening and reading, is that the basis of most political thinking is try and figure out what not to say. The man who can be elected is the man who stands for less. A man with a forthright attitude is run out of the party.

In fact, there aren't any politicians anymore that I can think of; there are only political parties. The party behind the politician is like somebody who works a ventriloquist's dummy and that dummy is like Eisenhower, like Nixon, and like Stevenson became in the second campaign he ran. I don't think there's a man with guts enough to stand up and let out anything he thinks in this country, politically.

I would love it if our politicians were given no time on television. I think we have enough nonsense in the world without being compounded by these political bombinating clichés, which as far as I can see or hear or make out, mean nothing. I've not yet heard a politician say anything I didn't know well or hadn't heard when I was twelve.

In politics its very rare to find a humanitarian. Our government and all its institutions don't appeal to people of high human calibre. They appeal usually to job hungry ventriloquist dummy types. Humanitarianism is a very rare thing. There are very few people who are able to get an appointment who are also able to remain human.

Drew Pearson and Ben Hecht: *The Collapse of America*

October 13, 1958: Ben's guest Drew Pearson was no stranger to controversy. His syndicated newspaper column, "Washington Merry-Go-Round," which he co-wrote with protégé Jack Anderson, helped him gain a reputation as one of the country's most influential political columnists for more than thirty-five years. Pearson was considered the principal practitioner of journalism's highest calling — scourging the venal and corrupt in public life. Occasionally faulted for inaccuracies, throughout his distinguished career he compiled an imposing record of exposing wrongdoing. Pearson's detractors repeatedly attacked him for character assassination of selfless public servants employing falsehood and distortion but his network of sources throughout the government more often than not provided him with the truth.

Fearless, opinionated and self assured, Drew Pearson proved the perfect partner to dissect America's maladies with Ben Hecht.

BH: Do you think our present form of democracy can survive and can compete with the Russian form of government as it's being run now?

DP: It can't, Ben, unless we are really diligent, unless we really wake up. And that is going to be tough.

BH: Who's got to wake up?

DP: Mr. and Mrs. America and they're not doing it at the present moment.

BH: Do you think our people have been reduced to sort of a dreary silence by the fear that McCarthy and early Nixon and those boys pumped into the country? Do you think we've been taught almost not to protest?

DP: Yes. It's fear. People have been afraid to protest. They've been afraid to say too much. They've been afraid to admit Russia forged ahead because if you do that you were in serious danger of being called a Communist.

BH: Do you think in addition to Russia forging ahead of us technically and scientifically, it is also way ahead of us morally? Do you think the Russian officials are more honest, more idealistic, more devoted to their country than our elected officials?

DP: Ben I wouldn't say that because I haven't been over there in a long, long time. I just don't know. The CIA is writing a report to prove that there is graft over in Russia, as well as there is here. But certainly there is a compulsion, a determination, a drive over there. There's propaganda all over the place with the slogan of "Let's beat America, economically and every other way."

BH: Do you think we're no longer a capitalistic country, a democracy, but sort of a corporation run country? I read in your column where two-thirds of government money is spent on corporations.

DP: That's a fair inference and that is a fact. I think the figure is one hundred corporations, three-quarters of the defense money, about thirty billion dollars. And of course, television and magazines are influenced very heavily by the advertising of these corporations and so on down the line.

BH: In one of your more recent columns you mentioned that a great percentage of our long term admirals, colonels, generals and statesmen, who work in the Pentagon and around Washington are sort of at the economic mercy of the lobbyists who promise them jobs upon their retirement, thereby using them as stooges for their lobby work. Is that generally true today in Washington?

DP: I think its perhaps more true than ever. There are very few people in the military or government who don't leave and join some big corporation. And although they don't do too much, they have the entrée. They go back to the fellow whom they promoted. He's giving out the contracts and the favors and he helps them get in.

BH: Are the lobbyists more and more powerful? Do they run the Pentagon?

DP: They have a very important influence on the Pentagon. Yes, the lobbyists plus the corporations they represent.
BH: We used to think of free enterprise as the glory of this country and it's turned out that free enterprise consists of big corporations intent on looting the government, and hardly any small businesses. Has free enterprise decreased?
DP: Very decidedly. Little businesses are having an extremely tough time in Washington and if you get a contract to little business, why its a miracle.
BH: They have no chance at all then because they can't hire any admirals or generals or statesman.
DP: They can't afford to have regular lobbyists there.
BH: Doesn't Mr. Eisenhower look at all the gifts that were showered on him, from his first day of his presidency, as a form of bribery from these corporations. Like that house he was given, all the land.
DP: He should. But he doesn't. That's the funny thing.
BH: Do you think this administration is corrupt?
DP: I regret to say that if you look at some of the things that went on, well history will show that it has been. This administration hasn't gotten that much publicity from corruption. That will come later on. That's a sweeping and very damning statement but I think it will prove true.
BH: Is there any guilt complex on the part of people like Nixon, who's a bright young fellow and should know what he's doing. Is he aware that he's a stooge for big business? You interviewed him, didn't you?
DP: Not for some time. He doesn't approve of the things I've written.
BH: I recall.
DP: Nixon has a very pliable character. And he has a very pliable point of view. He can change his point of view. As I described him, he's a young man with a wet finger in the wind.
BH: I remember that.
DP: I don't know that he has any deep moral convictions. I would say that he did not.
BH: Do you think the press has been negligent in calling attention to the flagrant doings of Washington people?
DP: Definitely negligent.
BH: We have a Republican press then?

DP: Yes, ninety percent Republican.
BH: Well it never seemed to have much influence in Roosevelt's time. It was ninety percent anti–Roosevelt, wasn't it?
DP: It was about that.
BH: It hasn't much influence now. It apparently doesn't influence the people who read it...
DP: I wouldn't agree with you on that. I think it does influence the people. I think that's one reason for our complacency. I must say that the press has become alert and aware of this, but not nearly enough as it should be.
BH: Don't you feel that the father image nonsense that Ike imposed on the country, or was imposed on his behalf, is still operating? We've got a myth there and not a man.
DP: Very definitely. It's very difficult to criticize him and make people believe that he isn't the father of the country.
BH: How much has the placid and complacent Mr. Eisenhower been responsible for crippling our war effort and our democratic feeling in this country?
DP: I think to a very considerable extent that's true. When a man is out playing golf all the time, the public doesn't worry. Take this weekend. Three big things happened this weekend in Washington and the world. The moonshot. Another was the prolongation of the cease-fire in Formosa, next to the China coast. And third, to me a very depressing happening. A school board from Clinton, Arkansas, came up to Washington to see Eisenhower to try and get some help. The school has been dynamited, and he wouldn't even see them. Instead he went up for three days of golf and bridge with some investment bankers and company presidents.
BH: The psychiatrists call that sort of thing, parapathetic flight. Do you think that Mr. Eisenhower is so discouraged and disillusioned with himself that he's yielding on all the major points of which he came into office? That he is eager to turn his back on things he doesn't approve of and has a real distaste for?
DP: I don't believe so. I think he has moments of worry. I know in fact that he's sometimes thought to himself and said to his friends that maybe he shouldn't have run for a second term. I think what's happened is this, that his assistants don't bring the problems to him. They don't want to irritate him and increase

	his blood pressure. And so they don't bring them to him until the problems become acute and then they're hard to solve. They wait too long.
BH:	He behaves then much like a foolish man might behave who hasn't got enough sense for the job he's in. Is he a bigger foolish fellow than Dulles in your mind?
DP:	Ben, they told me you would put me on the spot, but that's a hard question. Let me put it this way, Dulles has more brains, but he doesn't use them. Ike doesn't have as many brains but it's a zero either way. Well not a zero, but it isn't good either way.
BH:	You and your fellow journalists have been banging away at the horrors and faults and flaws of Washington for the past five or six years and you've made no progress, as far as I can feel, in the public consciousness.
DP:	I don't believe we have either.
BH:	I hear mostly people who believe this sort of talk is horrifying, subversive and deadly to the welfare of the state.
DP:	Yes, you're right. We'll get a flood of letters after this program.
BH:	You're old enough to know. Wasn't it different once? Didn't people rise on their hind legs, scream, cut loose, throw boulders once?
DP:	They did.
BH:	What happened to the American? What made him such a slug nutty, dopey fellow that he is today?
DP:	Two things. One is our leadership. The fact that we have this soothing syrup all the time. This constant ooze that everything is fine, everything is right. The second thing. Well this is understandable. I don't blame the American people too much. They feel that well these atom problems are so big, so difficult, that they can't solve them and so why worry about it.
BH:	You don't worry about the American people having had it? Having run their race and being on the way out sort of, as a great populace, just as the British are on the way out?
DP:	Sometimes I do worry a little bit.
BH:	It seems to me that is what's happened. I've lived long enough to see America change its entire voice, its entire brain, and become the most scaredy-cat country in the world.

DP: I think that's a fair estimate. You put it more bluntly and fearlessly than I have. But I don't think hope is entirely gone.
BH: Isn't it dastardly to have fellows like Eisenhower and Dulles sitting in positions of that sort?
DP: It certainly is.
BH: Don't you think we could better if we boarded up the White House entirely and picked up some sane, normal man to run the country? Someone without any emotional and political things in him. I've always been for boarding up the White House and even Congress at times.
DP: If you boarded up the White House and Congress, you'd put us newspapermen out of work, otherwise I'd be for it.

The Devil's Song

October 13, 1958: After his summit meeting with Drew Pearson, Ben told a Bedtime Story about a political scandal from his youth.

When I was young, once upon a time, this is how we reacted to low and crooked dealings in Washington. I wrote a rhyme that was printed on the front page of a newspaper, at the time of the Teapot Dome Scandal, when the oil barons were seemingly stealing our country from under the nose of our president, Mr. Harding, and some very crooked senators.
It's called the "Devil's Song." The devil sings:

My country 'tis of thee, land of high felony, I now am God. Land where the oafs preside, and freedom roped and tied; shrieks from each mountainside, who pinched my wad. I love thy patriots in whose foul clutches rots they pilgrim staff. These wily senators, greedy, frock coated bores, prowling thy corridors, hand me a laugh.
My country 'tis of thee, sweet land of villainy, I sing elate. Land of the hypocrite, land where Christ and Mammon split, on every holy writ, half of the gate. Whoever fathered thee, sweet land of felony, weep now and groan. Thy woods and templed hills, thy rocks and tender ills, my heart with rapture fills, they are my own.

Thus spoke the devil in my youth.

Westbrook Pegler and Ben Hecht:
They Call It Justice

October 9, 1958: Newspaper columnist Westbrook Pegler was Ben's guest. Even though he won a Pulitzer Prize in 1941 for his exposé on labor union racketeering, Pegler alienated many readers with his ultraconservative point of view and scathing, often malevolent style of writing. But Pegler's columns were widely syndicated, and his work also appeared in the John Birch Society's American Opinion *magazine.*

Hecht may have not been in total agreement with all of Pegler's views, but he certainly admired the man's writing. Before the topic at hand, the American judiciary, Ben opened the program with a few choice words about his guest.

When I was a young reporter on the Chicago papers, one of my idols was a man of middle years named Arthur James Pegler. He wore a bow tie, a McCann overcoat, a rakish fedora, sported a cane and a pair of yellow gloves. He spoke with a cockney accent in a voice like a snare drum. Arthur James could hold a barroom mute with a flow of whiplash anecdote and crackling epithets.

Years after I left Chicago the name Pegler caught my eye in the New York sport columns. Only it wasn't Arthur James, it was Westbrook, son and heir to the banging Peglerian phrases. I'd never run into Westbrook in Chicago. All I recall of him is his father Arthur holding forth in Stilson's Saloon about a son he was trying to keep in knee pants but who kept sneaking out of the house after dark in a tuxedo.

Since first noting son Westbrook in print, I read a thousand Pegler columns, a mere fraction of his produce. In toto the Pegler column is as large a spate of tirade, lampoons, scoop and philosophy as exists in journalistic record. I read them through thick and thin. Even when they were socking away at some of my mental pets or chanting lyrically about swivel heads I wouldn't be found dead with. But I read them always with a grin. However I might dispute with this writer, there was always one thing I had in common with him, a love of language.

Westbrook Pegler was, and after thirty years remains, the best writer produced by the American press. This is not too glittering a compliment. The American press, with a few exceptions offers readers sentences like sleeping pills. We are a nation of limp print. Our journalists are seemingly fascinated by everything except writing. Mr. Pegler is different. He hands in his reports in a consistently fresh language. He is as opinionated as a holy roller. His columns seem bug-eyed with wrath. They achieve often an air of mayhem reminiscent of the old testament.

Sometime ago a provoked magazine wrote him up on the headline, "God's angry man." The article missed the boat on Pegler. Not anger but a love of words is what distinguishes the Pegler fulminations. However high blown with anger they are, it is an anger lovingly put together with bull's-eye epithets and cunning imagery.

So much for Westbrook Pegler "the two gun poet." There are other qualities that have kept his columns shooting sparks for thirty years. Pegler is one of the few writers of "think pieces" who isn't anchored in a stuffed chair. He is as mobile as a bloodhound. He chases up and down the country as if he were on the heels of a kidnapper. There's also the quality of his ego. It is one of the few journalistic egos that American clichés and American pretenses haven't been able to flatten out.

Underlying Pegler's thirty years of fe-fi-fuming is an unwavering and serene philosophy. This is the bright belief that a man doesn't belong to a government, a tribe or a cause, but that a man belongs to himself. And that the only duty he owes to his nation or his maker is to go his own way if he has steam enough in him. In fact a Westbrook Pegler amuck among our smug or obtuse convictions is democracy in fine action. The only unquestionable virtue of democracy is that it can improve under attack just as the great unquestionable evil of Communism is that it can thrive only in silence.

Well, Pegler's on deck tonight with his jolly roger flying and full, I hope, of instruction for all patriots. Peg, you write very excitedly about goons and crooks that sometimes get involved in running unions. You expose thieves, villains and varmints, constantly. Have you ever been attacked back, physically? Slugged, shot at, mugged or anything by any of these characters?

WP: I've had a couple of little parties, but nothing serious. I did all right.
BH: Do you get a lot of mail from the stuff you write?
WP: Yes, I get a great many letters. I've had thousands and thousands of them.

BH: What's the nature of this mail?
WP: Mostly affectionate. They approve of me highly.
BH: Maybe you can instruct me a bit. I don't get that kind of mail, Peg.
WP: You've got to have the right sort of clientele. Mine are very intelligent people.
BH: Let's talk about judges tonight. What about our judiciary? From the point of their use of power, and their mental equipment?
WP: Morally, they're a bit below the average citizenry, because they're politicians and they're selected for political reasons. Naturally, politicians are not superior men in morals. Mentally, they may be a little more cunning than your average citizen, otherwise they might have to work.
BH: How does the average judge compare morally and mentally with the average New York cop?
WP: No judge, no jurisprudence in this country lives up to the exacting standards by which the New York police force is chosen. They are very superior men. The requirements for their conduct are much more severe than judges. Judges can drink. But a cop better not. A cop is on duty all the time. He must maintain decorum.
BH: And judges don't. Do you think judges are inclined to abuse their power? Do their positions go to their heads?
WP: Oh yes, some of them are brutally arrogant. They maintain an austerity, an arrogance in their court which puts people in fear. You walk into a federal court especially, you tiptoe. These fellows up there are drunk with power.
BH: They wear costumes.
WP: They wear that European robe which was in the color of doom. It's an ominous, threatening thing to put people in fear because these judges themselves haven't got the dignity to command respect as men up on the bench. Even though they're clothed with these awful powers. This costume is not an American thing. There's nothing in any statute that provides that a federal or any other judge should wear that black robe.
BH: Have you come across any cases where judges abused their sense of power in hauling up people for contempt of court.
WP: Oh yes. I investigated a case recently in which an AP story said that a judge had given a man ninety days for contempt in

addition to eighteen months for violating of the Dyre Act. That was passed for the benefit of insurance companies, solely, to prevent the interstate transportation of stolen cars. It's no more immoral to transport a car from one state to another than it is from one precinct to another. But insurance companies got that put over to reduce their losses. Well, the man got eighteen months for that and as he was going back to the can some deputy marshall reportedly tattled to the judge that the fellow had called him an "old something." The judge hauled him back and gave him three more months. The story said the judge had remarked, "I didn't mind the blank part." I don't know what that epithet was, but I surmised. "But I do object to being called old," he said. I looked up the judge and he's sixty-six. Now that's old. I'm sixty-four and that's old. And he's older than I am. I wrote the judge and I got no answer. Today I telephoned to his law secretary and he said, "The case is moot, the man has purged himself by a written apology." I said, "No it's not moot. If that judge did sentence him because he objected to being called old, it was not legitimate. It sounds as though the judge was malicious."

BH: What would they do to critics if they got a hold of them?

WP: This law clerk said to me, "All the women in the back of the room heard it." I said, "What women? Did you swear any of them in?" "No." I said, "Did you swear the deputy?" "Well," he said. "It's all on the record." I don't know whether he swore in the witnesses or not. I don't know whether the man had any defense, but he lost three months of his life like that. Now of course he's forgiven him. The clerk said the sentence is suspended. Well, in my view, a suspended sentence is still hanging over him.

BH: Who makes up all these laws which the judges apply and the lawyers keep maintaining?

WP: You can't say "oh, these laws." Congress makes many laws, but the judges themselves go into a huddle called a "judicial conference" and they pass many laws which amount to absolute outrageous persecution of the individual. These are then supported by many essays and arguments in the law journals.

BH: And the lawyers of course delight in the more laws there are, the more clients there must be.

WP: Certainly. And the more money they make.
BH: That's true.
WP: Of course they need more judges because nobody knows what the law is. The Supreme Court is constantly changing the law. If it can't remain consistent and adhere to the law how is the rest of the country going to know?
BH: What about the Supreme Court judges? Are they of a higher calibre than the judges who function in the lower court?
WP: No. I think they're a good cut below the speed trap or parlor judge. On the whole. I think that Tom Clark is a pretty good fellow.
BH: What kind of language do they use? Is their language intelligible to you as a reporter?
WP: Absolutely unintelligible. Nobody can understand a judicial decision Even lawyers can't. They have to get people to interpret it for them. And then they disagree. This court was split five to four on a case which involves the vital rights of a citizen. You wouldn't want a ball game that way.
BH: Do you have any examples of the judicial words with you?
WP: Old weenie here, Frankfurter. This is textual. Here is exactly how Mr. Frankfurter's remarks appear in the stenographic record. Justice Frankfurter: "Mr. Butler, why aren't the two decisions of this court, the first one which laid down as constitutional requirement that this court unanimously felt compelled to agreed upon and the second opinion recognizing that this was a change of what had been supposed to be the provisions of the constitution and recognizing that and the kind of life that had been built under the contrary conception said, as equity has also said, you must make appropriate accommodation to the specific circumstances of this situation instead of having a procrustean bed where everybody's legs are cut off or stretched to fit the length of the bed and who is better to decide that than local United States judges, why isn't that a national policy?" And that is all one sentence.
BH: What would happen if you turned that kind of copy in?
WP: I wouldn't turn it in. They'd say I was drunk.
BH: Peg, what do you think of the United States of America?
WP: I love my country devotedly, I don't know whether that means the Alleghenies or the Hudson River or the Mississippi but I

despise and oppose the administration of the government of many departments of this country. I despise the Supreme Court and most of the federal judiciary. The Internal Revenue, the Department of Justice. I've been down there and seen these things work. I've seen the most evil conduct in the Internal Revenue. The Department of Justice too, I have no faith in it.

Why the Troops Froze

October 9, 1958: Following Westbrook Pegler's denunciation of the American judiciary, Ben told a Bedtime Story which epitomized his distaste for bureaucracy American style. His interest in John Paul Jones may have been piqued while he was doctoring the script of the film John Paul Jones, *released in 1959.*

This story illustrates my dislike of politics. It's about John Paul Jones, the father of our navy. Actually John Paul Jones had an awfully tough time getting a boat to fight in. After he arrived in Philadelphia in 1776 he finally got a boat.

He went out and encountered a British man-o'-war with a convoy of twelve ships. He sunk the man-o'-war by ripping its sails with his cannon and then captured the twelve ships. Mr. Jones took their cargo, sixteen thousand winter uniforms destined for the British soldiers in the colonies. He brought the uniforms triumphantly to Philadelphia and handed them over to our founding fathers, who were operating the first Continental Congress. And then his ship was taken away from him. He was told he couldn't do any more fighting.

He got very angry. He raged around looking for another ship and was finally told that only George Washington could get him a ship. He tracked George Washington down and found him in Valley Forge. Mr. Jones arrived at night. Mr. Washington was sitting around a campfire, sparsely clad. The soldiers, mostly in their underwear, were dying at the rate of two and three hundred a night, freezing to death. John Paul Jones said, "Mr. Washington, I captured sixteen thousand winter uniforms, this summer. Where are they?"

Washington said, "I heard about them. Those uniforms are being held by the statesmen in Philadelphia. They're being held in the hope of a rising market, then they'll be sold back to the British."

That drove John Paul Jones crazy. He raged against the duplicity, stupidity and skullduggery of the politicians and he said, "How can we possibly fight for such a country and cause when people such as that are behind it?"

George Washington told him, "There are two sides to the picture. There's one side of men that you see in Philadelphia who are eager to make profit and prestige out of an ideal. There's another side that you see here with me and my men who are eager to hunger, starve, freeze and die for the same ideal. You can take your choice as to which ideal you're fighting for."

Goose Steps in the Night

The Last of Quinn Lusk

November 17, 1958: Robert Briscoe, the lord mayor of Dublin, was Ben's guest. A decade earlier, both men were involved with the Irgun Zvai Leumi *(a group of Jewish guerrillas headed by Menachem Begin) in the fight to wrestle Palestine from the British and establish a Jewish state. Revolutions in Palestine and Ireland were the evening's topics. Ben told a Bedtime Story taken from his days as a foreign correspondent in post–World War I Germany.*

Hecht arrived in Berlin in 1918 at the age of twenty-four, spending eighteen months in Germany and Russia. Writing for the Chicago Daily News, *with his work syndicated to other newspapers around the country, Hecht used his reportorial expertise to try and clarify the events that transpired in Europe during these confusing times.*

This story illustrates the depth of one's love for one's country. I got wind of the story when I was a correspondent in Berlin, in January of 1919. The Germans had put out a lot of propaganda on what was called the infamous "Irish Brigade." The Germans said two thousand Irishmen had deserted the British Army during the First World War and they lined up as German soldiers and were fighting the British hand to hand. Sir Roger Casement, who was supposed to have led this treason was captured by the British, tried and hanged.

One day I came down to the lobby of the Adlon Hotel and found a letter, addressed to me. It said, "If you want to find out the truth about the Irish Brigade and the Sinn Fein movement in Germany, meet me in front of the Palast Cafe, at five o'clock. I'll be whistling 'Tipperary.'" It was signed, "One of the Irish Brigade."

Well, Harry Greenwald, a reporter for the *London Express* and I went to the Palast Cafe. It was snowing, and there were motor lorries in the street. You could also hear a little shooting, not uncommon for Germany at that time. The place was crowded with officers milling around in the snow, and we kept looking at the group. Suddenly I heard "Tipperary" being whistled. I looked and saw a young man in long gray-green German officer's coat. On the cuff of his coat was sewn the figure of a shamrock.

I said "Are you the fellow that wrote the letter?" He said, "Yes, let's go in here and get away from these swine." We went into the Cafe. He said his name was Quinn Lust and he sat down.

"I'm going to tell you the whole story" he told us. "But the first thing I want to tell you is that the Germans are the worst swine in the world. They're the biggest liars who were ever born." He talked like Luther himself. "There were only seventeen of us in the Irish Brigade and we never fought the English or the Irish. We killed more German officers and German men than any seventeen Irish men in the war. We were used as propaganda. We were given countesses and baronesses and marched through the streets with the poor flag of Ireland overhead. Now before I tell you the full story, I want three things from you. I want a promise of five hundred dollars. I want the promise of safe conduct back to Dublin and I want the promise that you won't use the story 'til I'm dead, which won't be very long because if I betray the Sinn Fein people, they won't let me live very long."

I said to him, "What do you want to go back to Dublin for?" He said, "I want to be among my own kind. Sit in a pub and feel the fog of Dublin in my nose again."

And then he proceeded to betray the Sinn Fein movement. He gave us pictures, letters, photographs, documentation of every kind. He had a suitcase full of it. And we gave him the five hundred dollars.

Quinn Lusk was a kind, happy looking fellow. He had a prize-fighter's easy grin and he was very grateful to us for getting him back to Dublin. The English colonel in Berlin agreed to put him on a ship and he left behind all his credentials, all his notes and documents, involving every member of the Sinn Fein movement in Germany, a lot of them in London and all of them in Dublin. And back went the traitor to Dublin to sit amongst his own kind. Harry Greenwall went back to London about three or four weeks later. I didn't use the story. I sat on it as I promised Quinn Lusk. I sat on it three months and then Harry Greenwall sent me a little clipping from an English paper. It said the character known as Quinn Lusk had been found dead on the outskirts of Dublin with seventeen knife wounds in him. Who was a traitor?

Who Really Won the War?

November 27, 1958: Ben's guest was his producer Mike Wallace, who he called the "King Cobra of television interviewers." Wallace had recently returned from a trip to the USSR and he shared his thoughts on Russian television, and the cold war. Ben returned to his days as foreign correspondent for a Bedtime Story about Communism.

When I was in Berlin in January of 1919, I interviewed General von Hoffmann, who was one of the four great German generals in the First World War. He'd been the general with von Hindenberg on the eastern front when they'd beaten the Russians. The Germans killed a million Russians and stalemated them for eight months. I interviewed the general and the first question I asked him was, "General, who won the war?"

And his answer was, "The Russians." This startled me because I know the Russians had been without guns, without food, without ammunition for eight months, lying in their trenches, and no fighting had gone on. I said, "How did the Russians win the war, General?"

"I received an order from General Ludendorff about a month before the end of the war," General von Hoffmann told me. "I was told to sign a peace treaty with the first Russian that could write his name. And I went to Bretzletoff and asked if there was such a talented type of Rusky around. I found one named Leon Trotsky with whom I signed the Bretzletoff's peace. Our objective was to release our million two hundred thousand troops from the Eastern front and send them to the Western front for the spring objective that was going to knock out the Allies."

"Well, when the peace was signed, we started moving our troops. We found out that during the eight months they'd been lying in the trenches, fraternizing with the Russian Bolsheviks, they'd been infected with this Bolshevism. We had to reorganize every regiment. We had to change the relationships of all the men and reorganize all the companies. We court-martialed seventeen hundred officers and executed almost as many. But we found after one month of wild effort that we couldn't move the one million two hundred thousand men because they would endanger the morale of the men we had on our western front. So they remained on the eastern front. This was winning a war by propagandizing soldiers, and it was what won the war for the Allies I'm sure."

Well, the general's story seems to be the story of the first great Russian victory in the Cold War that's going on today.

Dusseldorf's Dictator

> *December 4, 1958: Labor leader Mike Quill was Ben's guest. A colorful character who represented his men with great dedication, Quill was known to New Yorkers as the fellow who led the transit workers. Quill tried to explain the necessity of unions and their role in working America. Ben's Bedtime Story recounted a rendezvous with a labor leader that took place during his stay in Germany.*

This story is about a labor leader I once met whom I did understand. Practically the only one I understood fully, due not to the labor leader's stupidity but my own. This fellow was named Herr Eichhorn and he'd become dictator in a town in Germany named Dusseldorf.

There'd been an uprising and the Bolsheviks had captured the town. Eichhorn had been a street car conductor and now he found himself in the Burgomeister's Palace as dictator of whatever province Dusseldorf was in. He was running the works. I met him at the palace to talk. He was a very fine street car conductor who sat there beaming and happy at his desk. I asked him what he'd done since he'd become a dictator.

"Well the first thing I did is two days after I was dictator I doubled the salaries of all the street car employees." I said, "That's fine, what else do you do?"

"I doubled the salaries of the street cleaners, in fact I've doubled the salary of every man who works with his hands and the sweat of his brow in Dusseldorf." I was very young but a question did occur to me and I asked him, "Where do you get the money to pay all these double wages?"

He said, "I get it out of the Treasury of Dusseldorf." So I thought for a moment and I asked him, "What'll happen when you run out of the money in the Treasury of Dusseldorf? How are you going to pay these double wages?"

He grinned. "I'm not worried about that, by the time that happens I won't be dictator."

Rudy Hise's Demise

December 19, 1958: The Socialist Labor party's candidate for U.S. Senate, Stephen Emery, was Ben's guest. Although Emery had just lost an election, Hecht was still interested in airing his viewpoint. He considered Emery a fresh face on the political scene and wished there were a hundred men like him in Congress.

For his Bedtime Story, Ben remembered another German revolutionary.

This story concerns a revolutionist. I've known a lot of revolutionists but this particular revolutionist was even more certain, more sure of ultimate victory. It was in Bavaria, in March of 1918. Revolution had hit Bavaria and the Socialists had taken over. I arrived there as a foreign correspondent and met up with an amazing young fellow named Rudolph Hise. Rudy was eighteen or nineteen years old and a poet in Frankfurt. He was head of the Committee of Safety. This meant he had the job of disposing of traitors. Rudy carried two carbines, four or five pistols and about six hand grenades in his belt. And in addition to all his other military equipment he had a small bottle full of nitroglycerine. When we got to be friends Rudy explained to me in rather poetical words that he was sure of victory. That nothing could defeat this revolution. Because come what might, let the Prussians come in with General Noske and his troops, and that he, Rudy Hise, would win the revolution for the Soviets of Bavaria. He said, "The reason I'll win it is because of this little bottle in my hand. You watch what's going to happen."

I was there and I watched. The Prussian troops came in under General Noske and the one hundred thousand revolutionists dwindled to about a thousand when the guns started. The revolution was overthrown in a day or two. Rudy Hise was among those captured. They brought him to the Wittelsbacher palais where the Prussian soldiers and their generals had headquartered themselves. They brought Rudy Hise there to get the names of the revolutionists from him so they could capture and punish them.

Rudy waited about an hour until all the generals arrived. He stood there and listened to them. And then he suddenly smiled and said "Well, gentlemen, I am going to win this revolution. You who are here represent the pick and flower of Prussian militarism and you're all going to die with me in the revolution. The revolution is going to live because with you gone, there's no chance of Prussia winning over Bavaria again."

As they were about to shoot him, he took out his little bottle of nitroglycerine and he said, "If you shoot me, I drop this and you all go." Then, after about a minute's silence, Rudy said, "Long live the Soviets of Bavaria," and he hurled his bottle on the floor. The bottle broke, there was no explosion, and a hundred guns ripped Rudy to death.

The Dictator of Art

January 30, 1959: Ben's final broadcast featured surrealistic artist Salvador Dalí. Their no-holds-barred dialogue touched on sex, art and creativity. Ben's Bedtime Story remembered an incident concerning great art from his days as a foreign correspondent.

This story is about an artist I once knew in Munich. He was a marvelous artist from the point of view of political importance. His name was Titus Tautz and he was head of the Bolshevik state of Bavaria, when the Spartacists won it away for a while. They appointed Herr Tautz as dictator of art for the Soviets of Bavaria. Herr Tautz was also one of the founders of the Dadaist movement in Germany. The Dadaists were a group of artists who were engaged in ridiculing and deriding the civilization which had exploded the continent in the first world war.

Mr. Tautz staged a meeting after becoming the dictator of art and when he addressed the meeting, he said that the next night, he wanted all good patriots and all lovers of true art to assemble. They were going to march on the Rembrandt Museum in Munich, set fire to it and burn up all the Rembrandts because they were Kitsch. They were unworthy of remaining in the world. I was a newspaper correspondent and this news excited me. I joined the parade the next night about nine o'clock. There were about two thousand men and women, and myself, the only American correspondent. We started marching with flaming torches down the avenue towards the Rembrandt museum. I remember the first mile of our march we lost about a thousand of our paraders. The second mile, the parade began to thin out, more and more. When we finally got to the Rembrandt museum there were thirty or forty of us left and only three or four torches.

But Titus Tautz was still leading and I was still waiting for the great big scoop of the Rembrandt museum burning down. Mr. Tautz skipped up the steps, paused with torch in hand, and then turned to his few admiring followers said, "While marching along I have changed my mind about burning up Rembrandt. Rembrandt represents one of the lower watermarks of human endeavor. The worst possible kind of art but he has a certain historical value, and I think its wrong for Europeans to destroy historical stepping stones so we will not burn the museum tonight."

The museum remained, I lost my story, and Rembrandt is still intact.

Docility and Mass Murder

November 5, 1958: Ben's response to his voluminous mailbag included another statement of his attitude towards Germans (see "Viewer Letters," p. 195). For his Bedtime Story Ben vividly remembered a time when he experienced two distinctive German idiosyncrasies.

I was a foreign correspondent in Germany in 1919 and 1920. One great event occurred. I witnessed many great events but this was particularly important.

A revolution hit Berlin. The Spartacists, that was the name the Communists were using, the Spartacists staged a revolution. They captured the Polizeiprasidium in Alexanderplatz. There were eight thousand of them. They barricaded themselves behind boxes and behind crates and barbed wire and lay there with their guns. And they vowed they'd never surrender until they'd overthrown the capitalistic country of Germany.

It was a country which had just elected its first president, a social democrat called Fritz Ebert, who used to be a harness maker. Phillip Scheidemann was the prime minister and a preview Adolph Hitler named General Noske was in charge of their little army. So I went down to interview these revolutionists. I was a very young correspondent, I'd never seen revolutionists before. I was really impressed by them. I thought, these are really hot people, they're going to fight for something. They lay behind their barricades for three or four weeks.

One morning, Dick Little and I were coming home from someplace. Richard Henry Little was a real and famous correspondent with many datelines under his belt: Port Arthur, the Bohr War and the China Boxer Rebellion. It was six AM and we saw a strange group of men walking down under Der Linden. They were led by General Ludendorff, Admiral von Tirpitz, and General von Hoffmann, the German who signed the Bretzletoff peace. There were about fifty, sixty, seventy, I don't quite remember. They were all men of rank, colonels and over. They were in their parade uniforms and wore sidearms consisting of very ornamental swords. Rather heavy waisted, they walked a bit oddly. But they marched bravely down Der Linden, two or three miles to Alexanderplatz and there they confronted the eight thousand rabid revolutionists behind their barricades.

They ordered the revolutionists to surrender. Four of the men stepped out, General von Hoffmann among them, and in violent, exacerbated German demanded that these enemies of the state give up. And the enemies of the state gave up in ten minutes. Eight thousand German people surrendered to these seventy-five German officers.

A month later I received a tip about a story. It was about one in the morning and I got a pair of opera glasses and went to a place called Moabit Prison on the outskirts of Berlin. I climbed a tree because I knew they wouldn't let me in the prison. From the tree I was able to overlook the yard of Moabit Prison. I stayed in the tree for almost three hours and while there, I saw two thousand men, women and kids brought out. They were handcuffed together in groups of four. The two thousand were among the prisoners the seventy-five officers had taken. They had not been tried but on this night they were all killed. They were executed by four machine guns that went after them as they walked up and down the prison yard.

I reported this story and wrote it for the *Chicago Daily News* and ninety other newspapers. I was denounced and ordered out of Germany and had to go into hiding for ten days. Finally when they had their first national assembly in Weimar, I sneaked into Weimar and my story was verified. Hugo Haase, head of the Independent Social Party stood on the stage of the Stadt's theatre at the first meeting of the general assembly of Germany and his speech consisted of reciting the two thousand names of the men, women and children who'd been executed in Moabit Prison yard.

Now there were no Jews among those people who were killed. There was no anti-Semitism in the Germany that I covered for two years. But the Germans that night were happy to exercise their two favorite talents, one, docility, and two, mass murder.

Lotus Land Gold Miners

My First Oscar

December 12, 1958: Writer Budd Schulberg was Ben's guest (see "Ben Hecht and Budd Schulberg," p. 147).
By 1958, Hecht's screenwriting assignments were at a minimum. The studio system as he knew it had disintegrated. Although he wrote or doctored one or two scripts a year, Hecht was essentially Hollywood history.
Ben told a Bedtime Story concerning Schulberg's father, B.P. Schulberg, who was head of production for Paramount Pictures when Hecht got his start in motion pictures, in 1926. The first film he wrote, Underworld, *was an immediate hit.*

When I came to Hollywood I was a novelist. I fancied myself as a literary fellow and thought I was going to startle this silent movie town. I'd written *Erik Dorn, Gargoyles, Humpty Dumpty* and eight or ten other books. However, when I arrived in Hollywood I discovered it was a land of tremendous genius and literature. Everybody's library was full of Marcel Proust, Remy de Gourmont, Gide was current, Cocteau, and Dostoyevsky was lying around on the floor. I quickly realized I would make no impression as a literary man.

On my third day in Hollywood, I announced myself as an expert on crime. This did startle the town because there had never been any crime movies done in Hollywood. Nervously, they allowed me to write a movie called *Underworld*. I wrote the picture for B.P. Schulberg. Budd's father was the very talented producer in charge of Paramount production at the time.

I wrote my first screenplay exactly as I would write a short story that I wouldn't care to sign. I used to write those kinds of stories for *Argosy* and *Blackcat* magazine in an afternoon in a newspaper office to pick up another two hundred dollars. After I wrote *Underworld* I left town.

About six months later I was told it was opening at the Paramount Theatre. I went to see it and was horrified because there'd been a few changes made. They may have been for the better or not, I don't know, but a change to an author is like the removal of an arm or the growing of another head. I wired Mr. Schulberg who up to that time had been a great pal of mine. "Dear B.P., read my telegram. I saw *Underworld*. You poor hams."

The next step in *Underworld* was that I was notified I'd won an Oscar, as they got be called, from the Academy. I was the first writer to win an Oscar. This further outraged me. The idea of receiving a prize for this piece of good hack work was annoying because I was a man of letters. I returned the Oscar with an indignant telegram saying I refused to be honored by Hollywood which I considered an outhouse on the Parnassus. Doug Fairbanks who was president of the Academy of Arts and Sciences, or whatever they called themselves, was a very nice fellow. He sent me the Oscar regardless and I still have it. It's one of three that I won. I use it as a doorstop.

Now, the idea that I was responsible to a considerable extent, as much as any writer, in starting this low grade renaissance of gunplay that has swept the screens of the world has made me feel a little guilty during the thirty years that have passed. Since *Underworld* there have been possibly five thousand gangster pictures.

I used to rail against Hollywood because four-fifths of the work I did for Hollywood would have been better had I not signed it. It would have been better had it not been done. But it made a lot of money. Some people got rich and it had one good value. People who couldn't read, couldn't go to the theatre, did find something to enjoy.

I once had a conversation with Adolph Zukor, the man behind Paramount Pictures that proves all my railing against Hollywood was unnecessary. Mr. Zukor sat by in Miami Beach one night listening to me rage against somebody, I forget who it was. I told of all his horrible flaws, his vital idiocies. How the man should have been put in a loony bin or an idiot farm. Mr. Zukor sat and listened to me. In fact, he was the only one at the table listening. When I got all through, he said, "I'm surprised at your being so stupid Mr. Hecht."

"Why Mr. Zukor?"

"If this man is half as bad as you're making out he is, why are you wasting time pushing him down. He'll fall down. You don't need to push."

That seems to me what's happened to Hollywood. It would have disappeared without my attacks on it.

S.J. Perelman and Ben Hecht: *The Hollywood System*

November 6, 1958: Humorist S.J. Perelman, who once described Hollywood as "a dreary industrial town controlled by hoodlums of enormous wealth," was Ben's guest. Mr. Perelman, whose writing made people laugh out loud, also paid some Hollywood screenwriting dues, including several memorable films for the Marx Brothers. Perelman was one of the writers on the 1931 classic Monkey Business, *which was taken from a story by Ben. (In 1952, Hecht co-wrote another comedy named* Monkey Business, *directed by Howard Hawks and starring Cary Grant and Marilyn Monroe.)*

Hecht welcomed Perelman enthusiastically, always savoring an opportunity to further lambaste his former antagonists.

BH: What Hollywood horrors that we met stand out in your memory?

SP: Principally the producers. I remember them with a sort of hard, gemlike loathing. Whom do you remember?

BH: I too remember the producers as being a stone wall between me and achievement of every kind. Do you remember any producers that ever helped you any?

SP: Not in the slightest. In fact I can say without qualification that every dreadful memory that I have circles around a producer.

BH: I found the reason for this partly due to the writers. I remember noticing the writers were being shoved out of Hollywood in the early days because they had small chins and big heads. Because they had girl children and couldn't speak up in a baritone in story conference. The fellow with the baritone and the instant decision took over. This usually turned out to be an ex–junk man or ex-salesman of some kind.

SP: Or a vaudeville booker. There were a great many vaudeville bookers in those days.

BH: They were the ones that could speak, as they called it, off the cuff. What was your attitude towards the Hollywood bosses? Did they frighten you when you were working in Hollywood?

SP: Completely. I was tongue-tied walking on my heels. I was never able to offer a constructive suggestion. In other words a mensch who did not belong there, let's face it.

BH: Well nevertheless, they kept paying us. I know they paid us quite well. Why do you suppose they paid us so much money when they despised us so?

SP: Was it real money though? I found that it was sort of Coney Island candy.

BH: It melted.

SP: That's right. It would disappear when you reached San Bernadino. Do you ever notice that?

BH: I never got that far. I can remember it disappearing when a member of the family went shopping and usually came back with a chateau, a yacht or some unprincipled piece of property.

SP: Yes it was an ugly fact that while you sat in those hot little cells your wife was out at I. Magnins or the Broadway Hollywood store buying acres, whole floors full of French provincial furniture. Stuff that you never saw because it was repossessed before you even got home.

BH: I also remember spending a lot of money on cigars. The only thing I ever bought in Hollywood that I'd been unaccustomed to was cigars. I discovered they had dollar cigars in Hollywood. It was fun to go out and buy five hundred of them and distribute them to the people on the set. Did the Hollywood major factotums leave an indelible memory on you as they did on me? Do you still remember them with this firm loathing of yours?

SP: Yes. Everything else changes. But I find there are still three or four individuals at Metro and Paramount and 20th who are kind of monsters in memory. They stand there looking at me with their basilisk eyes whenever I wake up at three or four in the morning. I let out quite a shriek because there they are at the foot of my bed.

BH: They destroyed more than the writers and this was poetic justice of a sort. They finally ended up destroying themselves and the studios.

SP: But oddly enough, they arose phoenix-like from their own ashes. These producers became agents and the agents turned into producers. It's some sort of strange biological reproductive process.

BH: Well there's another thing, the money they got wasn't melting money. Somehow they kept it.

SP: You're so right.

BH: I have never known a poor producer like I've known a poor writer. In fact, two of them are sitting here.

SP: You're so right. Let's wrap a shawl around the pair of us and sell matches, shall we?

BH: If we can buy any matches. What were the chief fears in Hollywood when you worked there? Aside from the producers, did you have any other ugly fears? Did you tremble at the thought of the critics, the thought of misusing your talent? You weren't a member of that group who thought of themselves as geniuses in bondage though, were you? You had other places to sell your wares.

SP: I was constantly heartened by the fact that I knew I could always get a passport to Europe on whatever remained of this money. And I immediately fled for France or wherever.

BH: But before we seem to be a little too fat-headed about our own calling as writers...

SP: Yes there's a little note of self-congratulations in here, isn't there.

BH: Let's remember what sort of writers there were in Hollywood. I can remember out of a hundred writers, possibly five who could write a legible letter. I can remember writers who got a thousand to two thousand dollars a week who couldn't sell a piece to a magazine for fifty bucks or twenty-five cents. That's my memory of the writers.

SP: Yes, and their letters when they wrote them were masterpieces full of what was called the Hollywood subjunctive: I'm writing you about a man which he has undoubtedly the greatest personality of our time...

BH: What do you think the producers had in mind, if they had a mind? What was the mental image they had in mind that they called box office? To whom were they selling this stuff that we were writing?

SP: Well, the eleven-year-old mind. Remember the well-known

BH: eleven-year-old mind that we were always supposed to be writing for?
BH: I never could reach that high.
SP: I recall that Groucho Marx, in the days that I worked for him, always used to ask us, "Do you think that the barber in Peru will understand?" He meant the barber in Peru, Indiana. Would the jokes get through to this putative tonsorial artist.
BH: It's harder working for comedians. I worked for one, Bob Hope. It was like working for a thrashing machine with yourself inside. You couldn't get much writing done.
SP: But an insecure thrashing machine because most of these bravos believed they were all through and washed up and that your jokes wouldn't help them. Do you recall?
BH: I remember that. Did you ever have any contact with an organization of literati known as the Screenwriters Guild?
SP: What are you saying? We were all union members of same. We had to belong to it.
BH: It's strange though because my memory of the place is that next to the producer, the most implacable enemy I had in Hollywood was the Screenwriters Guild. Did you have any troubles with them? Did they ever help you?
SP: Searching my memory, and believe me I'm searching it faithfully, I can tell you I don't recall any such occasion.
BH: I wrote a book called *Child of the Century* and there were some mild remarks in there about movies and what might be wrong with them. The book was hardly off the presses when a statement came out from the Screenwriters Guild signed by its president saying that I should be barred from Hollywood. That I had bitten the hand that fed me, which is a fine dog-and-master psychology for a writer to have. I was thrown out on every credit grab I tried. I never was upheld by them. Were you?
SP: Not that I can recall. In fact, au contraire. If you also recall, there was a point when the president of this organization was a man named Borden Chase. He had taken the name Borden from the New York milk company and Chase from the national bank. What his real name was nobody ever knew.
BH: Do you remember Ricardo Cortez who was named after two cigars by a director? The Ricardo cigar and the Cortez cigar? They picked it out in the commissary at Paramount and gave

him this name, which he's made good on ever since. I hear, we all hear who read papers, that movies are becoming our best ambassadors abroad. That they present an America to the world which makes the whole world envious of us, and hopes to become like us. You've travelled an awful lot. Is this true?

SP: Well if you mean that any given Siamese sitting in Bangkok and looking at a "B gunman picture" made in Hollywood regards this as symptomatic of our civilization, I can tell you he does. Regrettably, far and wide across the world, pictures of just this type are regarded as accurate pictures of our society.

BH: I'm glad somebody thinks they're accurate.

SP: That's something else to worry about at night.

BH: When we were young, do you remember the movies and the movie people beginning with Harry Langdon and Ben Turpin, Buster Keaton, Harold Lloyd, Charlie Chaplin, a dozen other great comedians? Where are they, what shows have they joined and why?

SP: I don't know. Like everyone else, in my quest for entertainment, I visit the my local show shop. The nabe as it's called. I'm continually and constantly appalled by the garbage that peers out at me from the screen.

BH: I'm smarter than you. I haven't been inside a movie theatre for two years. I've preserved my original admiration for them by keeping away. Now you've had some combat duty on television. As compared to Hollywood, how does television work seem?

SP: I would say that in comparison with, I might describe motion pictures as the work of a Raphael, as the Madonna for example, as compared to television. I think they bear the same relation. The two mediums.

BH: What would the other comparison be.

SP: Well the comic book.

BH: You were reluctant. I'm glad we got that out of you.

SP: I don't know why you had to squeeze me, Ben; I had it in mind all the time.

BH: What type of fellow are you as a television viewer? Do you feel compelled to rush out and buy things TV commercials exploit or do you try to organize boycotts against them?

SP: Yes, we have a boycott at home. If I catch my wife or any

member of my family responding to the appeal from the television screen, I get out the knout and conduct an onslaught that is memorable. I've pitted myself against this form of advertising and so far, I think I'm winning.
BH: Here's a parlor game question, Sid. What words would you select to describe, (A) Eisenhower, (B) Khrushchev, and (C) America?
SP: On the first I would say bland, on the second, sinister and on the third, status quo.
BH: Well, we'll give you ten points. When I worked in Hollywood, I worked a lot at Metro. You worked there, didn't you?
SP: Indeed.
BH: You came under the interesting influence of L.B. Mayer, didn't you?
SP: I did. A great man.
BH: I remember Mr. Mayer calling a conference one night after an ugly preview, they were all pretty ugly, where he said he would show us how to rewrite the movie. We got into the room, six depressed creative spirits, and Mr. Mayer looked at us for about three minutes in silence. Mr. Mayer then walked over to his grand piano where there stood a single rose in a vase. It was sort of in the dark. He lifted the rose out and brought it to his desk where it was light and put it in another vase. And then he said, that's what I want you to do with the movie. This was the height of producer education I got in Hollywood.
SP: Well I think one of the great comments that was ever made about pictures was the reputed deathbed statement of Marcus Loew. It was said that just before he died, he turned to his family and said, "Boys, this is a five-and-ten-cent business."
BH: I'm afraid he was right.

Harry Cohn's Boat

October 1, 1958: Ben's guest was actress Gloria Swanson. On the heels of a pleasant evening of Hollywood memories and some choice words on Hollywood morals and morality, Ben told a Bedtime Story that involved one of Hollywood's greatest sex sirens and one of its most feared studio bosses.

I know two or three famous, international movie sex symbols. They're all frigid as ice cakes. They haven't had a sensation since they were last spanked by their mother at the age of six. These goddesses put over tremendous sex for the world because they're narcissists, not because they're sensual. They are so in love with themselves that the audience looks at them swooning over themselves and swoons with them. They're nothing compared to the average normal housewife who is a gal of fireworks sensuality alongside of a Hollywood sex symbol.

Marilyn Monroe was an exception. I once wrote a book with Marilyn Monroe, an autobiography of sorts which disappeared. We wrote the book before she got married. Then she married Joe DiMaggio, who read the book and started screaming. While we were writing, she told me about the most wonderful hour of her life.

Miss Monroe went to entertain the troops in Korea. It was wintertime, something like five below zero. She came out on the stage in an evening gown with bare shoulders, bare everything. There were twenty thousand troops and she sang for them. It was snowing, snowing to pieces like Jessel would say. But the snow never touched her body. Miss Monroe's warmth melted the entire snowfall for yards around. When the troops cheered, she was so warm she almost caused the snowstorm to disappear.

I have a story about Miss Monroe, before she became a sensation. One of the great moguls of Hollywood, a very fearsome fellow who created some of the greatest pictures and headaches Hollywood ever saw, was Harry Cohn. Mr. Cohn, who died recently, was the president of Columbia Pictures. He was not a popular man although he was very bright and dedicated. His funeral was attended by more people than any producer had yet been able to muster up. And one of the wags of the town said, looking at the enormous crowd, "Give the people what they want and they'll come."

At the beginning of her career, Miss Monroe was dropped by 20th Century-Fox. The head of 20th Century, Mr. Zanuck, had looked at some rushes and decided that Miss Monroe had no future at all and threw her out of the studio.

Somehow, she got a small job at Columbia. Miss Monroe was told by the casting department to sit at her phone and wait, and she would be summoned. She sat glued to the phone for two weeks. It finally rang and she was summoned to see the boss.

Miss Monroe arrived and was ushered into Mr. Cohn's office. It was as big as a grand ballroom with a desk like a small ocean liner at one end of it. Miss Monroe stood there all alone. After a pause, a mysterious door opened and Mr. Cohn emerged.

He looked at her carefully, circling her two or three times, and studying her vantage points. Then he hopped over to his enormous desk and came back with a photograph. It was a photograph of a yacht and he said to Miss Monroe, "How do you like this boat?" Miss Monroe said, "I think it's very nice."

"Would you like to take a ride on it?" She said, "Oh, I'd love that."

"All right, we leave at six o'clock today and we'll be back Monday morning." Miss Monroe, who hadn't expected this sort of proposition, got a little nervous but managed to think of something. "I'd be very glad to go on cruise with you and Mrs. Harry Cohn, sir."

At these words Harry Cohn blew his top. He threw the photograph on the floor and screamed, "How dare you mention my wife? I never referred to her. You know I'm not bringing her. How dare you take that name in your mouth. Get out of here!"

Miss Monroe, still shaking and still hoping to keep her job, tripped lightly towards the door and paused with an exit line which she hoped would ingratiate her. Her exit line was, "Well, I hope you invite me again sometime, Mr. Cohn."

This clinched it. Harry Cohn yelled, "You're fired," and that was the end of Miss Monroe at Columbia. A rather happy end because without the aid of yachts she won her great success in her field.

The Soul of a Hollywood Producer

October 14, 1958: Ben spent the evening telling Hollywood stories about screenwriters and their battles with producers. Hecht always derided his bosses but he was never ostracized for his opinions concerning the management. His politics, however, elicited a somewhat different response. When Ben tried to solicit money and support from the rich and influential Hollywood moguls on behalf of the dying Jews of Europe, he was angrily rejected. It took the British boycott on his films to finally curb the demand for his screenwriting services. As result, he had to cut his price dramatically, and use pseudonyms to keep working.

For his Bedtime Story, he told a tale that portrayed the inner workings of a typical producer.

I'll tell a story about a Hollywood producer, a precise and definite story omitting his name, however, because he's still alive and still a great producer. In Hollywood, the motion picture producer was the fellow who got to this high state because he could talk more firmly and quickly in a big bass baritone voice than the author could. This was the big fight originally in Hollywood. The authors weren't able to compete with the high class, floorwalker, stylish manners of the fellows who became producers. They became bosses because they were furious looking fellows. They knew nothing but they could talk fast.

About twenty years ago, one of the great theater talents of New York, Julius Tannen, rushed to Hollywood to make his fame and fortune as a movie star. Tannen was quite a talented performer. But he was one of those hard luck boys on whom not the star is drawn but some black mark is chalked. When he couldn't get a job people would that say, "Julius Tannen, now he's not working, he's no good," for no reason at all. We who were his friends tried desperately year in and year out to get Julius a job. We got him a couple of small parts and walk-ons but we knew he was a star and he could function as one.

About fifteen years passed and Julius supported his family by playing in little stock companies for sixty dollars a week, doing this and that. He had been making three or four thousand when he was a star on Broadway. Finally we got a very important producer at Paramount to consider Julius for a big part in a movie that was being prepared. We told Julius this producer was a great friend of ours and that he was practically hired.

Now, Julius was bald as an egg. He wore a wig but he was a very proud and finicky fellow and it took him about an hour to put this wig on. He pasted it on carefully in half a dozen places. All bewigged and all bespangled with perfume and whatnot he arrived at the producer's office. The producer sat down and looked at him, talked to him for three, four minutes and said, "Mr. Tannen, I'm very sorry, I don't think you'll do for this part." Julius said, "Am I too short, too tall, or too fat? What's wrong with me?"

The producer said, "It's the part of the city editor. You have to play a newspaperman and I don't visualize you as a newspaperman." Julius smiled and said, "It just so happens I was assistant to the editor in a Connecticut town for five years before I became a monologist. I know all about newspaper offices."

"I'm terribly sorry," said the producer, "because this particular editor is bald-headed, and we've got to have a bald-headed man for the part." Julius smiled rather triumphantly, lifted his hands to his head and slowly tore off his wig. And then, with his head completely bald and trickles of blood running down from where the plaster had injured the skin, he looked at the producer and said, "Well, I guess I'm your man."

The producer looked at him attentively for some time and said, "I'm sorry, Mr. Tannen. I cannot visualize you as a bald-headed man."

And that is the soul of the Hollywood producer.

Screenwriters' Victories

November 6, 1958: Following his animated exchange with S.J. Perelman, Ben told a Bedtime Story about the revenge his collaborators Gene Fowler, Charles MacArthur and Charles Lederer sometimes extracted from their employers.

This story is about the joy and wonderful times we writers had in Hollywood. For the first time in the history of the world, Hollywood created writers who owned yachts, ran busy harems, bought swimming pools, and rolled in gold. Of course we ended up with none of the money because we didn't really know how to spend it. But we had some victories, some literary victories in Hollywood.

I remember one victory by Gene Fowler who was then writing scenarios. He wrote a picture called *This Is Hollywood* in which Constance Bennett starred. The picture was pretty well mangled by the time it got on the set and Gene stood by a little moodily. Finally, he struck. The big scene was one in which Miss Bennett picked up her child from the perambulator, held it to her bosom, wept, kissed it and then dashed out in the snow and left her husband.

The cameras were rolling when Miss Bennett picked up the child and it was the Negro baby that Gene had put in the baby carriage. Gene had switched kids. She stood there about three minutes emoting over this child without noticing its different color. That was Gene's victory.

There was another victory that Charlie MacArthur won one day. He was coming to work a little moody about everything. When he stopped to get some gas, he noticed the attendant spoke in a heavy English brogue. MacArthur asked him how much he was making a week and the attendant said "Thirty dollars." Charlie told him to get in the car, that he had a better job for him.

By the afternoon, he had introduced the fellow as a well known novelist from England, a close friend of Bernard Shaw, and sold him to the bosses, Bernie Hyman and Mr. Mayer for one thousand dollars a week, telling them he was a very, very promising writer. The fellow, of course, had never written anything. Charlie told the bosses that the man didn't want to sell out his talents and perhaps they could convince him. An hour later he signed a contract.

Charlie instructed this fellow, whose name was Peter Winston, never to say anything in conference except, "I'd like to take that home and brood a bit," or, "that doesn't go with me." And to say it in very thick English accent. This boy stayed for one year at Metro, writing absolutely nothing and collecting his thousand a week. None of the producers or directors who had conferred with the gentlemen ever found out the man could not write so much as a postcard.

The third writers' victory was won by Charlie Lederer, who was having one of his one man battles with MGM. He kept being thrown out of the place, three or four times a day. Lederer finally struck. With the aid of Leo McCarey the director, he entered Metro. Leo boosted him up on his shoulder. Charlie lit a copy of the Sunday *New York Times* with a match, held it against the water sprinklers until the heat of the burning paper melted the gadgets on the pipe and Metro was flooded from one end to another. All the producers at MGM were up to their knees in water, arthritis set in, and Lederer won a great victory. These were a few of the happy things we writers did.

The Blue Couch

October 14, 1958: On an evening devoted to Hollywood, Ben told a story about his friend and collaborator Gene Fowler. Fowler was also a former newspaperman who'd been seduced by the financial opportunities Hollywood offered. And like Hecht, Gene Fowler wasn't afraid to stand up to the bosses.

I have another story about a marvelous battle won by one of our best writers, Gene Fowler. Mr. Fowler and I were once signed to do a script together for David O. Selznick. The "O" stands for Oliver. He made that initial up himself. He said he wanted to have very stylish stationary.

We occupied a suite of offices in what was the Selznick unit. At least they called it a suite. Actually, David occupied the entire lower floor, as befitted a man of his stature. Fowler and I were shoe-horned into a tiny office, as befitted movie writers of our stature. Next to our office was a broom closet of sorts in which the required secretary was to turn our scribbling into readable pages.

Our last collaboration was *The Great Magoo*, which opened and closed on Broadway rather abruptly thanks to the New York critics. So Fowler suggested we decorate our office in a way that would stimulate our creativity. We chose a brothel decor, complete with red velvet curtains, pornographic photographs and drawings on the walls, and an atomizer that pumped perfume regularly.

Of course Mr. Selznick insisted we have a secretary, in accordance with the MGM rules that each movie writer must have a female secretary. We called central casting and found a beauty contest queen from Texas, whom we named "Bunny." We dressed her in a red ball gown, instructed her to bring her favorite reading matter every day, and to inform callers that we were out of the city.

Bunny couldn't read or write, but her explosive contours were sweet honey to all the boys in the studio. She had about two hundred people in the outer office, day and night.

The second week we were working on this script, I discovered that Mr. Fowler had malaria. Each day at one o'clock, Fowler would get one of his head cooking spells, just for an hour. He had to lie down. But Fowler couldn't lie down in our office, because there was a rule at Metro that authors couldn't have any couches. Fowler said the rule was enforced because the studio efficiency expert, Major Funkwhiler, thought that if writers were exposed to a couch, they be overcome with lewd thoughts and unable to function at maximum efficiency. The major, a retired regular army officer hired by Mr. Mayer to keep things on the up and up, had ordered that all writer's couches be removed.

I suggested buying a couch, but Fowler had another idea. He told the major that if we didn't have a couch by four o'clock, he was going to throw all the furniture out of the window, set fire to the building and destroy the backlot, that contained Jerusalem, Peking, Old New York, and all the sets that were standing. The major laughed this off.

After we did some more work, Gene got a little restive. At four o'clock, as promised, he opened both windows and started throwing the furniture out. He threw a desk out, three chairs and emptied our office. Then he ran into several other offices and got more furniture. I had seen Fowler do this before, when he emptied hotel rooms in like fashion after heated discussions with the management. This was his pattern of revolt.

MGM was in an uproar. As he continued to unleash his fury, a crowd of about two thousand stars and extras gathered. The studio security called out the fire department, but we'd locked the downstairs doors so they couldn't get up. They tried to squirt Gene with a firehose through the window and even that didn't stop him.

This went on for about an hour and Gene was about ready to put a torch to the building when down the road came a truck with a wonderful, big, blue couch in it. This was one of the rare victories I can think of an author winning in Hollywood.

A Goldwyn Conference

October 14, 1958: Ben's evening of Hollywood memories spotlighted several stories featuring his dear friend and sometime collaborator, Charles Lederer. Mr. Lederer, who was the producer and co-author of the Broadway musical hit Kismet, *co-wrote such classic films as* His Girl Friday, Ride the Pink Horse, *and* The Thing *with Ben Hecht. Lederer's wit and humor, as well as his practical jokes, were highly regarded in literary and theater circles.*

Charles Lederer is a native born marvel in Hollywood. He's one of the only writers in Hollywood who's able to hold the bosses at bay. He didn't strike once as Fowler did, he struck often and keeps on striking to this day. Mr. Lederer is the most feared writer in town. He's the only writer that the Hollywood bosses stand either in awe of, or in terror of.

Charlie came into my life as a young man. I didn't know much about him. He was about eighteen and the lover of the highest paid musical comedy star in New York. Charlie was making no money and wanting to make no money at the time. In fact, throughout his career, he loathed employment. One day this star took him to the Colony

Restaurant for lunch. As they ate, she explained that he didn't live right. That a man should get up before noon. That a man should go around looking for a job. That a man should find a job. That a man should work. He shouldn't take baths, hot baths, three hours a day like young Lederer did. She kept on talking like this to Charlie and when she got through, Charlie rose and handed her his trousers which he had taken off during the conversation. "Here my dear, you wear them," he told her. And he walked out of her life. This was my first acquaintance with Charlie.

In Hollywood, when Charlie was about nineteen, I was employed by Sam Goldwyn at the enormous sum of five thousand a week to try and think up a movie. Sam is one of the few people in Hollywood who thought a little beyond profits. Although he was a man who could squeeze a dollar harder than anybody, Sam was a fine producer with no head. He had small brain power but a very intellectual stomach. It would react at a distance of fifty paces. If you were reading him a script and it had a wrong passage in it, Sam's stomach would react. He would turn pale and green.

Mr. Goldwyn understood the importance of the screenwriter. In fact, he once told me, "the writer is most important. If you have rich dialogue with rich characters, you have the mucus of a great movie."

And so I sat around in my wood lined office for two or three weeks and thought of nothing to write because Mr. Goldwyn was calling me into conference all the time. A Goldwyn conference was something in those days.

I said to him, "Sam, I need a collaborator." This horrified Sam because for five thousand dollars a week he thought a man should be able to think by himself. I said I didn't need someone to help me think but to relax me playing cards. I suggested he hire Charles Lederer for five hundred dollars a week as my collaborator. And he did. Sam was an awfully nice fellow, always.

I told Charlie what his duties were. They consisted of him being within ten minutes' call of the office. Two days later when Mr. Goldwyn called me to conference, I summoned Mr. Lederer, who as my collaborator had full rights to enter the office with me. Mr. Lederer used to dress oddly: he wore a T-shirt with holes in it, had a tie for a belt, very broken down pants, no socks and sneakers. He looked like sort of a decadent Huck Finn.

He arrived within ten minutes and I said to him, "Now Charlie, your duties are very simple. When we go in to see Mr. Goldwyn, as we go in, you lie down on the couch and fall asleep, instantly." We walked in, Charlie laid down on the couch, fell asleep, and began to snore.

This sort of confused Mr. Goldwyn. He said, "We don't want him here." I said, "He has to be here according to the Screenwriters Guild. He's my collaborator."

We only had two conferences. Mr. Goldwyn stop calling and I started writing.

The Lederer Wars

October 14, 1958: Hecht's Lederer stories continued with several more anecdotes about Charlie's unique brand of revenge.

Charlie Lederer was always having these amazing fracases. The boss, in Charlie's eyes as in mine (this wasn't true about Selznick from my point of view but it was from Charlie's), the boss was a pompous, fat head with nothing on the ball, but with powers exceeding that of Khrushchev in Russia.

Hollywood inspires a lot of things, but chiefly adulation and obsequiousness. It very seldom inspires revolt because it's hard to revolt. Charlie now makes two or three thousand dollars a week as a scenario writer. I'm glad to say his manners and habits haven't changed. He's still inspired to hit back.

All I know about the fracas with Selznick is that he'd been kicked out. He'd worked for Selznick and something happened. I was with Mr. Selznick one Christmas morning when David was unwrapping his Christmas presents. He was saving up the biggest one for last because it was an enormous thing about twelve feet long. David unwrapped it and had to unscrew all kinds of screws to get to it. He finally got it opened and there lay a big long pole with a card attached to it which read: "Mr. Selznick, this is the ten foot pole I wouldn't touch you with. Charles Lederer."

Charlie Lederer just couldn't stand to be bossed. And if you can't stand to be bossed, Hollywood is the last place you must be. The first requirement of everyone in Hollywood is to always have twenty superiors, no matter who they are. There are twenty people who are your boss. Charlie was a philosopher. He fought the boss with ridicule.

There was another producer he got involved with, again I don't know what the cause of fracas was. Sam Zimbalist was a very nice fellow who produced *Ben Hur*. Charlie got in a terrible ruckus with Sam. He wouldn't tell me what it was about but I knew he'd left Metro. He used to brood on these things. Charlie was like Monte Crisco, he'd rise every morning with the cry of, "I shall be avenged." On New Year's Day four or five years after his ruckus with Sam Zimbalist, an ad appeared in the Los Angeles papers which read, "Will pay $2 for your used Christmas trees." It was signed Sam Zimbalist and it contained his address. Something like eight hundred old Christmas trees were dropped on Sam's lawn. He had to leave the house and flee Hollywood for a week until they cleaned it up.

Barrymore's Hamlet

October 3, 1958: Ben told stories about Charlie Chaplin and the man he believed was the greatest actor of his era, his friend John Barrymore. Hecht wrote a number of Barrymore films, and they were close until the actor's death in 1942. When Hecht and MacArthur's second stage hit Twentieth Century *was made into a film in 1934, it was Barrymore starring as Oscar Jaffe, a flamboyantly Napoleonic theatrical producer. With its hilarious script and Howard Hawks' flawless direction, the film helped define the screwball comedy genre in American films.*

The Barrymore family included brother Lionel and sister Ethel. John was always a great womanizer, and his career was plagued by alcohol abuse.

My friend John Barrymore wasn't tragic. He had a marvelous life. Instead of living the usual one or two lives that people usually live, Barrymore lived a hundred. He lived through one adventure after another and had a marvelous time.

I once asked him if he thought he was a great actor. Jack thought there was no such thing as great acting, just a deluded public. I told him he was noted for being the greatest Hamlet of his age. He said that the only press notice he ever kept was from his performance as Hamlet.

"I've kept them to keep me humble and remind me that there's no such thing as art in acting. I'll tell you what sort of a Hamlet I performed then I'll let you read the notices," he told me. "When I arrived in London I fell madly in love with a Duchess the second day there. The lady was the most frigid Duchess the British had yet hatched. She wouldn't look at me, wouldn't let me get near her. I wooed her madly for the three or four weeks of rehearsal and got nowhere. On the day we were supposed to open, a uniformed servant arrived with a great big message saying the Duchess was awaiting me in her castle for lunch. It was about thirty miles outside of London, but I got there forthwith.

"It was a brilliant, magnificent day. I drank two or three quarts of Scotch and ten or fifteen bottles of wine. We made wild, passionate love. At seven o'clock they carried me in the car unconscious and brought me to my dressing room in the London theater. I was completely out. Somehow, they woke me with ice cakes, coffee and electric shocks. They got me into my tights.

"The curtain went up. Then I heard my cue to come on. I staggered out on the stage, the footlights hit me with their warmth, I got sick to my stomach and ran back and relieved myself. Through the whole show I tottered in and out of that stage. I fell down on a couch, I couldn't recite standing up. But," he said, "I never missed a line."

"I did everything as a drunk would do it. I made ten or twelve unexpected exits because I was again sick to my stomach. I recited my major speeches lying in a half coma. And the next morning these notices," he said holding the clippings. "The greatest Hamlet of our age. It taught me that it's an audience delusion, not actor's art."

A Forgotten Speech

October 3, 1958: Ben continued his Barrymore stories with a tale taken from the actor's declining years, when years of alcoholism had finally taken its toll. No one wanted to hire Mr. Barrymore in his final days, but his friends, Hecht, MacArthur and Fowler, never stopped trying to help him land acting assignments.

In his later years, Barrymore had difficulty finding work. An actor has a thing called a front lobe, where he gets his memory. It's the place where he stores his lines, his dialogue. Barrymore's frontal lobe began to melt out of his head and he couldn't remember lines. But Gene Fowler and I decided we'd get him a job. I'd written a script for David Selznick called *Nothing Sacred*. I wanted Jack to play the part of the editor. David Selznick adored Barrymore. His was the only picture David had hanging in his waiting room. Handsome Jack with his profile. So, David said if we could get Barrymore to memorize one speech, a half a page long, without going up on his lines, he could have the part.

Fowler and I rehearsed Barrymore for about eight or nine days on this one speech. Finally Jack arrived on a Monday morning in the Selznick office looking like all people in trouble look. His sleeves had shrunk, his pants were up, he looked like he had been out in the rain a long time, but still with that lovely face. After considerable reminiscences, we said, "Jack, let's have the speech." "Yes," said Jack. And he stood up to recite the speech, an address at a banquet. He recited a speech no one had ever heard before. A brilliant speech that I wrote down as fast as he said it. It was much better than the speech I'd written for the film. At the end, David shook his head and said "Jack, I'm sorry. We can't use you, you didn't do the speech."

We didn't use Jack but his speech ended up in the movie. Walter Connolly recited it in Jack's stead. It was sad, but Jack adored it. He thought it was a great joke.

Tryst at the Chicken Farm

December 8, 1958: Ben's guest was Diana Barrymore, who inherited her father's profession, and alcohol problem. Her appearance on the show was a somewhat eleemosynary gesture on Hecht's part, perhaps in memory of his long departed friend. Ben told a Bedtime Story about an attempt to reform Miss Barrymore's father.

The story illustrates the fact that sometimes egos do not reform. Because Mr. Jack Barrymore never quite reformed, he got laid out and silenced. There was a time when we tried to reform Jack. Gene Fowler, Tommy Mitchell, Roland Young, Charlie MacArthur and I figured out it was time for Jack to stop drinking. So we persuaded Barrymore to retire to a chicken ranch about a hundred and fifty miles south of Hollywood in the desert. We arranged with the owner of the chicken ranch to keep Mr. Barrymore on it for two weeks. The chicken ranch was completely isolated. There were no roads, no automobiles, no neighbors and not a drop of liquor on the place. We promised the chicken ranch owner double pay if Mr. Barrymore was kept there for two weeks. We drove Jack down there and he said a very sad goodbye to us from behind the chicken wire.

After about two days, MacArthur received a desperate phone call, with the charges reversed of course. It was from Mr. Barrymore. He said, "I understand your noble hearts, all of you. I understand how you're looking out for my interests and you've isolated and marooned me on this incredible, insane, maniacal chicken ranch and there's not a human being except the old chicken farmer within a hundred miles. It's unfair. I'm willing to stay here but in the name of manhood and honor, I demand you send me a girl."

We talked it over and decided it would be a little difficult, not only to find a girl for Jack, but one who could drive an automobile. It took about two days of searching to find such a talented type in Hollywood. We finally got a girl who could drive a rented flivver. MacArthur warned her that Barrymore was very convincing and she mustn't let him talk her into returning to Hollywood. Charlie cautioned her that she wouldn't be paid for her services until she returned, alone.

Armed with maps of how to get there, we sent her down to this chicken ranch. Well, we got the story from the girl later. She arrived at the chicken ranch and a most gallant, gracious Jack Barrymore came out to greet her. He helped her out of the car and as she stepped on the burning sands and he said, "My dear, this is much against my character but terribly necessary" and he popped her on the chin, knocking her cold. Then he hopped into the car and drove back to Hollywood.

On Monday morning we picked up the paper and there was Jack Barrymore on the front page, leering drunkenly at a black diva, holding a wine glass and being toasted as the guest of honor at the opening of Earl Caroll's new nightclub. And that's how Jack Barrymore never reformed.

Barrymore's Death Scene

October 3, 1958: Ben's final Jack Barrymore story on a night of Hollywood reminiscences revealed Hecht was witness to the actor's deathbed performance.

Barrymore was very dangerous to get into contact with socially. Jack was unhousebroken. He had no inhibitions. He was wild, fascinating, brilliant and entertaining, but liable to fall in love with the hostess, the wife, or your grandmother. Any dame he looked at could easily become the light of his life.

I was at Jack's bedside when he died. Jack had a marvelous love for women. He loved them as a miser loves gold. He adored women. It wasn't just a lecherous adulation. It was because they were wonderful and beautiful. And when he was dying, we all took care that his nurses wouldn't be anybody that would distract him and probably hasten his death. Gene Fowler was one of the group and he made sure that no one would excite our friend's devotion to the female species.

One of his nurses was a girl who weighed about a hundred and eighty-five pounds, five feet tall, had a very odd, sad, homely face, full of warts and was a spinster. We knew that Jack couldn't pull any hanky-panky with this kind of nurse. Finally, when he was dying, we sent for a priest.

When the priest arrived he asked Jack if there was anything he wanted to tell him. And Jack said, "I want to make a confession, Father." "What is it my son?" said the priest. "I have had carnal thoughts father," Barrymore replied. "You have?" said the priest. "Of whom?"

Raising his head with great difficulty, Barrymore rolled his eyes toward the massive woman, and smiled with that classic Barrymore leer. A few moments later, he died. It was the biggest gift this girl ever got. It was a nice death. Very gallant.

The Ladies' Man

October 3, 1958: After his Barrymore banquet, Ben continued with Chaplin stories. As with any popular hero, Chaplin's persona was shrouded in myth. Hecht knew the real Chaplin.

Since our kings and queens have disappeared, the only royalty remaining are our actors. They are now the only living embodiment of the daydreams of people. They're not really people themselves, they're the daydreams of the public. They're romance, lust, pleasure, love, greed, courage and everything else. They walk around on the stage but they're actually inside of people's heads. In the early days of Hollywood, Chaplin was a king of the highest order.

Charlie Chaplin had a reputation as being a ladies' man. Not only a reputation but a thousand seven-column headlines in the press of all his amours. The truth was that he wasn't a ladies' man at all. First he was too stingy, second he was too famous, and third he was too great an artist. Chaplin was a performer. I remember a story about Charlie showing how much more a performer he was than a ladies' man.

Sid Grauman, the fellow who built the Chinese theater in Hollywood, ran into a salesman one afternoon who was selling stockings in a very exciting way. He had a life-size female dummy, a very voluptuous looking waxen figure. The salesman would lift up her dress, put the stockings on, and show it to the buyer. He was selling loads of stockings. Sid said he'd like to rent this dummy for an evening.

He rented the dummy and took her to a suite in the Biltmore hotel, got her in bed and put an amazing nightgown on her. There she was smiling and looking very happy. He called up Chaplin and said a woman had come all the way across the country, a great admirer of his, and that he had promised the woman that he would produce Chaplin for the evening. So Chaplin said he'd come over and have dinner. It was in fact after dinner.

Chaplin came over and Grauman introduced him to the lady who was lying in bed. Chaplin saw her smile but didn't notice she was a dummy. He began to talk to her, began to perform, began to tell jokes, began to do all his tricks that he was going to do in his next picture. He put a lamp shade on, performed for thirty minutes, laughing and giggling, never noticing he was performing for a waxen dummy.

That was Chaplin's interest in women. Sort of symbolic of his relations to the world too.

Chaplin's Vocabulary

October 3, 1958: Ben's next Chaplin story returned to a familiar theme — the all-powerful boss.

Charlie Chaplin had practically no intellect. He had great talent. Which is like being able to walk a tightrope. Intellect is a matter of words. Charlie didn't have it until later in life. When he was almost at his peak, he began to learn words out of a dictionary. He had one hidden in his bathroom in the studio and whenever he was in the bathroom for any reason he would sit and study twenty words, memorize them very carefully. Then come swaggering out on the set and use these long words on people.

He had an assistant named Chuck Reisner who later became a great director. One day on the set, Chaplin asked Chuck for a gag. He'd been thrown out of saloon in the scene and he said, "I want to pick myself up here and do something." So Chuck said, "You pick up a cobblestone and you take it in your hand. You're going to hurl it right through the window and as you go to hurl you feel something. You touch a cop, you feel his buttons. Instead of hurling the cobblestone you put it in your hands and rock it as a baby and walk away." And Chaplin says no, "That's too outre."

Now Chuck Reisner was not very learned and he thought Chaplin was talking pig Latin. He said, "What's wrong with it if it's true, that don't make it a bad gag." "I didn't say it was true," Chaplin replied, "I said it was outre." And then Chaplin began to rag Chuck about his stupidity, about being an ignoramus, about having no brains at all. This reduced a very tough fellow almost to tears.

Reisner went to a fellow called Tom Geraghty, a poet from Dublin working at the studio. Geraghty used to sit in his office writing letters all the time. He'd stamp the letter, address it, and throw it out the window because people would always pick it up and mail it. He went to Geraghty and said to him, "You've got to tell Charlie to stop picking on me because he makes me feel so stupid."

"I'll tell you what to do," Geraghty said, "Next time he picks on you, just call him a quidnunc. I'm sure it's a word he's hasn't come on yet in the dictionary."

The next day Charlie started riding Reisner again, and Reisner said "There's no use listening to you, you're a quidnunc, you're the worst quidnunc, you're most quidnuncious quidnunc in the whole of California." Chaplin stared at him, his eyes fogged and he said, "I've got a slight stomach ache. I'll talk to you in a minute." He ran back to the bathroom, opened the dictionary and found the word quidnunc but the definition had been rubbed out with ink. Chaplin tried desperately to find the word quidnunc. He called up about eight people, nobody had heard of it. Finally, he went to his office and did what a boss in Hollywood always does, he fired Chuck Reisner. It was a big thing for Reisner because he went to Metro and became a director and producer and did the "Min and Bill" stories with Marie Dressler and Wally Beery.

A Christmas Gift

> *October 3, 1958: Ben's Bedtime Story for his evening of Barrymore and Chaplin memories featured Charles Lederer in a much more reflective mood than his usual rebellious self.*

When my friend Charlie Lederer was fifteen, he was one of Chaplin's only friends. Lederer used to play tennis with him. Chaplin used to take him to dinner at a swanky restaurant and of course Charlie had to pay his own dinner check. Chaplin never bought anything for anyone, great artiste he was.

He was walking with Charlie one night, on Christmas Eve, down Santa Claus Lane in Hollywood, where they have fake snow and fake reindeers and the whole thing is lit up like it's Norway or Pittsburgh. Charlie suddenly stopped in front of a window displaying a LaSalle automobile, which was a precursor of the Cadillac. Lederer stared at it with wide eyes. Chaplin came to him and asked him if he liked the car. And Charlie said, "Oh, that's wonderful."

"Would you like a car like that?" Chaplin asked. "Oh, I can't even dream of such a car," Lederer said.

"I don't know," Chaplin said. "It's Christmas Eve and things happen on Christmas Eve, Santa Claus you know." And Charlie said, "Oh, nobody's going to give me a car like that."

And Chaplin said, "Don't be too sure, Charlie. I think you'll find it in your stocking tomorrow morning." Tears ran down young

Lederer's eyes and he walked on. He went home. He waited all night, didn't sleep, he waited all Christmas day, no car came.

After the episode I said to Charlie, "That was a pretty dirty trick to play on you." Charlie said, "No, it was the best gift I ever got. Chaplin gave me more hope than I've ever had in my life since."

The Music Lesson

November 15, 1958: Ben's guest was humorist and television personality Henry Morgan, for an evening on the role of humor in contemporary life. Ben's Bedtime Story recalled a rather comic episode from the thirties.

While Hecht and MacArthur were writing the screenplay of Wuthering Heights *for Sam Goldwyn, they vacationed on a tiny Vermont island owned by Alexander Woollcott. The Emily Brontë book was a Woollcott favorite, and as a result he tried to oversee their adaptation. Hecht and MacArthur, up to their usual tricks, left phony pages for him to find, which had Heathcliff as an Old West cowboy, complete with sixguns and Indian foe.*

One of Woollcott's other house guests was Harpo Marx.

I have a small story to tell about comedy. It proves how comedy can be the most effective thing in the world. We used to go as guests, very honored guests to Alexander Woollcott's island in Lake Bombazine, Vermont. Woollcott in his prime was one of the most fierce, arrogant, wild spoken, almost unbearable hosts you could run into. He ran his little island as if he were Kublai Khan and Xanadu. Nobody was allowed on the island, Woollcott was fiercely possessive.

One day he looked out of his window and saw a launch with twelve prim and proper schoolteachers arriving with picnic baskets. They carefully unloaded their food and sat down to eat. Woollcott went down to the water's edge and denounced the schoolteachers as no one was ever denounced before in language that may have frightened mere mortals. To his dismay, they ignored him and continued to unwrap their sandwiches. Woollcott almost had apoplexy. He returned to his house, was about to lie down and die when Harpo Marx, who was one of the house guests, said he would take the matter over.

About fifteen minutes later, Harpo appeared out of the bushes, stark naked with a ribbon in his hair and a little fife in his mouth. He played Pan, jumping up and down, pretending he was a fawn. The schoolteachers dove into Lake Champlain and vanished. Harpo continued dancing around with his fife all afternoon to the delight of Mr. Woollcott. This was one of the most effective comic bits I've ever seen. Particularly against schoolteachers.

Yes Man Says No

> *January 7, 1959: Ben answered mail and offered his thoughts on success. Making the transition from the premier Hollywood screenwriter to an outcast within the space of ten years gave Hecht a unique perspective on the ups and downs of show business.*
>
> *For his Bedtime Story, Hecht spoke about actor/director Gregory Ratoff. Born in Russia, Ratoff was known as "Gregory the Great," a man with a reputation for sartorial flamboyance. When directing, he sported a bright blue polo shirt, a gold-braided yacht cap, and broad-checked suit. He carried a cane and a whistle, the latter for directorial emphasis.*

This is about a friend of mine who's one of the most exuberant actors, producers, directors in the entertainment field. His name is Gregory Ratoff. Many years ago Mr. Ratoff arrived in Hollywood under very unfavorable circumstances. He had no money and no job. The play he was acting in had folded. And he hung around Hollywood for some time. He was rather large, as he always is, and his clothes began getting bigger and bigger because he wasn't eating much. In the midst of his darkness, when he had despaired of ever finding employment again, a hand reached out and pulled Mr. Ratoff into the 20th Century–Fox studios. The hand belonged to Mr. Darryl F. Zanuck. Gregory was overwhelmed with the wonder of being rescued and given a whole new life.

His devotion to Mr. Zanuck was really one of the most charming things in Hollywood. He adored him. In those days Darryl was a great poobah. We used to call him White Fang. He was one of these heads of a great studio who was always surrounded by ten or twelve yes men who acted exactly as if he were the ruler of the universe. The chief of these yes men, but sincerely so, was Mr. Ratoff.

One night they were in the projection room showing a rough cut of a movie starring Sonja Henie, the ice skater. It was the second movie of hers that 20th Century had made. After the movie was over and the lights went up, Mr. Zanuck stepped out of the projection room for a moment. There was a silence. No yes man dared speak. Finally Mr. Ratoff spoke. And Mr. Ratoff tells the story, "I heard an ugly voice, the most horrible voice saying the most horrible thing in my life. It was me and what I was saying was, 'It's not as good as the first Sonja Henie picture.'" There was a silence. The other yes men were stunned.

Then Mr. Zanuck returned. He said, "Well, boys?" They all pointed to Mr. Ratoff and as Gregory told it, "I heard that same ugly voice once more speaking to this wonderful man who had done these wonderful things for me. Again I said, 'it's not as good as the first Sonja Henie picture.'" There was a hush. Nobody spoke.

Mr. Ratoff left Zanuck and his yes men. He went to a hamburger stand where he used to retire to have a bite of food after a run in the projection room. He thought they would join him and all would be forgiven. But he sat alone eating his hamburger. They all passed him by. He knew his end had come. He returned to his home and told his wife, Eugenie, "These walls, these paintings, these new rugs, they are all gone. Everything is over. We are back where we were, on the sidewalk. I will not have anything to eat again."

He sat bemoaning the fate of a collapsed yes man until about three in the morning when the telephone rang. It was Darryl Zanuck on the phone. And he said, "Gregory, I'm calling to tell you I am making you a director because you proved tonight you're exactly the sort of man I want in the studio. A man who will say no."

Jessel and Ratoff Live!

November 21, 1958: Writer and lyricist Abe Burrows was Ben's guest. They compared battle scars from the show business wars.

For a Bedtime Story with a life and death twist, Ben remembered an evening in Hollywood with a rather imposing cast: Charlie Lederer, Orson Welles, Gregory Ratoff, and one George Jessel. Mr. Jessel, who billed himself as the Toastmaster General of the United States, was another Hecht favorite. Hecht based the main character of his controversial novel A Jew in Love *on the more revolting facets of Jessel's intense persona.*

This story is about two of the wittiest men in the world. One is Gregory Ratoff, the other George Jessel. One evening I was sitting in Romanoff's with Mr. Orson Welles and Mr. Charles Lederer when Mr. Jessel appeared at our booth. He had a flushed face and a very tense manner. Mr. Jessel held out his hand and started saying goodbye. He said goodbye to Mr. Welles, Mr. Lederer and to me. Then he told us how much he admired us and that he would always remember us to the last moment. We asked him where he was going. Jessel paused and told us he was going to somewhat from which no traveller returneth. He said he was going to commit suicide at eleven-thirty. It was only about ten and we had some time so I said to George, "Why don't you come over to the house and we'll discuss why you're committing suicide? It'll be interesting to find out why a bright man like you is going to kill himself. I can tell good stories about it."

We all went over to Mr. Lederer's house. As always, with Jessel at the time was a beautiful tall blond that he'd met about thirty-two minutes before deciding to commit suicide. When we entered the house, Gregory Ratoff was there in a moody, fat man's slouch. He hardly said hello to us. George then, in reply to our questions, told us why he was committing suicide. He recited a list of calamities, disasters, heartbreaks, and failures that Voltaire couldn't have matched. No one could touch the list of monstrosities that happened to Mr. Jessel during his life.

During this recitation, Mr. Ratoff sat inattentively, his head down, his eyes heavy. Finally, when Mr. Jessel concluded, Mr. Ratoff said, "Georgie, that whole list of troubles is just a picnic in my life. I have come here tonight to say goodbye to my friends Charlie Lederer and Ben Hecht because I cannot live any longer. I wanted to say goodbye to people I have loved. I've been in the hospital for three months with a heart condition and they've robbed me of every penny I've got. I'm an absolute pauper, there's no use for me to live."

He started out and Jessel went with him. I thought both lads were going to Lover's Leap, which is in Capistrano, and jump off. Jessel left the beautiful blond behind and I called a taxi for her. As we were shaking hands with her, I noticed that her wrists were scarified. I asked her what had happened. She said she had tried to cut her wrists about five weeks before but somebody had interfered. So she was still alive.

Well, the climax of this story is that George Jessel today, which is about two years after this suicide leap, is a very successful television performer in Los Angeles. And Gregory Ratoff is again a very successful moviemaker in Switzerland.

Memories of C.B. DeMille

January 21, 1959: Once again, Ben spent the evening responding to viewer correspondence. Cecil B. DeMille died earlier in the day, so Ben chose to remember him in the evening's Bedtime Story.

Cecil B. DeMille was one of the founders of the motion picture industry. I never liked his pictures very much. They seemed to be made with horses and for horses chiefly, but he himself was a man of great potency and wild imagination.

In the beginning, Sam Goldwyn, Jesse Lasky and DeMille decided to do some pictures. They didn't know where to go. Mr. DeMille was the literary member of the trio. He'd written some plays in New York. Lasky was a cornet player and Goldwyn had been a glove salesman. They engaged Dusty Farnham for a picture that was to be called *The Squaw Man*. Mr. Farnham had a codicil in his contract that if any news of his being employed as a motion picture actor leaked out, he would be paid in full without having to act. This was because there was a great shame in those days attached to being a movie actor.

They sent Mr. DeMille out west to find a location where they could shoot the picture rather cheaply. He was supposed to get off in Kansas City or Denver but he kept idling in the train playing cards. He finally fell asleep and missed his destination.

DeMille got off the train ten hours later and walked around this strange little town. He found a barn in a place called Vine Street and negotiated for its rental at $10 a month. Then he wired Mr. Goldwyn: "Have found an ideal place to shoot a picture. It's a fine barn, we can get it for $10 a month. The name of the town is Hollywood." This was the first time it was put in the dispatches.

I remember a second story about Mr. DeMille. His second picture was called *The Great Divide* and was shot by DeMille with some strange notions about art. He decided he wouldn't use artificial lighting. He used only natural lighting. If a person was reading by lamp, there'd be no Kleig lights thrown on them. So the picture was shot that way.

In those days, there were no rushes. You shot the whole picture and looked at it when it was cut and finished. And there was no projection room in the newly hatched outfit of Lasky, Goldwyn and DeMille. Mr. DeMille took the tin cans with film to Chicago where Colonel Selig was atop the industry, such as it was. Selig put it on the projector and threw it on the screen and they couldn't see it. With this natural lighting, the people sitting by the floor lamp trying to read were practically invisible. Mr. Goldwyn was put out no end because their entire fortune was wrapped up in this picture. He called up Mr. DeMille, and said, "We got a bad print Cecil, we have to print it over again. Can't see the picture at all." Mr. DeMille answered, "That's exactly the way I wanted it. That's Rembrandt lighting. Advertise it as Hollywood's first art opus."

They did and it sold like hotcakes.

The Collapse of Hollywood

December 26, 1958: Ben swapped Hollywood stories with director Otto Preminger. They worked together on a number of films. Preminger hired Hecht to write two films during the British boycott, Where the Sidewalk Ends, *and* Whirlpool. *For the British release, the screenwriting credits went to Rex Connor, and Lester Barstow, who was Ben's chauffeur. And when Preminger made* The Moon Is Blue, *he agreed to release the film on a double bill with a motion picture Hecht wrote and directed entitled* Actors and Sin. *A character in Hecht's film was based on L.B. Mayer, MGM's resident poobah. When Mr. Mayer got word of Hecht's parody, he made sure the film never received general distribution.*

For his Bedtime Story, *Ben delivered a Hollywood post mortem.*

I seem to be becoming an expert on collapses. Perhaps I shall soon possibly discuss my own.

Hollywood is giving out a rather pretty death rattle these days. The long love affair between Hollywood and the movie makers is almost at an end. It was a fifty-year honeymoon of stupidity. Not that Americans are stupid in ninety million lots, but all people seem to have an infantile streak in them. A sort of a wish not to improve, a wish to go backwards. They want to get back to the apes. Hollywood quickly realized that anthropological fact and threw out about fifty thousand movies catering to this human flaw. It served the infantile side of the country no end and without stop for millions and billions of dollars worth of profit.

Who was to blame? Well, the public is always to blame because the public always makes the lowest demands. If the demands of the public were listened to we would have never gotten beyond sideshows and carnival tents. They like only that because it's relaxing and easy to take. The human being always wants to go back to his childhood and remain a half idiot, and very happy enjoying life.

In Hollywood itself, the writers were chiefly to blame. Writers, perhaps myself included, are not very pugnacious fellows. They usually have small chins and big heads and they talk weirdly. They cannot win an argument. They have to have a pencil in their hand before they can function. And also, they're kind of greedy. Writers usually get very little money. In Hollywood we got tons of money and this soothed us. It made us eager to bend our heads to the knout. We were like Siberian prisoners but in guilt gilded cages.

Hollywood was finally sunk by its egos. Its talents might have saved it, I don't know. If they had cut the salaries of all the writers down to nothing, and if they'd reduced the salaries of the stars to nothing, and the directors to nothing, they might have had a great industry, a great motion picture business.

The three great virtues of old Hollywood were high salaries, production of mass entertainment, and the accumulation of beautiful women. They were also its greatest sins.

The Writer's Craft

Advice to Young Writers

October 6, 1958: Ben's guests were two students from the Columbia University School of Journalism. Somewhat in awe of their host, they began by asking the elderly sage where a young hopeful might find the best training for a writing career.

Start as writers always start. By either loving or hating something too much. By thinking that everything in the world is wrong. The world's out of step and you know the answer. You start by being the most fat headed, objectionable, difficult-to-get-along-with young person there is. If you're that in the beginning, you can only hope to improve. That is, to tame down. To get less and less. That's called improvement.

Writing is the best training for a writer. I used to look down on people who wasted their time learning things in college. That was possibly very wrong. Those years of youth, where you express yourself to the irritation of your folks, betters and elders, are very vital ones. I used to think that all you could learn in college was to be a critic. That college gave you education, culture and taste. These are fatal to a writer. A writer will never write if he learns taste ahead of expression. The good writers I knew were abominable in their first five or ten years. They wrote like Hemingway or Sherwood Anderson. Unreadable.

You don't have to be angry. You have to have emotions. There are two kinds of writing, two ideas about literary art. One is the idea that the man who writes has. The other is the idea that the man who doesn't write has. The man who writes has no ideas at all about what he's angry at, what he's going to say. He has a desire to express something. Sort of a mental bellyache. The ideal in the critics' mind is somebody who will be a great writer and yet not be cleverer than they are. And that's why most of our great writers are pretty dull.

There can be no such word in a writer's mind as integrity. A man who speaks of integrity is speaking from the enemy's camp. A writer only knows himself. It's just as important to write badly as to write well. The only thing that's dangerous to a writer is not to write. If you write advertisements, if you write doggerel, limericks, movies, whatever you write, it loosens up your brain cells a bit. It's like shadowboxing, you get limber and facile. You're able to work and when you come to your good work, you find that your mind has been made creative by your bad work.

Anatole France said that "literature is the dreams of sick men." Sickness is perhaps another word for anger. You have to be angry when you enter the world because it's a pretty horrid place. It gets worse every ten years. The only fun you can have is to assert yourself, not to be taken in by it. To be amused at its horrors.

What Influences a Writer

>*October 6, 1958: Although he lacked the academic credentials his young guests from Columbia University were about to receive, Ben Hecht was an avid reader throughout his life. He could quote from the classics, Shakespeare or any number of modern writers.*
>
>*His guests were curious about what had the greatest influence on his career as a writer.*

Two things have influenced me. Women and other writers.

Many writers are stopped by a woman. As soon as a woman hears you're a writer, she has visions of you selling stories to the *Saturday Evening Post*. Visions of you making lots of money. The moment you write your first story, which is usually about a beggar full of vermin, she gets horrified. Disillusioned. She begins to holler at you.

Of course sex is more important to a writer than to any other type of performer. A bedfellow can do more for your style and more for your future than any critic or editor.

The chief influence you have to look for as a writer is someone who'll not be too angry if you're yourself. This requires a cunning, strange woman because to be yourself is to be annoying to everybody else. People don't like to be contradicted. They don't like to have their basic beliefs contradicted. It hurts them a great deal. In the home, it's very painful.

As far as writers, I used to read the French and Russians. I used to love any writer who touched on the theme called the soul of man. The emotions of greed, hate and violence. I also used to love any writer that wrote fancy phrases. Like Weisman the Frenchman, or Remy de Gourmont.

Writing for Hollywood

> *October 6, 1958: Movie writing provided Ben Hecht with a rich man's bankroll. He did what he called his serious writing in books and for the theater. Ben's young guests from Columbia University that night wanted to know more about the relationship between his work for films, and his prose.*

During the time I spent writing Hollywood movies, I also wrote twenty-three books, ten plays, two hundred short stories and sixty or seventy movies. Hollywood was to me like the publishing business was once to an author. Charles Dickens used to write serials for his publisher, Dostoyevsky used to write serials. Of course you couldn't write like those boys for Hollywood but you got paid the same way.

I spent so much time in Hollywood in order to make money. Hollywood was the greatest encourager of writers that I ever knew. It overpaid a writer. Instead of paying a writer one hundred dollars a week, it paid him five thousand dollars a week, ten thousand dollars a week. And nothing you ever wrote for Hollywood ever hurt you because no writing ever hurts you. The only thing that hurts you is idleness, rustiness and sleeping too late in the morning. You don't do that in Hollywood.

Money is an awfully good thing to work for because it makes you happy. I've always regarded money as applause. When I got a hundred thousand dollars for doing a job, I thought people were clapping hands. But I never kept the money, I never bought a stock or bond or life insurance. The moment I got enough money in the bank to last six months, I retired from work instantly. I couldn't imagine anybody working who had any money.

You see money can sometimes stop a writer. That's the dreadful thing about Hollywood. Whenever I made a lot of money in Hollywood, I quit writing 'til the money was gone. I was never able to write anything if I had a bank account. This becomes sort of a tug of war with yourself. You make some money, put it in the bank, then you wait until it's gone.

I don't think any writer every wrote anything except under the prod of needing to eat, needing to live. You can write movies when you're rich but you can't write novels when you're rich. You can't go that deep into yourself if you're secure and happy.

A writer just can't make any compromises. Talent is like your looks. You get old, your teeth fall out, your hair disappears and your talent wanes. A good writer isn't conscious of compromises or non-compromises. He just works.

A good writer is the same as a good fiddler. He gets up in the morning and he practices. For almost thirty years, when I get up in the morning, I've written four to eight hours a day as if I were employed as a plasterer. Where the compromise came in, I don't know. I just remember working hard all the time. Sometimes you worked on things you adored, sometimes you expressed yourself, sometimes you contrived plots, sometimes you made up childish stories. Sometimes you worked on one short story for a month and got fifty dollars and sometimes you worked a week on a movie and got twenty-five thousand dollars. There was no sense of difference in the work. You just kept on working.

There never is any motive for working. It's like drug addiction, its like boozing. You get started to work, and you get started like a canary bird in a cage to chirp, sing, yodel, flap your wings and you keep doing it. You pretend you're doing it for money. You pretend you're doing it for fame. You even pretend you're doing for people's anti-attitude, for non-fame, for indignation. What you actually do it for is yourself. You breathe, you walk and you work.

I'm proud of my prose work. I've done some movies that I like very much. When I see them, I'm surprised that they still exist. But movies can't give you everything. You can only get money from movies. You get very little money from books, comparatively. I worked four years on a book called *Child of the Century* and made maybe fifteen or twenty thousand dollars for the four years' work. I've done a movie in a week for which I had a hundred thousand dollars. You shouldn't ask for everything from one source.

I wasn't ashamed of working in Hollywood. I didn't despise, except intellectually, anything in Hollywood. It was a Garden of Eden for anybody who wanted to live a life of lotus eating. In addition to being a maniacal workman, I was always a terribly lazy man who liked to lie on a pier and do nothing. Hollywood permitted you to work violently, and idle violently. It paid you equally well for either, working or idling.

Budd Schulberg and Ben Hecht: *The Writer's Dilemma*

December 12, 1958: Ben's guest, Budd Schulberg, wrote such memorable films as On the Waterfront *and* A Face in the Crowd. *With so much in common with his guest, Ben sounded off on movies, writing, literature and politics, using Schulberg as an adversary. With every vitriolic Hecht comment, Schulberg seemed to retreat deeper into his shell.*

BH: You are the only American I can think of who is as mis-fortunate as I, being engaged in providing writing on all the fronts. You've been a movie writer, television writer, play writer, book writer, newspaper writer, essay writer and short story writer. Me too.

BS: Ben, maybe we can make it yet.

BH: Think we can? Well you must have as big an elephant's hide as I had, 'cause when you're on all fronts, you meet a lot of Sherman tanks called critics. I wanted to ask you one general question and see if we can gabble on from there. Culture, or high class provender for the mind is at a pretty low state in this country. What think you, sir?

BS: This is one of the great cultures, Ben. It sounds like we thicked it up, but we didn't. I think this is one of the great cultures of all time.

BH: For the mob, the crowd, or for the high class hermit who knows what's best. Are we a democratic or an aristocratic culture?

BS: Both I would say.

BH: Where's the second? I keep looking for it. Who? Where?

BS: Well, Ben, you must know, you've written it. It isn't only today

or last night, it's a couple of fellows in Chicago, they weren't too bad. Sandburg or Sherwood Anderson.
BH: Yes, very good.
BS: A few others. I could go on with a lot of others.
BH: Carl and Sherwood Anderson sang their songs thirty years ago. You're talking about my generation, that is the last half of my life. What has happened to the high class, slam banging protesting artist we used to have? Do you find them around still?
BS: Ben, we're sort of contemporaries.
BH: We ran across each other quite a bit in Hollywood.
BS: Yes, we did.
BH: Your father was my first boss, B.P. Schulberg.
BS: I remember it.
BH: And you worked on a picture I once did, didn't ya?
BS: Ben, I did.
BH: Confess, whatdya do to it? Ruin it?
BS: Since you couldn't help it, I didn't improve it.
BH: It was *Nothing Sacred*. I walked off it because the producer, Mr. David Selznick, and the director, Mr. Willy Wellman, had figured out they couldn't shoot the whole picture. They just shot half and wanted a new ending. I screamed and left and you did the new ending. Well, I forgive you.
BS: I don't entirely forgive you for walking off. Once you take a job you should see it through to the end.
BH: When you talk about culture for the masses, don't you think of movies as providing culture? You think movies are pretty hot, don't you?
BS: Ben, I think most movies are pretty cold but every once in a while there are one or two or three percent that are pretty hot. I really didn't come tonight to defend movies. I don't think you realize this because you were raised in a more cynical age. I'm not a romanticist. I'm almost as mean as you are. But I do think that we have a very encouraging culture that the Europeans, the English haven't begun to realize.
BH: The English have these roaring young men who are protesting about the Queen not being descended from God and the monarchy being on its last legs. Do you like them?
BS: We have a morals angry culture that goes much deeper.
BH: We have anger in this country? You had it, I remember. You

wrote a book called *What Makes Sammy Run*. There was a good right hook in that book.
BS: Thank you, Ben.
BH: And you wrote a nice book, *Waterfront*, and you wrote a movie called *Waterfront* where you watered it down at the end, with the cologne that's necessary to be sprinkled on work in Hollywood.
BS: That was a pretty tough picture.
BH: It was a lovely picture, but it wasn't as lovely as the book. It would have died had it been as good as the book because I don't think a good picture can sell a lot of tickets. I have never known of a picture that I admired as a first class picture, even the picture you wrote, *A Face in the Crowd*, that was a very good picture. It didn't sell.
BS: True.
BH: *The Informer* was a tremendous picture. It grossed seven hundred thousand dollars. You know of any good picture that made a fortune?
BS: It reminds me of the old argument about Goldwyn and Shaw. When Goldwyn saw Shaw he was talking about art and Shaw said well you're only interested in art and I'm only interested in money. You sound to me as if you're only interested in money. The fact that *The Informer* was made is something. The fact that we made *On the Waterfront* when for several years no film company would do it is something. The fact that *A Face in the Crowd* didn't make money and that we're proud we did it is something. You made a few like that.
BH: I had no pride in them. I did *The Scoundrel*, *Specter of the Rose*, *Crime Without Passion*, all kinds of rather good pictures. But, I had no pride in them because I saw them as entertainment. I never spent more than ten days writing one. And you had a consecrated attitude towards movies because you came out of Hollywood. I came out of a very tough town that loathed Hollywood and loathed New York and Paris, too.
BS: I came out of a tough town called Hollywood.
BH: What anger do you see in this country? Who are the angry writers? I'm a little petulant on this program here from night to night. There's a fellow called Collins in London who wrote *Memos of Public Baby*. Did you run into that?

BS: No, I'm sorry. I read about it, but...
BH: Well he's a screaming, screaming writer. He's not too good but he screams. Who have we got that complains, that yells? Take Mencken as a standard.
BS: By God that's a good standard.
BH: Have we got anybody?
BS: Ben, I feel this about Mencken and about our anger. Our anger is deep and the anger I feel that's come out of England is very recent and is rather shrill. I think that we're getting over our anger now, but we've learned from Mencken, we've learned from Dreiser. We've got the best line of angry old men from Mark Twain and Dreiser and Mencken and Lewis. I don't consider myself but just a tiny little cog in that tradition right up to Norman Mailer and on to Arthur Miller. But there is finally a thrust forward. It's like a line. Have you ever seen football played? You know sometimes there's a weak guard or a weak tackle but the line is pretty good. I feel our line is pretty good.
BH: I love your optimism. I'll try and share it. I find nothing true in what you're trying to say, but I find the line was wonderful. I find from Melville on way down to Red Lewis, wonderful, but suddenly I find this country turning into will of the mill. Its writers, I don't mean its public. The public has improved. Readers are better. The masses are much higher class, everything is higher class, except the writer. He has become a vanishing fellow to me. There was a scare thrown into this country about ten or fifteen years ago. If you expressed yourself as being pro–Russian or pro–Communist or pro-anything that wasn't pro-administration, they moved you off to hoosegow. They did this to a lot of the boys. Do you suppose that scared our writers a little? We had a wonderful writer, Dalton Trumbo, was one of the boys in trouble. A fine writer who went under a cloud.
BS: He wrote one excellent book, that book about the basket case, *Johnny Got His Gun*. But there was nothing in our country that would stop him from writing another book. And on the other hand Ben, I don't think that we were scared. I think maybe you got a little bit scared.
BH: Me scared? No way, I don't get scared. I kept yelling. I yelled all the time. I was even threatened with deportation until they discovered I was a New York boy.

BS: Do you know where you would have been deported to? Right back where you came from. Wisconsin. Truly, Ben, I do think this: that we have a very honest country, and we have a country where you can speak your mind, you could be in a little trouble and maybe you won't get hired. I think you're wrong about McCarthy.

BH: I liked McCarthy. I thought he was a great irritant and he made me happy although I was sorry when he lost his punch. You've got to have a villain in the country, a writer can't function without a target. I liked McCarthy. A very important fellow. Now we have nobody. No anti–McCarthy, there's no excitement to me as there used to be. I have an idea you can speak your mind in this country theoretically, but oddly don't hear any minds speaking. I read the press, of course I know about newspaper writers. They write what they think the boss in a lucid or sober moment would like to read. I think that we uniform ourselves here out of an inner police that we have much more than any country.

BS: Do you really think I do, and I don't consider myself great, but do you think that I sit down and say, "What are they going to like?" Do you really, Ben?

BH: I don't think you do it on purpose. I think you're a new kind of writer that this country has hatched. First you're very facile, you're very talented and I like your books, but without knowing it, you trim your sails to a certain audience. You trim them for instance when you write a different movie, then you write a book. Whether you say yes or no, I know that your dedication towards a book is five times more than it is towards a movie, no matter how hard you work on a movie. Nobody can tell you to change a phrase in a book. You'd shoot them. And lots of people have told you, and you haven't shot them, to change scenes in movies.

BS: I don't agree with you.

BH: You think you're as dedicated as a movie writer?

BS: When I try, yes. When I talked to Kazan about a movie and I said "I'll do it if it is like a play," and then if that picture is wrong, it's also my fault. It is not Sam Speigel's, it is not Kazan's, it is all of us together. I do think this, in our country we can fight for that. I don't think that you, except for a few times, in the East, really fought for that. And you could . . .

BH: For the movies you mean? To me movies were dime novels, I had one attitude...
BS: They're a powerful medium that you could have influenced...
BH: Not for expression. They were a powerful medium for an audience, not for an artist. They made fine audiences, they improved the dishwashing element of our hinterland. Instead of sitting around with nothing to do, people had some place to go except for church and it was a big improvement.
BS: Then why did you do so many? I think that's shameful.
BH: I don't think what we call art belongs to people, I think art, like religion, belongs to the few. The few who can see the vision, who can see the miracle. I think art's become part of the advertising mania in this country, but you like advertising too. You have a noble heart, Budd.
BS: You're really begging the question. I haven't advertised anything, I assume they will. I like my play.
BH: Your play is very good. I haven't seen it, but I read the book and I hope it's as good as the book. If we had a fellow like Pasternak in this country, do you think we would treat him any better than the Russians treated him?
BS: (pauses to think)
BH: No answer.
BS: You mustn't say no answer, Ben. You know for a long time I was amazed that I even heard myself speaking. I feel a very strong answer, but I want to think about it a moment. I think it's a very good question and I think the answer is black and white. The answer is, do you think we would have forbidden Arthur Miller from winning a prize for a work that everybody recognizes? And Arthur Miller has won prizes and his politics have not always been completely constant, not with me or with the population. This Pasternak thing is very sad and points up the difference between our countries.
BH: No, I think it points up in favor of Russia. We don't forbid Arthur Miller from winning prizes but we so depress, harass, annoy and vicerate his soul that he can't write for a period of two, three, four years. When you put such gloom and doom on a writer and you make him feel he's a traitor, you don't help a writer. You don't have to stop him from winning prizes.

BS: Ben, I think of myself as a writer and a very selfish writer and therefore I bring myself to the breaking point. Which is, would I rather be here writing, trying to say what I want? Or, would I rather be somewhere else? You know lots of them disappear.

BH: Yes, lots of them get killed. But I'd like to go to Russia and see what would happen. I loathe Russia because as a writer you can't write. But I'd like to see if that were true.

Art and Literature

November 26, 1958: Ben pulled out the mail bag and answered a number of viewer inquiries concerning modern literature, in particular, the work of Ernest Hemingway. In 1956, Hecht wrote the screenplay for Hemingway's novel A Farewell to Arms.

What is "art"? This word has caused even more bad writing and general confusion than the words "religion," "God" or "politics." To me art is a male version of childbearing. It's an expression. You have something you have to say. You groan, you moan, and you say it. You paint it, you dance it, you sing it. You express it out of your own soul.

"Non-art" is where you please people. Non-art is where you have very little to say. Where you have a great aptitude for mimicry, stealing, adapting, repeating and parodying. This is non-art, which covers most of our popular media like the movies, television and a great percentage of Broadway.

I have a sad feeling that we so-called writers and artists have sort of run our course. We haven't done very badly. In twenty-five hundred years we managed to pump a very fine sky of words into the world in which man adventured. But the fellow who expresses himself is not so important anymore. He's given his news to the world. The new artist today is the fellow who has the information that the poet hasn't. He's the scientist. He's the man sending covered wagons to the moon in next generation. He's going to be the new John Keats. The Shakespeare. He's going to show us real tricks that we didn't hear about. He's going to tell actually what our souls are and even bring back a photograph of God. He's the new artist.

I don't think too highly of today's writers. Novel writing has come on bad days. Modern novels are sort of an extension of true confession magazines, of movies, television shows. The novelists that began around the 1890s with Mark Twain, that included Sherwood Anderson and Dreiser, Thornton Wilder, Sinclair Lewis, were remarkable people. They had brains. They were looking at society and human beings and doing their best to report intellectually on these subjects.

All of this came to an unhappy end with the arrival of Ernest Hemingway on the scene, who was a writer without a brain but with a very fine camera lens. He introduced the business of writing baby talk. Novels that were beautifully reported by a camera.

Hemingway was the best of the bunch that came along after Sherwood Anderson and the difference chiefly is that in the Hemingway books, there's no effort to look into people. The dialogue is almost inept. It has been hailed as the greatest dialogue of our time. It's really baby talk. Phony, odd and cultish. It has no reality in it, no truth in it, and worse than that, it doesn't pry into the people that are talking. Everything is from the outside, beautifully done. All of Hemingway's books make fine movies without any change in them at all. They're all stereotyped people and journalistic situations.

His reputation is an odd thing. Intellectuals are usually represented by college professors and literary critics. And these boys are sort of odd. They're the armchair brigade who suddenly found a man who was able to give them a vicarious sense of fantasy sex and sight seeing. Most of the writers writing about America are writing about Podunk. Suddenly a man started writing about faraway places. He became sort of a Fitzgerald travelogue and they adored him for it.

In Hemingway's first successful book, *The Sun Also Rises*, he presented the college professors and the critics with a hero who was sexually impotent due to the fact that he had been wounded nobly while serving his country in the war. Despite his impotence he was a man of tremendous derring-do. This seemed to give the boys a hero they could kowtow to. His second successful book, *A Farewell to Arms*, had a fantasy sex story that you'd hardly read outside of an old fashioned true confession magazine. It was about a hero almost unable to talk, except baby talk. He was so powerful and marvelous a man that the woman he fell in love with, called Catherine Barkley, used to crawl around on her hands and knees. She was the most curried dog type of female ever put in fiction. She looked on this non-speaking, non-thinking man as a god. And this also inflamed the college professors and armchair literary brigade. They hailed this as one of the great Romeo and Juliet stories of the world. I had to do the movie adaptation so I read it fourteen times. It's a terrible book.

Nietzsche in Plano

November 26, 1958: After his mail, which was devoted to contemporary American literature, Ben told a Bedtime Story concerning the literary marketplace.

Great literature can sometimes sneak in on people and be embraced. I was covering a coal miner's strike in Carlinville, Illinois, some years ago. There'd been a great uprising in Herrin, Illinois, where the militia had shot down a number of miners and killed them. So, we expected high doings in Carlinville and I went there prepared for bloodshed.

It was a hot day. Middle Illinois can get hotter than the Sahara. I was walking down the street which was like an ironing board with a red hot iron in the sky. As I walked, I happened to glance into the window of the general store of Carlinville. The window was full of odd objects. It had plowshares, shivs, calico shirts, alarm clocks, all kinds of physics, jackknives, tools, and weapons.

There was also a row of eight books standing oddly in the midst of all this clutter. I looked at these books and they were all the same, copies of *Thus Spake Zarathustra* by the philosopher Friedrich Wilhelm Nietzsche. I couldn't believe my eyes. What Nietzsche was doing in Carlinville, I couldn't imagine. Mr. Nietzsche at that time, and today too, is the most explosive and wildly exciting anti-social, anti-conventional, anti-Christian, anti-Jewish, anti-everything philosopher that Europe has hatched.

I entered the store and asked for a copy of the book and the proprietor, a typical Lincolnesque, middle-Illinois looking fellow, gave it to me. He made the change very furtively, and looked oddly at me as I put the money in my pocket. Then I said to him, "How many of these books have you sold?" He said, "I've sold four of them." So I said to him, "How is that you happened to have stocked twelve volumes of *Thus Spake Zarathustra* in your store?"

He told me. "Well, um, it was kind of a funny thing that happened.

I came down one day and saw an advertisement. I must have had a hangover or something. I thought they were advertising a sequel to Tarzan so I sent away for twelve copies because Tarzan always went big in this part of the country. When I got it I saw it wasn't Tarzan but I was stuck with them. And of the four books I sold, one of them was returned to me but the three others the fellows have kept them. I think they're pretending to read them, I don't know."

That's one way in which a great philosopher can enter the soul of a country. By mistake.

The Writer's Antagonists

September 19, 1958: Drama critic Richard Watts was Ben's guest. Some of Ben's most intense opinions concerned critics. Before his interview with Mr. Watts, who was the drama critic for the New York Post, *Hecht delivered a sermon on the playwright's chief nemesis.*

Anatole France once said that "literature is the dreams of sick men." I think criticism is a few steps lower than that in the ailment department.

In any fracas between playwright and critic, the critic must always sound like a winner. A critic's "tut tut" can be a disaster for the playwright. The playwright's most devastating answers can only add importance to the critic. One reason perhaps is that a critic never gets licked. One reason that he never gets licked is that he is never in the ring with anybody. He can become a champion just shadowboxing.

Every time I have written a book, play, essay or pageant, critics have emerged like Indians around a covered wagon with bows and arrows. Sometimes they didn't shoot, but waved hello. But, when I look back I'm inclined to forget the friendly Indians. I remember only the ones who were after my scalp.

I never had much feeling for the thousands of critics popping merrily away throughout the republic. I read these far off critics of my work with a steady hand for they are critics without power. However hot or cold they blow they influence no one.

There is only one civilized spot. One single city in the U.S. and possibly Christendom where critics are all powerful. This blighted area is our city of New York. The critics of power are the seven men who lurk in the drama pages of the New York press. Occasionally one of these seven writes a piece cooling disclaiming any such power. The fate of a play he purrs to Little Red Riding Hood, depends on the public and of course on the play. This is false modesty because "Oh what big teeth you have, Grandma."

The power of the New York morning-after review to bankrupt or enrich the many people involved in a play is a statistical fact. The critics can bowl over plays like nine pins. On the other hand, their non-guilty verdicts are equally potent. A blessing from these grand poobahs brings gold to the box office.

In my eyes, the actual reviews that exercise such life and death power in our theater are usually stale bits of writing full of weary sentences, repetition and monotonous righteousness. Our critics are literate, but determinedly on the dull side. They write the way Perry Como sings. Appearing anywhere but the New York papers, their combined findings would not influence a field mouse. They are seldom power conscious, they have a low sadism content.

Put together, today's drama critic boys are the least murderous and cunning lot to line up against playwrights and actors since the 1920s. You'll find among them no Bruin, Woollcott, Benchley, Percy Hammond or Miss Dorothy Parker.

Bob Benchley, for instance, listened one opening night to the native heroine of *White Cargo* recite, "Mc Nube. Me bad girl. Me stay." Rising from his aisle seat, Mr. Benchley announced, "Me Bobby. Me bad boy. Me go."

And there was the time Heywood Broun was sued by an actor for stating in print, "Mr. O is the world's worst actor." The judge awarded actor "O" one dollar in damages and warned Bruin sternly about repeating such libel. When the actor appeared in a new play the next season Bruin wrote cautiously, "Mr. O is not up to his usual standards."

There are a hundred such tales which reveal the superior viciousness, wit and egomania of the yesterday critics, yet their power to make or break a play was small beside our present reviews. Then how is it that these milder dull fellows hold a city captive with their opinions? The answer seems obvious to me. Their power is derived from a new quality in their readers rather than in themselves.

New Yorkers, the most numerous mass of citizens in the world, have developed a strong "herd instinct." They do not move in trickles here and there, they flock. They look for the shepherd's signal and jam only the approved lobbies. Point the way and they swarm where they are told, ba-ba-ing for tickets. Tell them it's a bad or so so play and they remain in their home pastures.

But there's an older reason for the power of critics. It's that they're the people's representatives and not the artists. They're in the world to preserve its cultural status quo and keep the human herd feeling comfortable that it's going in the right direction. The critic must always further the idea that the world is flat. The artist must always try to prove it's cylindrical or cone shaped. As for the hallmark of the critics, the seeming smugness, the certainty that always knows what's what; the certainty that always sits in judgement and never questions itself; well, God evidently saw fit in handing out his gifts to men to give the poet wonder, the novelist confusion, the playwright search, all he had left for the critic was certainty and oblivion.

I have another notion about criticism. When I was on the papers in Chicago, I tried to put this over. The drama section of a paper is run differently than the literary section. In the literary section, a child's book is not given to some old spinster and a mystery thriller is not handed to some fellow infatuated with Marcel Proust. Reviews are assigned into their natural niches and result is that we get literary criticism based on the intent of the writer who was writing the particular work. On dramatic criticism we have one slightly tiring fellow who keeps being shagged to all the battlefronts, whether it's a farce, whether it's O'Neill, whether it's a song and dance song. Would it be better if there was a group of critics?

Flavius Is a Dirty Dog

September 19, 1958: Ben's intense feelings about critics did not frighten his guest, drama critic Richard Watts. He seemed to enjoy the intensity of Hecht's anger, but chose not to serve as spokesmen for his fellow judges. For his Bedtime Story, Ben decided to end the evening with a note of levity.

This is a sort of shaggy dog story about the power of critics. It's about a Roman patrician BC named Flavius who was one of the most famous fellows in the Roman empire. He rivaled Trimalcio as a feast giver. He used to give dinner parties that involved three to five hundred diners, with a hundred dancing girls, fifty poets, acrobats, sword swallowers, everything he could dig up to entertain his party. Flavius wanted to be known as the most lavish and generous host of his time. A fellow whom everybody loved.

Things were going along swimmingly until one night at one of his biggest parties, his cook got angry. The cook and Flavius had an awful row. Flavius fired the cook and the cook left.

In leaving the grounds, the cook paused to write an inscription on a wall. The inscription read, "Flavius is a dirty dog." About ten minutes later Vesuvius erupted, buried the wall, buried Flavius and buried all the grandeur and glory that was Pompeii.

About eighteen hundred years later when they were digging up Pompeii, one of the first things they came upon was a wall that had this mysterious statement on it, "Flavius is a dirty dog." And to this day, nothing more is known of Mr. Flavius.

Let the Critics Live

October 7, 1958: Billy Rose was Ben's guest. The great showman worked on a number of projects with Hecht, including the epic theater piece Jumbo, *and* The Great Magoo, *a play by Hecht and Gene Fowler. The Great Magoo closed in eleven days. Popular with audiences, its frank, juicy language offended the critics.*

Ben remembered its demise and the reaction of several of its financial backers.

We used to hole up in the Algonquin Hotel when we had to write. Gene Fowler was in his suite one simmering July evening after a day of pounding pencil into page. He was brushing his teeth and while gargling, the glass slipped out of his hand, exploded on the sink, and some of its sharper projectiles made their way to Mr. Fowler's exposed member. He was untouched except for his reproductive organ, which was spurting blood like a geyser. Somehow he summoned a physician who stitched the lacerated projectile as if it were a baseball.

I was on the town that night and stopped by to see Gene before going home to Nyack. After learning of the details of this rather unique accident, I suggested Fowler spend some time in the hospital, but he was concerned that some snoopy visitors might get the wrong idea about the nature of his ailment. Gene decided it was time for us to write a play we'd already plotted. So, he came with me back to Nyack, where we wrote *The Great Magoo*.

The play opened six months later and the critics gave us their version of the broken gargle glass. It seems they found our drama too lewd a tale for the Great White Way. The morning after the opening, Mr. Fowler and I were sitting around, tarred and feathered by the critics, unable to move. We were backstage with our producer, Billy Rose when three rather stocky fellows arrived and asked for the owner of the show. They said they represented a certain union, an underworld organization who had helped back the show. Our visitors wanted to know which three of the nine anti-Magoo critics Mr. Rose wanted knocked off. "Just give us the names of the ones you think are the worst guilty. When we leave, you never saw us and we never saw you." Fowler told them to wait outside while we deliberated.

Now we were of two minds about it. Billy was firmly against any carnage. Gene spoke out for the score of playwrights who had crosses to bear against Percy Hammond, Burns Mantle, Alexander Woollcott and their fellow fault finders. I reasoned that critics were in the world to preserve its cultural status quo and keep the human herd feeling comfortable that it's going in the right direction.

We were facing quite a problem. After nearly two hours of debate we finally decided to let the critics live. It's a deed I've sometimes regretted.

My Semitic Brothers

The Broken Vase

October 14, 1958: On an evening of Hollywood memories, Ben told a story about his friend Charlie Lederer's brush with anti-Semitism, the subject of Hecht's 1944 book, A Guide for the Bedeviled.

This story takes place in India, where my friend Charles Lederer was stationed during World War II. After some time, Charlie was promoted to the rank of major. It seems that a certain British colonel asked for his help in wooing an English lady in Calcutta. Charlie was very whimsical and could be no end of service for him. So, Charlie accompanied the couple for an evening.

During the evening the British lady kept denouncing Jews all the time.

Now Charlie is half Jewish. His father was a Jew, George Lederer, the producer. His mother however was a Catholic, Rene Davis, a singer who popularized *Every Little Movement Has Meaning of Its Own*. She was quite a prima donna. And so Charlie listened with his very owl-like eyes to the denunciation of Jews that transpired during the evening.

They came to the lady's home in Calcutta, a very well furnished home. A very elegant home. There was a cabinet in the home that contained liquor, and the lady asked Charlie if he would get the drinks out. Charlie went to the cabinet on top of which was perched a very expensive jade vase. He put his hand on the cabinet door and said to the lady for the first time, "By the way, what have you got against Jews?" And the lady said "Why, I have nothing against Jews, nothing at all."

Charlie jerked the cabinet, knocked the vase over, smashed it to pieces and said, "You have now."

Jews for Sale

October 23, 1958: Peter Bergson was Ben's guest. Bergson, née Hillel Kook, was Hecht's captain in the fight to save the dying Jews of Europe. As the Irgun commander in America, Bergson was an important catalyst in the battle for an independent Hebrew nation.

Ben Hecht's Jewish awakening occurred when he learned of Hitler's extermination plans. In 1941, as the German anaconda was swallowing Europe, Hecht and collaborator Charles MacArthur wrote Fun to Be Free, *a pageant which advocated U.S. participation in the war. Hecht also wrote magazine articles about the threat to European Jews, and a regular newspaper column for* PM, *a New York afternoon daily. Hecht's columns, which attempted to sound an alarm, caught the attention of a group of men dedicated to action: Bergson, Yitsaq Ben-Ami, and Samuel Merlin. They contacted him and they quickly joined forces.*

The Committee, as Hecht called it in his autobiography, encountered enormous obstacles in their attempts to awaken American opinion on behalf of the Nazi victims. Even when they had proof of impending disaster, their impassioned cries were largely ignored by the allied governments. A rift rapidly developed between the group and the Jewish establishment, who favored a more conciliatory approach. Rabbi Stephen Wise, whom Hecht called "the King of American Jews," claimed Mr. Bergson was "a greater danger than Hitler," because he felt the Committee's outspoken activities would generate even more anti-Semitism in America.

The storm center of Jewish international life, the Committee mobilized the sympathy and active support of at least a million people. Hecht wrote a series of newspaper advertisements that helped the Committee raise millions of dollars and call attention to the massacre. He also tried, unsuccessfully, to raise money in Hollywood. All of the rich, influential studio bosses were Jewish and Hecht repeatedly tried to solicit their support on behalf of their European brethren. But for the successful Jews of America, the nightmare on the other side of the world had little immediacy. Not one Hollywood film produced during World War II ever mentioned what was happening to the Jews in Europe.

Ben's Bedtime Story recalled one of his printed bombs of freedom that set off a firestorm of controversy.

One night while walking on Fifth Avenue at midnight, Kurt

Weill the composer showed me a clipping from a Swiss newspaper stating that the government of Romania had offered the governments of the United States and Great Britain seventy thousand Jews it had within its borders. It wanted fifty dollars a piece to transport these Jews outside the Romanian borders. The reason it was making this offer was because the Germans hadn't yet come in. There were only twelve German battalions in all of Romania and they were going to pour in any week and murder the seventy thousand Jews.

Our group, led by Peter Bergson, dashed all over the place. We rushed to Washington and we tried to get verification of this offer. We were told by the State Department, the White House and all official quarters that no such offer had been made by any government, Romania or anybody else.

We investigated further and discovered the offer had been made. And so I wrote an ad which we printed as a full page in many of the big newspapers of the country. The ads proclaimed in large type: "For Sale to Humanity, 70,000 Jews, Guaranteed Human Beings, $50 a piece."

We tried to provoke and startle the Jewry of the country into giving money and getting these Jews out and believing that such a thing was going on. We failed.

All the officials in Washington, including Mr. Roosevelt, Mr. Morganthau, Mr. Hull, denied there was any truth in the thing. About three, four months later, the Germans came into Romania; the seventy thousand Jews, including some thirty thousand children, were killed and murdered.

After the war, numerous books were written, among them Mr. Morgenthau's and other officials' memoirs and reminiscences. In these books you can find today the truth that such an offer was made by Romania, such an offer was received by our president, by our State Department, and such an offer was spiked in order to prevent the noise getting abroad that Jews were being murdered and thus keeping the ports of Palestine closed against any possible refugees.

Fifty Rabbis Can't Say No

October 7, 1958: Billy Rose was Ben's guest. Following an an evening of show business memories, Ben told a Bedtime Story concerning a pageant that the Committee presented at Madison

> *Square Garden and in other cities around the country in 1943. Hecht wrote* We Will Never Die, *Rose produced the show, Kurt Weill of* Threepenny Opera *fame composed the music and Moss Hart, later who staged* My Fair Lady, *served as director. Two standing room only performances were given at Madison Square Garden on March 9 and 10, 1943, with thousands listening to the pageant over loudspeakers in the freezing cold.*

One of the big adventures Billy Rose and I had was producing *We Will Never Die* at Madison Square Garden, to protest against the massacre of the Jews in Europe. Those were tough days. Most Jews were very silent on the subject and we had a lot of trouble.

One of the acts Billy and I put on in the Garden that night consisted of fifty rabbis from the old country, refugees. The youngest was about seventy-five. They were bearded, and strangely dressed. My notion was that we'd open the show by having them come out and recite a Hebrew prayer that begins "Shimai Israel." A day before the show went on I discovered that the rabbis couldn't do this because it was sacrilegious for a Jewish rabbi to come into a theater and recite this ancient prayer.

We called a meeting of the rabbis and I was to address them. I couldn't think of what to say to them. One of the rabbis stepped up and asked if he could speak to the rabbis on my behalf. I told him he certainly could. I've never forgotten the speech he made to his fellow rabbis.

He was an old man about eighty years old with a beard down to his knees. He spoke in Yiddish, a language I half remember from my youth. He said, "Dear fellow rabbis. I can tell you very little you don't know about God. And you know as much as I do about Jews, I think you know as much as I do. But the town of Bubberick where I was born and until recently lived, I don't think you know so much.

"Well in this town we built a theater some years ago. People came from all over, as far as ten miles away to attend the opening. On the steps of the theater sat a beggar. He watched a horde of people go in but he couldn't understand it.

"He waited until the show was over, until they came out, and he said to one member of the audience, 'What went on in there?' And the audience member said, 'Oh, a great tenor sang.' The beggar said, 'What did he sing?' and the audience member said, 'He sang beggar's songs.' The beggar looked at him and said, playing his little accordion, 'Did he sing this song?' And he sang a snatch. The man said, 'Yes he sang that.' The beggar said, 'Did he sing this song?' and he sang a snatch. The man said, 'Yes he sang that too.'"

Then my rabbi with the long beard said to the other fifty rabbis, "We are the beggar on the steps with the true song, and this gentlemen is asking us to go in and sing it for the world."

The next night the fifty rabbis appeared and committed sacrilege and recited Shimai Israel for our pageant, *We Will Never Die*.

They Will Not Be Forgotten

October 22, 1958: Ben's mail call was peppered with comments about Germans. He told a Bedtime Story concerning the Warsaw ghetto. In the midst of an era that has seen the fusion of technology and news, it seems rather unbelievable that the battle fought by the Jews of Warsaw went unnoticed.

This story is about a Jewish Thermopylae that has remained unknown and unremembered. It was a battle that the Jews fought in the early forties, ten times more bloody and violent than the battle the Hungarians fought so well against the Soviets in Budapest in nineteen-fifty-six.

During the war, the Germans were in Warsaw and their fun was going to be to kill the forty-five thousand Jews in the Warsaw ghetto. They intended to get the Jews as if they were shooting deer in a deer park. They had already exterminated, gassed and quick-limed some million and a half Jews in the concentration camps around Treblinka.

Well, the Jews decided to put up a fight. The Germans came marching into the ghetto and were met by the forty-five thousand Jews who were armed with hand-made grenades, old pipes full of dynamite, staffs, plumbers' supplies, kitchen knives, anything they could find. And with these they had at the Germans. They stood the Germans off for five weeks and the Germans began to think that it was a little more than shooting deer in a deer park. They sent their tanks in, they sent their airplanes over.

The Jews stood and fought and while they were fighting, they had a radio station going. One radio transmitter, where they were able to talk to the world. They didn't complain or ask for any approval. All they wanted was a few more guns. A little more powder for their tin cans. They broadcast an appeal once an hour. And while they sent this appeal out, the forty-five thousand died, to a man and to a woman. There wasn't a Jew left alive when the Nazis finally came in. All the dead Jews were quickly thrown into the lime pits and in prepared graves.

The odd thing about this Thermopylae that the Jews fought was that despite their daily appeal to the democracies and to their fellow Jews all over the world, and despite their watch of the skies day and night for something to drop, not even a cap pistol was dropped to them. They didn't even get an audible round of applause when their Thermopylae was over. They died, they were buried, and they've been more or less forgotten. I remember them.

A Frenchman's Gallantry

October 30, 1958: Ben's guest was the French actress Lilo for a discussion of love and fidelity. Hecht turned serious for a Bedtime Story about a Frenchman who stood up to the Nazis. While Hecht, Bergson and their Committee comrades waged a war against public indifference, there were a few isolated instances of support for the Jews.

French culture represents half the bright thinking and beauty of this whole world. It's backed up by a succession of authors beginning way back. In its present generation there are dozens of them, Cocteau, de Gourmont, Gide, France, Proust, and they read like a roster of genius. They also have painters, everything beautiful in France. But in addition to its beauty-making people, France is noted for the fact that gallantry reaches its height in the French nation. I don't think that any nation has a better record of gallantry than the French.

One of the stories that most thrilled me during the war was the story of Dr. Thierry de Martel who was the greatest surgeon of France. Dr. Martel was in charge of the American hospital in France while they were fighting the war. All of the wounded were under his care. The Germans, of course, came in and took Paris at the beginning of the war. And when this great doctor who'd also been a "war hero" saw the Germans come in, he didn't see Germans. He saw people with the mist of murder hanging over them. He smelled the stench of six million Jews, three million Poles, ten million civilian Russians, all murdered. All killed in cold blood.

He watched the Germans come into his hospital. They threw out all the French wounded and put in the German wounded instead. And they approached Dr. Martel. They approached him with their fat necks, watery eyes, and no ankles. But they always had the grease of politeness in their waists. They bowed to Dr. Martel and they said they knew what a great scientist he was. They wouldn't think of depriving him of his post. They wanted his genius and they wanted it to serve them.

Dr. Martel asked for a half hour to think over this fine offer. He retired to his office where he sat for a few minutes. And when the Germans came in, forty-five minutes later, Dr. Martel was dead; he had killed himself. He refused to give his genius to the murderers who had taken over his country. This is one of the most gallant things I know of a Frenchman doing.

What the Allies Did

October 22, 1958: Ben answered his mail and discussed the Allied reaction to the meticulous slaughter of millions of people during World War II. Throughout the war, the Committee kept running ads written by Hecht to try and get a response from the Roosevelt administration. After the president, Mr. Churchill and Mr. Stalin composed a 1943 Moscow declaration of other atrocities which ignored the Jewish murders, Hecht himself wrote to Roosevelt as co-chairman of the Emergency Committee to Save the Jewish People of Europe. He said, "There is not one word about the slaughter of more than two million Jewish men, women and children! That this, the darkest crime in all the annals of history, is not mentioned specifically and stressed in a statement on Nazi atrocities, must be considered as a fatal oversight or else a grave injustice, not only to the Jewish people, but to humanity itself." Hecht received no reply from the president.

One Hecht ad did provoke a response from FDR. "My Uncle Abraham Reports" ran in several newspapers around the country. In the advertisement, Hecht told of a deceased uncle, a ghost who was now sitting on the window sill two feet from Mr. Roosevelt, waiting to see what the president would do on behalf of the Jews. Presidential adviser Bernard Baruch called Hecht and

> told him that the president was very upset about the ad, and that in the next few weeks the president was going to take some definite action. Ben and the Committee agreed to stop all advertisements concerning the president. Roosevelt went to the Middle East, where he met with Saudi leader Ibn Saud. When he returned, he told a press conference that he learned more about the "Jewish problem" from five minutes with the Arab leader than the exchange of two or three dozen letters. Roosevelt then continued his policy of silence. Hecht called Baruch to tell him the Roosevelt amnesty was over. The Committee resumed its advertisements.

After the war, the Nuremberg war crimes trials took place. I think they did something very bad. The Nuremberg trials exonerated and freed the German of guilt, at very small expense to Germany. And they enabled the United States, Britain and the rest of the world to put its arm around the German murderer because he'd paid for his atrocity. Our leaders could once again become very chummy with the people who had committed a crime against the human race the like of which is not known in history.

The men in the camps and those who organized the murders were merely carrying on a tradition Franklin Roosevelt and Winston Churchill and Joe Stalin started. The tradition was that Jews were not privileged to become corpses even. They were not privileged to live, they were not privileged to die.

In 1943 there was a pact in Moscow signed by Roosevelt, Churchill and Stalin. It listed more than fifty crimes for which the Germans were going to be punished after the war. They were called atrocities. They mentioned the killing of some Polish officers, Norwegian officers, Greeks, all sorts of people. They did not mention the word Jew. Already there had been four million Jews killed. Put in boxcars, burned to death, killed alive, shot down in huge masses with machine guns, burned in fires. Women, children. These were not mentioned.

To mention the Jews would be to call attention to the fact that there were two more million waiting to be murdered and to call attention to that fact would be to have to save them and to have to save them would be to wreck their little tiddlywink oil policy they were playing with the Arabs in Palestine. So, our President Roosevelt, Mr. Churchill and Stalin locked the last two million Jews in with their murderer, and let them all be killed.

During the war, I worked with Mr. Peter Bergson to get a statement from the White House denouncing the German murder of Jews. We tried to get the leader of the most powerful and respected nation on the face of the earth to condemn the Germans' "let's kill all the Jews campaign." We never got one.

The Irgun

November 17, 1958: Robert Briscoe, a former mayor of Dublin, was Ben's guest. Mr. Briscoe was a Jew, and in addition to fighting the British in Ireland, he fought alongside the Irgun in Palestine.

During World War II, England refused to open the gates of Palestine to European refugees fleeing certain death. Fearing a large settlement of Jews would threaten control of the region, Great Britain continually sabotaged any attempt to relocate any more than a handful of Jews to their rightful homeland. With the support of President Roosevelt and other Allied leaders, free world ports were closed to all but a handful of escapees. The Irgun smuggled Jews out of Europe and into Palestine during the war although many of their boats were sunk or turned away by the English navy.

Once Hitler was defeated and the six million had perished, the Committee turned its efforts to establishing a Jewish state. With Menachem Begin commanding the Irgun in Palestine, Bergson and company tried to enlist American backing. Ben wrote a play entitled A Flag Is Born *which starred Paul Muni and featured a young Marlon Brando. It ran for several months on Broadway and other cities. Profits from the production financed a boat, rechristened the* SS Ben Hecht, *which tried to transport refugees from Europe to Palestine. The vessel was seized by the British navy, the refugees were relocated to Cyprus, and its crew was detained. When he learned of the news, Ben Hecht declared, "The British can capture ships to their heart's content but there are more where they came from."*

On June 19, 1947, Hecht's "Letter to the Terrorists of Palestine" appeared as a full page advertisement in prominent American newspapers. The ad praised the Irgun freedom fighters for battling the British by any means possible, including terrorism. And it accused the Zionists worldwide of a slipshod commitment to establishing a Jewish state.

A firestorm quickly errupted. Throughout Hecht's tenure as a Jewish propagandist, he had encountered intense resistance from all quarters. His Hollywood card-playing cronies warned him repeatedly of involvement with the Jewish rabble rousers. By the time the "Letter" appeared, he was already a pariah in the entertainment community, with former friends refusing to acknowledge him in public.

Repercussions in the Jewish community were even more vociferous. During the Second World War many Jews thought Ben Hecht a troublemaker. Rabbi Stephen Wise tried to squash Hecht's pageant, We Will Never Die, and after Peter Bergson formed the Hebrew Committee of National Liberation, Wise testified to a congressional committee that Bergson deserved deportation. With Hecht's plays and ads for the Irgun, he became an object of outright scorn—even more vilified in the Jewish press. Natham Goldmann, a Jewish leader who became a force in the Ben-Gurion Israeli government, proclaimed that Hecht was "very insignificant and he does not represent even a small section of American Jewry." There may have been more truth in the statement than Mr. Goldmann realized.

At the time there was a schism in Jewish leadership. The majority of important Jews were Zionists, led by Wise in America and Chaim Weitzmann in Palestine. They too wanted a Jewish homeland, but it was to be a showplace for select Jews, not the uneducated European masses. During the Second World War, they supported the British by informing on their Irgun brothers. Hecht believed that through their lack of forceful action, the Jewish establishment had served as silent partners in the German butchery. In Palestine, the Zionists and their Hagganah army tried to bring about the establishment of the Jewish statement by peaceful means.

Committed to the violent overthrow of British rule in Palestine because they knew that was the only way to achieve statehood, the Irgun Zvai Leumi were considered radical guerrillas. Hecht's "Letter" only served to reaffirm the spirit and determination of the Irgun to their enemies. Great Britain had a lynch mob reaction to the "Letter," with English newspapers calling for Hecht's immediate arrest. Instead they thrust a dagger into his career, banning his films in the British Empire, which at that time represented a sizable share of worldwide distribution.

As for the Irgun, it was their dogged tenacity that brought the matter of Jewish statehood before the United Nations. In 1948, Israel was born.

A revolution is an explosion of the heart and it's the only gauge by which people can rid themselves of a tyrant's institutions that are too top heavy. Its always a minority who fights a revolution. I admire them because they're the most active of human beings.

Most revolutionists usually get to run the country after their victories. It has always been true except in one case. The American revolutionists ran the country. The French, the Russian, the Irish revolutionists got some sort of powers. But the Jewish revolutionists, the Irgun, the ones who began the fight for freedom in Palestine and turned it into Israel, they got their comeuppance. They not only fought the British, they also fought the Zionists and the members of the Jewish Agency.

The Zionists and the members of the Jewish Agency officials acted as an informer group for the British and turned over hundreds and hundreds of them to the British, to hang, and to put in the British concentration camps.

In Palestine, the British had on their side all the Jews belonging to the Zionist movement, and all the Jews belonging to the Jewish Agency who functioned as sort of an auxiliary informer group. Yes, these Jews championed the British. I remember Chaim Weitzman saying he suffered more over the killing of some British mayor than he had over the death of his own son. His pro-Britishness used to startle me because I was new in the business. I thought the Jews were anti-British. It turned out only about two percent of them were.

And when the Irgun had raised eight million dollars' worth of armaments and was bringing them in a boat called the Altalena to Palestine, Mr. Ben-Gurion's government came down to the pier where the boat that Begin commandeered was anchored, fired on it, blew it up and killed twenty-six of the patriots that were coming there. He was afraid the Irgun would have a little power after the revolution was won and so he tried to kill off its leaders. He succeeded. He killed off the best of them. They have no power now.

From Where I Sit

The State of Our Country

January 21, 1959: Ben answered his mail. A number of letters that night focused on the state of America. As usual, Ben rose to the occasion and delivered a sermon revealing his heartfelt view.

We've accomplished nothing but to create bigger messes for each succeeding generation.

I read about a philosopher recently named Carl Krauss, a mysterious fellow who wrote in Vienna some years ago and whose works have long disappeared and whom Eric Heller writes is "the greatest of all modern thinkers." One quote I read from him fascinated me. He wrote long before our present situation, "We are trapped in a tragedy and unable to recognize our guilt."

Americans have become afraid of the word "people." Anytime people do anything, it's as if lepers, monsters and communists are doing it. They don't mind killings when they're done by policemen, authorities or dictators. They can't stand people doing anything. It's very odd that Americans should be frightened of people because we were originally a people. Our humanitarianism has become a little askew. The best we can do now as Americans is love our crooked neighbors with our crooked hearts.

It seems our glorious land specializes in turning out assembly line human beings. Radicalism, which was once the keynote of American life, is gone from our country. The worst thing the Russians have done to our country as yet, is to rob us of radicalism. It used to be a lively hearted, healthy outcry against corruption, injustice and bigotry, all the things people can't stand. Today radicalism is a sort of a synonym for treason. Instead of the good old fashioned American radicals, we have a tribe of journalistic pipsqueaks who make a mockery of courage by hurling thunderbolts at alleged little ex-commies who are no more harmful to our country than june bugs.

Our former radicals were stout hearted but not quite stout hearted enough. The media eventually became closed to them. Most of television, the newspapers, the magazines, radio dried up on them. The only place open for a radical became a publishing house because radicals are smart enough to write books.

They also subsided because there's an economic factor involved. You lose your job. You get boycotted. You get blacklisted, you get pushed around all over the place if you speak up against something a little too loudly.

They kept the country in a happy ferment. They actually improved the country. Little by little they made it a better place to live in. It was a much gayer and exciting place than it is now under our cabalas of silence, conformity and belief only in platitudes.

Censorship

December 15, 1958: Actress Monique van Vooren was Ben's guest. A well educated woman, she touched a number of bases with Ben in what proved to a provocative interview. After soliciting her views on censorship, Ben expressed his opinion.

As you mature, which is a synonym for decomposing, you get a more open view of the things that have been. Of their charms and their failings. And one of the great failings in my young life was a mistake we all made. By we, I mean a lot of mighty fellows who jumped at the Victorian era and laid it to rest. There was Theodore Dreiser, Sherwood Anderson, H.L. Mencken, George Nathan—lord, there was dozens of us. I was among them.

We carried cutlasses and we removed censorship. We knocked out all the asterisks from the novels. We opened the stage. We put pregnant women, unmarried, on the stage and we called them heroines. We did everything we thought would be happy and our cry was, "Let joy be unconfined and if confined pray God it be a girl." This was our battle cry against the censors.

What has happened I think as the result of all this was that we made a big mistake. It seems to me that by removing censorship, we also took a fall out of sex. The sexual coloration of our time today is much more pallid. It's much more lackadaisical. By removing God and the devil both from outside the bedroom we reduced sex to sort of a casual dubious exercise. It's lost its great excitement, its great pull. I think we should have let censorship stay. We would have had more fun.

Look at what happened when censorship was most effectively applied in this country. Prohibition. Prohibition practically turned the entire country into drunkards. Think of what would happen if sex censorship was applied like it used to be.

What is it that makes nearly all our programs the same? What is it that makes all our acting, all our stories, all our objectives the same. Who is the censor in this country? Is it the stupidity or mediocrity of the people at work?

It used to be normal for a fellow to dislike Nick Carter and Liberty Boys of '76, and Deadeye Dick in the old days. A normal man with normal intelligence could dislike it. But today disliking a movie with the same intellectual content stamps you as a madman and I don't know why that should be.

Censorship is much easier than sanity. Sanity takes a lot of work. My feelings about censorship usually get me tongue-tied. I've been angry at it since I was nine years old. I think censorship is a device to insure the well being of the feebleminded. If we have a country that has more morons and cretins in it than normal people, we should have a censor to take care of them. But I think we have a country that can take care of itself. I don't remember anything depraved or even violent happening as the result of outside forces.

Individualism

December 30, 1958: Ben devoted an evening to himself. As a young reporter, he held H.L. Mencken as one of his idols. It was Mencken who published Hecht's first short story and had a profound influence on his thinking. Hecht remained a Mencken supporter throughout his life. One of Mencken's recurring themes was the individual versus society. That struck a responsive chord with Hecht, especially in light of the Cold War.

The modern world is witnessing the decline and death of individuality. Individual man is being made a faceless part of democracy, socialism, communism and fascism. Although at variance in mood and practice, all modern political systems make for the same goal posts — how to run most conveniently for the crowd.

My feeling is that Americans frighten themselves into regimentation. We don't have to be clubbed into line like the Russians do. We have no policeman telling me or you what to do, but instinctively we do the thing that's least harmful to our cowardice. The United States is muzzling itself out of an overwhelming, foolish respect for Russia.

One of my heroes was H.L. Mencken. I think Mencken sowed more deeply than ever he imagined. There's a tremendous percentage of people in this country who have fed at the Mencken fountain; people who are individualistic and who are not taken in by the shambling bombastic platitudes of the day.

Mencken told me when I was very young, about seventeen or eighteen, that the fight so far, the first fight, has been between human desire for original sin and the expression thereof, and the human desire to get to heaven. This fight has lasted about a thousand years and the preachers have lost. Nobody wants to go to heaven anymore. They've given that up. There's no such place and they've forgotten it.

Now the fight, and this was long, long before communism or anything, now the fight he told me, is been between society and the individual. Society is going to repress the individual just as the preachers tried to repress the animal. It's going to take away his decency. It's going to take away his ability to speak the truth out of his own feelings and his own responses to life. In this fight, Mencken told me, the victory is going to the wrong side. Society is going to win. The human being will end up without a truth of his own to speak. He'll end up as a mouthpiece for the herd and only say those things he's told to say, as is now going on Russia and is going to happen here, perhaps.

Ultimately, Mencken told me, he sees the disappearance of poets, writers, all people with individualistic expression with the possible exception of toe dancers, whom he always claimed were harmless to the state. They will all disappear and there will be no human being left with the capacity or the will to speak the truth.

I've listened to that statement in my mind for forty, almost fifty years. Once in a while I remember what Mencken said and I say to myself that I must be awfully careful not to be captured by the herd.

Prostitution

December 23, 1958: Judge John Murtagh was Ben's guest. Murtagh was billed as an expert of sorts on prostitution, having tried a number of cases involving whoredom. Ben professed to having no knowledge of the present-day streetwalker, but fond memories of the disease-free ladies of long ago.

A prostitute to me is a very vague and pleasant memory. It goes back to when I was a teenager, seventeen and a veteran journalist in Chicago. The only lady friends I knew in those days, the only ones that most journalists knew, were the blithe, fancy girls. I remember them as women full of kindliness and charm. We drank and danced with them. It was much like going to the Stork Club or El Morocco. You made whoopee, you told stories.

I remember I even used to write plays that they would perform when their chores were over, at four or five in the morning. They'd come on and all fight over playing the character that was supposed to enter in the nude. I know nothing of today's prostitutes, only a wistful memory of my own youth.

My favorite was a girl called Queen Lil, the head of a great house. She used to attend the opening day of the Washington Park Race Track in a tallyho. The madam would have sixteen girls dressed in lavender ball gowns on the top and fellows in knickerbocker pants blowing horns. Queen Lil, with a wide pompadour, would sit in front, and whomever she nodded to on the Michigan Avenue pavement considered themselves honored. These were the girls I knew.

Today, the fact that call girls are being used by high class businessmen is kind of disturbing, to me at least. It used to be a very Jewish enterprise. I remember my own family, my uncles, and my father. All the people who in the garment trade used to use models. My uncle had twenty-eight of them and they were available for all customers. The backbone of the garment industry was the obligingness of the ladies who paraded in front of the buyers. That the gentiles have become aware of this kind of disturbs me a little but it has a good side. If the gentiles stick around long enough in New York, they may learn how to do business in the correct way.

Audiences

October 8, 1958: Ben answered his mail. Aside from his days as Jewish propagandist, the letters he received on The Ben Hecht Show *were the closest Ben got to his public. He found his audience a rather curious lot and for his Bedtime Story, he remembered an assembly from his Chicago days.*

I've been thinking considerably about audiences since I've been in this rather exposed spot. When you're a performer, particularly an amateur one like I am, audiences are a very mysterious and deceitful outfit. You can't quite figure out what they're all about.

I have a startling memory of one audience, which frightens me when I remember it. When I was a reporter I did some publicity business on the side. One of my accounts was the Chinese Famine Fund. My bosses were J.P. Morgan and Thomas Lamont. Everything we did went along swimmingly. We did no work and collected considerable money for it.

One day we got a notification from Mr. Lamont that Ambassador Sze, the Chinese ambassador, was coming to Chicago to deliver a speech at Orchestra Hall on Chinese history and Chinese politics. On the morning of his arrival, he was greeted by a cloudburst. An end-of-the-world storm hit Chicago with fifty-mile-an-hour winds and more rain than I'd ever seen in my life. We realized around noon that nobody would be in Orchestra Hall to listen to the learned and philosophical ambassador from China.

At one o'clock I was terrified. I knew it would be horrible if our Chinese ambassador spoke to a completely empty hall so I went to see a fellow called Colonel Walters, head of the Boy Scouts of Illinois. I put my problem to him and the colonel said, "Don't worry, Mr. Hecht. Everything will be fine tonight. Just go back and wait."

At about eight-fifteen, the Chinese ambassador and his entourage of statesmen arrived at Orchestra Hall. We escorted him backstage and put the gentlemen on chairs on the stage. But the hall itself was entirely empty. We stood out in the rain, which was still beating down like mad. At eight twenty-five a troop of twelve hundred Boy Scouts came around the corner, aged from twelve to fourteen, in ponchos. They were blowing fifes and beating drums and marching valiantly through the storm. We led them into Orchestra Hall, where they all sat down. I imagined they expected to see a Chinese magician, I don't know what Col. Walters had told them.

But, at the appointed hour the ambassador came out and delivered a very complicated harangue on Chinese history, Chinese politics, global politics, etc., and the little boys sat there very obediently applauding when the colonel indicated that applause was necessary. At the end of the oration, the happy Chinese ambassador bowed. The twelve hundred little boys applauded like mad, and the Chinese ambassador left.

Since I've become a performer, this memory has acquired overtones for me. One of the overtones is, I used to look back on this incident with sort of a grin of irony. Now I would settle for twelve hundred well behaved, well mannered Boy Scouts aged twelve to fourteen as an audience.

Television Commercials

September 15, 1958: On Ben's first show, his guest was advertising executive Bob Foreman. Ben was fearless, not afraid to bite the hand that fed him. Before a rather heated interview, in which he chastised modern advertising, he delivered a sermon condemning television commercials.

The television commercial and the atom bomb are the two grand new signatures of progress. To date they run neck and neck in unpopularity.

The mysterious thing about television commercials is how they sell anything. As far as I can make out, the only public reaction to television commercials is, I can't stand them.

There was always an outcry against advertising even in the halcyon days when it wore only the modest mask of print. The more sensitive citizens used to bellow against the pollution of the landscape by vulgar billboards. Later the public had a chance to rage against the increased horrors of radio advertising. But sensitivity is never a match for progress.

The arrival of television made all the peddler hullabaloo of the past seem like the chirping of robins. Nearly all of the human noises have been drowned out by the advertiser, except, of course, the eternal noise of the politician. The American citizen today is equally surrounded by threats of disaster and new hair rinses.

But to return to the mystery, I have not witnessed anything in my time as wildly unpopular as television advertising. I've seldom met any human of any age group who didn't groan at the word commercials. Who didn't wince when a commercial whoop-de-dood on the screen. Who didn't curse the sponsor for interrupting his diversion. I've seen people jump up, snap off the television set and keep the screen darkened for a whole evening as revenge against one commercial too many.

A large segment of the television audience not given to physical protest has developed a sort of home made catatonia toward commercials. Instead of turning off the set, they turn off their senses. They neither see nor hear the commercial, but remain in an automatic coma until the late ululation has subsided. And yet, there's the mystery. Sponsors spend hundreds of thousands of dollars walloping the public with the peddler cries.

Whatever you might say of sponsors, you must admit financially they are very bright. Indeed one of the prides of the republic has always been the smartness of its moneymakers. When they spent money on something, they got more money back. Unless there's been an IQ breakdown among our tycoons, obviously their television commercials pay off. The millions spent on them bring more millions back. How? One explanation to the mystery may be that the facts are all wrong. That my observations have been confined to the small fringe of sensitive fellows like myself. But that doesn't sound to me like a solid explanation. There must be some more convincing and enlightening one.

A Toast to Television

December 31, 1958: Ben closed his New Year's Eve broadcast with his producer Ted Yates by toasting the medium that employed him.

I want to propose a toast to television, the most completely infantile type of entertainment since the creation of the rattle. To television, that round the clock Santa Claus that machine-guns entertainment into fifty million parlors. That has on the bill art and idiocy, sagacity and feeble-mindedness. An entertainment run by con men, sideshow barkers, adolescent nitwits, traumatized nitwits and an infiltrating pack of D'Artagnans and Don Quixotes. And paid for by sponsors who vary from drooling avarice to bankrupting altruism.

My Favorite Quotations

December 25, 1958: Ben's Christmas broadcast featured his favorite quotations, which he recited from memory.

I hope the scholars will bear in mind that these sentences are from memory and they may be a bit askew as to ands, ifs, or buts. However, these sentences have kept me company through a lot of years.

The Golden Rule

Instead of the golden rule, I prefer the Arabian proverb that says: He who does not resent an insult deserves it.

Friendship

On friendship, I like Chilo, the Greek philosopher who said: Love a man as though you know someday you will hate him. And hate him knowing that one day you will love him. (It's more realistic than the golden rule. It says be cautious as well as sweet.)

Famous Last Words

During the French Revolution, the Duke Degeis, listening to the executioner reading his death warrant interrupted irritably and said: "Tut tut, the style of Diderot."

Another I like is King Charles I, of England, who with his head on the block waiting to be cut off said to the ax man: "One moment please, these curls have given no offense." He lifted his curls, as so they would not be hurt by the blade.

John de Roche, the champion archer of France who was condemned to death by Louis XI, was given a chance to win a pardon by shooting at a difficult target. He refused, saying: "Sire, under these conditions I am liable to miss and ruin my reputation." He preferred to lose his head.

And then there's Harry Greb the middleweight champion who used to say before throwing a knockout punch, "Here goes nothing." On his deathbed, his last words were: "Here goes nothing."

W.C. Fields, the irreverent comedian, faced death with a laugh. When he was dying in Palm Springs, I came up to him where he sat in the chair and he was reading the Bible. And I said to him, "What are you reading that book for?" And Bill Fields answered: "I'm lookin' for loopholes."

The Ideal Wife

Poetus, a Roman senator, ordered to commit suicide by the tyrant Nero, faltered with the sword in his hand, and he was afraid. His wife took the sword from his hand and ran it into herself and said: "See Poetus, it does not hurt."

Polite Husbands

The great black comedian Bert Williams, on leaving home after eight years of nagging marriage, left a note pinned on his pillow. It read: "Dear Liza, your troubles begin to amaze me."

Optimism

Dostoyevsky was a great optimist. He wrote: "Man survives where swine perish and laughs where gods go mad."

Modern Theology

Bertrand Russell said: "Religions commit suicide when they find their inspiration in their dogmas."

My old friend H.L. Mencken, a tumultuous man, wrote in his coda as follows: "The earth is a gigantic flywheel making ten thousand revolutions a minute. Man is a sick fly taking a dizzy ride on it. Religion is the theory that the wheel was designed and set spinning to give him a ride."

Cyril Connolly the London semi-mystic once said: "The perfect religion would consist of love, poetry and doubt."

The best example of doubt was made by Baudelaire in an antique shop with a friend. The friend looked at a statue of the Buddha with a big belly and forearms and burst into a laugh, and Baudelaire said: "Don't laugh. You may be in the presence of the true God."

The Devil

Saint Jerome said: "The power of the devil is in the loins."

In-Laws

Ring Lardner once wrote: "Rather than visit his mother-in-law for a weekend, he would prefer to row across Lake Michigan in a hollow tube."

Don Juan

Balzac wrote: "There was so much fire in the eyes, it was doubtful that it was duplicated elsewhere." That would fit ninety percent of the movie stars I have known.

Our Statesmen

Ted Cook, the American journalist wrote: "The narrower the mind, the broader our generality."

Jimmy Durante used to do a nightclub act where he was in a rowboat with his two pals, Clayton and Jackson. They'd be rowing for three days without water. Suddenly Jimmy yelled out: "There's land, pull for that." And Clayton said, "That's not land, that's the horizon." Jimmy answered, "Pull for that. It's better than nothin'."

Disarmament

Napoleon said: "If nations on the brink of war could go to bed as angry lovers do, we would have no need of armies."

Patriotism

Socrates, one of the wisest of men, was executed by the State. The Russians would have killed him pronto, and he probably would have been jailed in the U.S. He was a true subversive, to wit: "I look upon all mankind as my fellow countrymen. I prefer the common bond of humanity above all national ties."

Traitors

E.M. Forester, the author of *A Passage to India* and other gentile novels, wrote: "If I had to choose between betraying my country and betraying my friend, I hope I should have the guts to betray my country."

Governments

Citrobrian said: "Society rests on the acquiescence of the poor."

Pessimism

Lucretius, twenty-two hundred years ago, wrote: "This age is broken down. The earth, outworn."

Philosophers

Philosophers have always had one thing in common, they're inclined to mistake their own infirmities for those of the cosmos. Stendhal expressed it a little bit more sensibly and understandably when he said: "As we age, we outgrow the charms of love, sin, health and even living."

The Catskills

George Jessel is one of the modern, reportorial kind of philosophers, as all good comedians are. Returning from a visit to Grossingers Hotel in the Catskills, which are known as the Jewish Alps, George reported: "You can get snow-blind from the sour cream."

Movies

Sam Goldwyn once said to me: "The writer is the most important. If you have rich dialogue with rich characters you have the mucus of a great movie."

Critics

My two favorite observations on critics come from writers. Chesterton wrote: "Critics are midgets juggling cannonballs." Chekhov wrote: "Once a fly was attached to a bull while the bull was walking up and down a field plowing all day and when the fly came home his wife asked him what he was doing and he said, we were plowing." And finally Anatole France wrote: "Criticism is the adventure of the soul among masterpieces." An academic statement since there are few masterpieces, and fewer critics with souls.

Television

George Moore in describing the novels of Henry James said: "Right in front of you, bang, nothing happens."

For Café Goers

In George Bernard Shaw's *Caesar and Cleopatra*, when Cleopatra is fleeing her throne and she hesitates to enter a dirty barge, the captain speaks and he says: "Royalty lies in your foot madame, not in the barge."

American Ego

Herman Melville wrote in *Moby-Dick*: "Talk not to me about blasphemy, men. I'd strike the sun if it insulted me."

Newspapers

I once wrote in my youth: "Trying to determine what is going on in the world by reading the newspapers is like trying to tell time by watching the second hand of a clock."

Education

Bertrand Russell said: "In the schools of antiquity, philosophers tried to impart wisdom. In our colleges, our humbler aim is to teach subjects."

Ring Lardner on our modern educational system said: "'Shut up,' my father explained."

Writers

After a couple of weeks hunting with Ernest Hemingway, a Wyoming ranch foreman asked him: "Mr. Hemingway, do you buy your shirts that way or do you stuff them yourself?"

Love and Virtue

Fielding in the novel *Tom Jones* wrote: "Stopping at the inn were three northern girls of great virtue and two Irish lassies in the same predicament."

Ovid wrote: "What women like to give, they love to be robbed of."

Rabelais said; "Repentance is the sour grapes on which old age feasts."

Carnal Sin

The Greek philosopher Aristippus said, when caught by his pupils entering a brothel: "The vice lies not in going in, but in not coming out."

Theodore Dreiser said: "If marriage is only a license for lewdness, the license is too expensive."

When Socrates was asked if it was better to take a wife or not to, he answered: "Whichever you do, you will repenteth."

My friend John Barrymore had his view on male and female relationships, he said once: "If they ever dig up the hands of the missing Venus di Milo, they'll find a pair of boxing gloves on them."

H.G. Wells said: "Most husbands hate their wives because they themselves have wronged them."

Straparola, a fifteenth century Italian writer, said: "Never woo a woman on her birthday."

Keith Preston, the British comedian, said: "He must not laugh at his own whiz, a snuff box has no right to sneeze."

Advice to Politicians

Ambrose Bierce wrote: "A lie with a purpose is the worst kind and the most profitable."

The sage Professor Whitehead of Harvard wrote: "Old truths are useless, knowledge does not keep any better than fish."

Experts

Professor Strobert said: "An expert is a person who avoids small errors as he sweeps on to the grand fallacy."

My old friend Teddy Roosevelt said: "All men say silly things, but only silly men defend them." That would apply to the leaders of both the Democratic and Republican parties.

Materialism

The best comment on our materialistic civilization was made by one of two prospectors during the gold rush days. They were splitting up and he said to his pal: "You keep the gold mine, I'll take the frying pan."

A happier note was struck by my pal Billy Rose. He said once: "To a gal these days, a mink coat is not a garment. It's a diploma."

Time

Heraclitus wrote: "No man has entered twice the same river." A river is always flowing and it has different water in it. Time is also always flowing and has different moves and events in it. And for that reason, no man, statesman or husband, can ever enter twice, the same situation.

Life

Aremourje said: "He walked backward through life looking at the day he was 21." My biography in a sentence.

Aristotle again: "Happiness and not goodness is the aim of life." That should be the one line biography of the human race.

The gallant Sir Walter Raleigh wrote: "I dislike those gloomy moralists who allow the pleasures of life to pass them by and browse only on its miseries."

And Santayana sums it up in a line. He said: "Where happiness fails, existence is a lamentable experiment."

Women

Something from the *Arabian Nights* might best describe Lena Horne: "When she smiled it was as if the moon came out."

Juvenal wrote: "Male lust is impressive, women's lust is unconquerable."

Human Nature

Anatole France wrote: "We all find pleasure in the faults we deplore." That's a perfect description of our public. It hates gangsters but loves gangster movies. It hates juvenile delinquency, but the biggest motion picture hit in years was the *Blackboard Jungle*. It deplores and hates drug addicts, but two of the most successful films of recent years were *Man with the Golden Arm* and *Hat Full of Rain*. And it hates sexual promiscuity, but won't go to see a film that hasn't got it in it.

Memory

J.M. Barry wrote: "God gave us memory so we can have roses in December."

Modesty

Ovid wrote: "Modesty is useless save one feigned." Modesty is a lost art. I think it must have died with Ovid about 25 BC.

Women

Something nice about women. Nietschze said: "A woman's tongue is the stairway to calamity."

Courage

J.M. Barry again: "All goes if courage goes." That applies to all politicians blazing our new trail down the middle of the road to nowhere.

Cicero said: "Let him employ his passion who can make no use of his reason."

Love of Humanity

Bertrand Russell wrote: "The love of humanity is usually accompanied by a violent dislike of the next door neighbor." That might apply quite well to Governor Faubus of Arkansas, but maybe it's a little fancy for him.

A Wyoming sign is a little more to the point. It read: "No Trespassing, survivors will be prosecuted."

Beauty

Another by Theocritus. He said: "Beauty is a delightful prejudice." It means there is no beauty and that man has only a talent for deluding himself. But, on this talent rests marriage, art and infidelity.

Epitaph

My wife Rose and I have selected the following quote as our epitaph to be. Camille de Moulon, poet of the French Revolution who was beheaded, wrote: "There will be stars over the place forever, though the house we loved, and the street we loved, are lost."

To close the program, instead of his usual Bedtime Story, Hecht offered his viewers a Christmas message.

A Christmas Card for My Viewers

Time stands still and lets me feel my fugitive solidity. The stamp of moonlight and the seal of incandescent sun on me, so evanescent is the real, so endless is reality. Devouring time, let me forget your hunger while I grace your plate. Let's have no philosophic threat about a missing vertebrate who bore my name. I'm living yet, immortal and immune to fate.

The Mail

Viewer Letters

Every Wednesday night, Ben would answer his mail. By his third week on the air, the mail arrived by the sackful. Most of it was favorable. For entertainment purposes, Ben answered mostly negative letters on the air. The following is a selection of some of the best letters, and his responses.

I've always hated answering mail. When Charlie MacArthur and I were making pictures in Astoria, Long Island, mail was a big problem. We finally solved it by engaging a bald, fat poet named Alan Ross MacDougal as our secretary. He was the only one with courage enough for the job. He would come into our office every morning, with fifty or a hundred letters and dump them unopened into the lighted fireplace. This freed us for our work, we thought.

On this program, though, we have no fireplace.

September 17th

>Mr. Hecht: I like what you have written and as a sad friend what I'd like to know why, all of a sudden, at a not too tender age, you have decided to squander yourself on television. From things you've said and written, you don't have much respect for the medium. What possesses a writer to become a ham? — *Miss E.R., Scarsdale.*

Money. No further answer.

>Dear Mr. Hecht: You portray a sour attitude about life. I read your autobiography, *A Child of the Century*, and I think the life you describe in your book accounts for your jaded outlook. As a youth, you admit that your conduct with women was, to say the least, somewhat

> loose. You were a kind of an amoral, Bohemian newspaper man who rarely saw life at its cleanest and most decent. Is that why you are so antagonistic and bitter about everything? —*Miss A.P., Rockaway Beach.*

That letter bristles with inaccuracies. I wasn't a Bohemian newspaperman. I was a terribly hard-working newspaperman who usually worked fourteen hours a day. I hardly had time to get drunk. There is an error in this letter. It is not I who has the angry outlook towards life, but the letter writer.

These kind of letters are usually written by people who imagine if you have any fun in life you must end up full of remorse. This is never true. The only thing I've found in people who've had a lot of fun in life is that when they get old, they wish it hadn't ended. They have no remorse except for the passing of time. I've never met anyone who ever regretted any sort of fun, even if it was sinful.

> Dear Ben: In your book *Charlie*, you wrote: "We were all fools to have left Chicago. It was a town to play in, a town where you could stay yourself and where the hoots of the critics couldn't frighten your style or drain your soul." What happened to Chicago? —*Mr. I.K., Manhattan*

What happened to Chicago was that it turned into a sort of minor road company New York. It became a very, very big city full of a million miles of cement. There was hardly any place left for an individual to make an imprint. When Chicago was at its height, it had two million people. About 95 percent of whom where fascinated with what the other five percent were doing. Now it has six million people and nobody is fascinated by anything.

September 18th

> Dear Mr. Hecht: With all this controversy over whether or not birth control should be practiced, I would like to know what you think about birth control? —*Mrs. M.M., East 15th Street.*

I don't do too much thinking about it. Two things about birth control have always surprised me. One is that there should be people foolish enough to taboo against it, and the second is that there should be people foolish enough to obey that taboo. There's nothing much to worry about. Taboos against sex through the ages have not been markedly successful. The last taboo I can remember that worked for a while was three hundred BC, King Lycurgus of Sparta didn't like sex because it interfered with the workings of his military plans, so he didn't exactly taboo against it, he tried to outwit it. He passed a law compelling all women to cut their hair short and appear in public in the nude. After about ten years sex came practically to a standstill. But I still would have liked to have been in Sparta.

> Sir: Do you think Richard Nixon would make as good a president as President Eisenhower? — *Mr. D.F., Seaside Heights, NJ.*

That's a stumper. The Chinese have a proverb that sort of touches on that. The proverb runs, "Of two eagles who disappear beyond the clouds together, who shall say which flew the higher." Which means, it is very difficult to determine the difference between two great geniuses like Mr. Nixon and Mr. Eisenhower.

> Dear Ben Hecht: Why weren't you ever a Communist, particularly in the thirties when so many intellectuals were toying with Communism? — *Mr. N.Z., Sunnyside*

It be must due to my selfishness. I was always a self-centered fellow. I met Communism first in Europe in the twenties when I was war correspondent in Germany and Russia. It seemed a very exciting and compelling notion, but it also had two bad points. The two great targets of Communism seemed to be the rich man and the writer. I wasn't a rich man at the time but I always dreamed of being one. I was a writer so I didn't see any reason to hook up with an outfit that was against my daydream and my reality.

September 22nd

> Dear Mr. Hecht: I feel it was short-sighted of you to knock the sponsors. Don't you feel a sense of allegiance and intimidation to the people who pay the bills? — *Miss K.B., New York.*

No, I've had one credo all my life, "The boss is always wrong."

I've found the only way you can get ahead in the world is to be as big a nuisance as you can towards anybody who employs you.

> To the Management of WABC-TV: At this point in his career, Ben Hecht is not concerned with offending the people who supposedly constitute his audience. But his new television venture on WABC must take some nefarious pride as his most blatant effort of boorishness to date.
> His first show gave evidence of the two faces of its star. While lashing at television advertisers with his tongue, he gleefully accepted their money with his hands. — *Mr. J. N., Astoria.*

Mr. N. sounds very naive. If he's old enough to write such a letter, he should know that all writers are rascals and will take money from whatever hand they can find it in.

September 24th

> Mr. Hecht: What do you feel about Miss Jayne Mansfield as a talent and Hollywood product, now that she's back in the newspapers? Do you feel she's a later day Mae West? — *Mr. C. S. of Washington Heights.*

I don't know Miss Mansfield but I feel she's part of the great "bust renaissance" that has overtaken this country. From what I've seen of her on the screen, I'm afraid she'll lose her artistic standing when she loses her shape.

I did know Mae West a bit in Hollywood. Miss West wasn't dependent on her measurements for success. She was in her heyday a very witty, exciting gal, who knew how to put herself over and how to write. She wrote herself some fine jokes, and some fairly good low grade plays, which I enjoyed.

> Dear Mr. Hecht: The papers have been full of news about Gene Tierney, the actress, returning to Hollywood after a mental breakdown. Why do so many people in Hollywood apparently go to pieces in the brain works? — *Mrs. M. G., Princeton.*

That isn't true about people going to pieces and having mental breakdowns. I've been in Hollywood an awful lot of times. I never saw anybody have a mental breakdown or engage in mental activity much of any kind, breakdown or not. Hollywood people have been terribly misunderstood. They are the happiest, most charming, most blithe people I've ever known. They are as uninhibited as the Samoans and they live a life of great luxury, freedom. They have no frustrations and continue on into their eighties enjoying themselves. Their insanity is visible only on the screen.

October 3rd

> Mr. Hecht: You and Weegee glorified crime criminals and murder. You should be ashamed sir, and for that matter tossed off the air. — *Mr. B.C., Darien, CT.*

About being tossed off the air, that's not up to me. About being ashamed, that is up to me. About glorifying crime, I don't understand Mr. C. I'm sure that he looks at four hundred murders a week committed on television that don't glorify crime, but offer it as entertainment. I thought people would be rather amused or interested to hear what real crime was like. That they were in favor of crime because it is the backbone of the television industry.

I don't understand why people hate the thing they actually love the most.

> Dear Mr. Hecht: You owe the public an apology for a shocking eulogy for murder, murderers and crime. — *Mr. D.C., Hawthorne, NY.*

There are two ways of looking at that. I think the public owes me an apology for misunderstanding me and for not liking what I do.

People get a kick out of protesting. They could easily turn you off. That would solve their apoplexy. If that doesn't solve it, they can go see a doctor and save themselves a stamp.

I don't think anything can be done to improve the public. They're going to remain always as charming and protesting as they are.

October 8th

> Dear Ben: How do you like being a television star as compared to being a writer? — *Miss E.K., Forest Hills.*

A funny story. It's about a mouse. The mouse was put into the cone of a rocket ship that was fired to the moon. And the rocket ship hit the moon and came back. By some miracle, the cone got detached from the rocket ship, the mouse was recovered and brought back to the cage with the other mice, alive. The other mice gathered around it. They'd all been used for experimental purposes for some time and they said, "Sylvester, how was it?" Sylvester answered, "Well, it's better than cancer."

This is my present feeling.

> Dear Mr. Hecht: On Friday's program you discussed your friends Charlie Chaplin and John Barrymore. You described these men as "really living." How can anyone feel that leading an immoral and drunken life is really living? Don't you realize what a chaotic situation would arise if America followed your recipe for really living?
>
> You made Chaplin appear to be a great guy and one widely misunderstood by the American people. Doesn't you realize that Chaplin is a Communist sympathizer and could it be that you fall for the latter category and are using ABC to sound off your feelings for the matter? — *Miss M.C., Valley Stream, NY.*

That's an old story. That letter has been coming into my orbit for many, many years. They used to call these people the "little half dead" who tried to make rules for the living. They sit inside their little coffins and give out laws. They're depressing. The most wonderful thing about them is you never see them. Whatever social circle you circulate, you never meet them. This is quite a delight. They never leave home. They never get out of the grave.

This woman has obviously joined that tribe of spinsters who before retiring, look under the bed for a burglar. They're sad and foolish people and they think that the first requisite of a patriot is to lose his head. This is the idea. They try to propagandize themselves.

They're not entirely harmless, however, because they are the enemies' fifth column during peace time. They are the terrified ones. They yell "havoc." They yell "fire" when somebody lights a match.

They yell "havoc" when there's nothing going on but some poor sad fellow like Chaplin, who was morosely living out his last years in Europe, doing nobody any harm.

> Dear Sir: Is it true that Ben Hecht, given two drinks, will confess he missed his destiny? That he traded lives with Maxwell Bodenheim, the life of a bad but genuine poet, for a mediocre but money making novelist who ends as a TV wit? Hecht should be hung for his literary crimes. — *Mr. E.R., Long Island.*

That's possibly true. I have no denial to offer. He may be on the right side, who knows?

> Dear Mr. Hecht: Why is it so inconceivable to believe that Jonah actually lived in the belly of a whale or that Jesus Christ walked on water when scientists observe equally astounding miracles happening every day? Thank God there are those who adhere to God's word as absolute truth. — *Mrs. J.N., West Point.*

I thank God, too. There's no profit to arguing with people who are given to hallucinations. I think they have a much happier time than we who never have any hallucinations. I envy them. Anybody who can believe in *anything* is enviable. She shouldn't give up Jonah, but stick to him.

> Dear Mr. Hecht: It is my considered opinion that all misanthropes, cynics and pessimists are suffering from (a) continuous alcoholic hangovers or (b) chronic constipation. Do you agree? — *Mr. J.H., West 36th Street.*

That's another old pal. This lemonade and loose bowel champion I've met often. I envy them sort of. I can see this fellow sitting in front of his television set, grabbing his pen and wiping me off the earth. The delusions of power a letter writer gets are very enviable. An author never gets them because he has to sell his writing. This fellow has only got to pay two cents and mail it.

October 22nd

> Dear Sir: You made a very poor political blunder. You indicated

that Germans committed war atrocities. There were however millions of Germans who were put into concentration camps themselves for resisting Hitler. The Germans on the whole are good people. It was the Nazis who were bad. — *Mr. C.C., East 22nd Street.*

That's a very sad piece of idiocy. There weren't millions of Germans put in concentration camps. There were hundreds. And the atrocities, meaning the murder of six million Jewish men, women and children of all ages, that murder was performed by the German people, not by the Nazis.

The German people, the businessmen, the rotary clubs, the plumbers who fixed up the murder business in the crematoria. The lime pits that had to be arranged. The lime that had to be ordered. Freight cars that had to have lime in them so that the Jews could be burned alive in them. Graves that had to be dug so Jews wouldn't contaminate the landscape when they were dead. This was all done by Germans. The Nazis, meaning the army, had very little to do with it.

> Dear Ben: I've just had the unexpected delight of your conversation with Jack Kerouac. I'm holed up in this hotel while trying to get Bellevue Hospital to release my beatnik son who committed himself two weeks ago. He had been on this Zen Buddhism kick and given himself the horrors with it. He said he had become a dangerous schizophrenic and the doctors agreed. Can you help? I'm sure you could. Would you? — *Mr. B.K., New York, New York.*

Well this fellow seems to be boasting a little to me. Beatniks are inclined to boast. I wouldn't monkey with this fellow. Maybe a beatnik is a good place for him to stop. They're not very bad people. They're charming, harmless, they don't even write very much. I would allow a beatnik to stay a beatnik rather than to take a chance on turning into something worse.

> Dear Mr. Hecht: There is a way of handling such people as you, just tune out. Of course the same could be said of a showing of obscene or lecherous pictures on the air... — *Mr. I.F., Manhattan.*

This man regards Americans as imbeciles who have to be saved from themselves. There's another school of thought who regards them as imbeciles who are not able to please themselves as they wish. Me, I don't know. From the letters I'm getting, I wouldn't be able to vote which yet.

October 29th

> To the Program Department of the American Broadcasting Corporation: After listening to the Ben Hecht Show last night with Drew Pearson I will take an oath and swear never to see or listen to a program on this channel, network and station. Last night Mr. Hecht and Mr. Pearson stated that the president of the United States was below average intelligence, incompetent and lazy, in addition to stating that his administration was corrupt. Also on this program, they made it quite clear what they thought of Mr. Dulles, Mr. Nixon, the United States Navy, and the entire scientific organization of the government. It is ironic that this left of center broadcast took place on the eve of the president's 68th birthday. I can't understand how it was possibly permitted. I sincerely state that I will never listen or watch a program of news, public interest, or special events on Channel 7. — *Mr. X.*

A tremendous loss. Hard to face such a situation.

This fellow, or his prototype has been around in my life ever since I learned how to write with a pencil. He's the amoral neurotic. The queer sickly fellow who hides inside of all platitudes. He's the chap who has to worship institutions because they are fine places in which to conceal his own insufficiency. He's behind everything that's noble, successful and important.

Patriotism sometimes comes out of looniness more than out of love of country. It's a kind of pigeon called chauvinism. These loony bed-wetting oddities of human construction wrap themselves in any kind of flag, that serves both as a bandage and as a concealment for what they are.

They love institutions. They love a White House, the State House, a great hospital, a place where important people are functioning because they don't like people, because they don't like themselves. They are for government against humanity because judging by themselves, they think humanity is pretty low.

This Mr. X is sort of a grade B gooney wart because he really didn't go about the thing right. He sent this to the program department hoping to get my job. It shows he's a very ineffectual fellow, he should have sent it to the sponsor, and should also send copies to the

American Legion, the Watch and Ward Society, the Anti-Defamation League. As the underworld says, "Pick up a little strength before he hits."

> Dear Mr. Hecht: Several viewers of a recent telecast in which you participated have written to tell me how generously you spoke of me at that time. I want you to know of my appreciation. In the midst of a campaign period when brickbats are more often than not the order of the day, it was most heartening to learn of the bouquet which you threw my way. I can assure you that it provided a real morale builder during some long days of work. With every good wish, Richard Nixon.

That's very effective. It almost turns one instantly into an ardent Republican. It's a wonderful way to get one vote. My reaction is one of pleasure because I did admire Mr. Nixon's antics in South America. He was quite human, bold, brave, nice. But I also admire another thing about Mr. Nixon, that may induce him to write me another letter. He said the only intelligent thing that I've heard during the past six months of political caterwauling. Mr. Nixon said that his objective was to reduce government to a minimum. To remove as many politicians from the political scene as could be removed. And to work the country with a skeleton crew, instead of adding politicians. This is great philosophy, and I hope Mr. Nixon is sincere.

November 5th

> Dear Mr. Hecht: As a member of the Bed-Wetters League, I would like to protest your use of the term bed-wetters when you wish to deride someone. Granted our numbers are few but there are many among us who are sensitive, talented people. Therefore, to protect the anonymous bedwetter, it is not something one usually talks about, I would like to take this opportunity to ask you to refrain from using the term.
> —*Name Withheld.*

He's quite right. This is my first apology in seventeen years. I apologize to the bed-wetters of the U.S.A. and to nobody else.

> Dear Ben: With reference to the type who threaten to boycott ABC because of your comments, I think they have chosen the wrong

type of government. A totalitarian system would eliminate such freedom of expression for them. — *Mrs. E.O'B., Grove Street.*

Dear Sir: On the old democratic principal of one simpleton, one vote, I hereby cast my ballot with a view to counterbalancing the sad little men who want you expelled from TV. I hereby declare I will never tune into ABC unless your show is not only continued, but possibly lengthened. — *Mr. A.T.B., Boonton, NJ.*

A magnum of champagne to them.

Mr. Hecht: Again, you expressed your hatred for the Germans, calling them venom inspired epithets. As if the Germans were good people, and the French bad people. What nonsense. In that case, what are the Jews, good people or bad people? Shall we hate the Jews because a sizable portion of them are bores, egotistical and unspeakably selfish in business? Can't you see that you who will not stop blaming the German race for the fate of six million Jews are purveying that same kind of hatred and stereotype thinking that massacred the Jews? — *Mr. J.G., Staten Island.*

Fritzi boy is quite right. I have a hatred for Germans with fat necks and watery eyes and no ankles and a cold spot in their hearts that only murder can warm. But it's a kind of hatred that I don't think a German can understand. It's a hatred that doesn't dream of grabbing two million males from fifteen years to seventy and eighty years, stripping them of their clothes, pouring kerosene on them and burning them alive. It's a hatred that doesn't include a dream of grabbing two million women from youth to old age raping them by the thousands. Stripping them of their clothes, putting them into lime kilns and letting the lime eat them up alive. It's a hatred that doesn't include grabbing two million children from the age of one to the age of ten. Making them naked, putting them into gas chambers, suffocating them, killing them, putting excrement on their heads when they cried too much. Letting them be devastatingly, horribly, executed.

No, my hatred is Jewish hatred. It doesn't involve those things that Fritzi boy has. It also doesn't look forward with too much surprise to the Germans trying it again and perhaps conquering the world in their third try. But when they do, there's one little civilized area in which they'll never thrive and that's my brain. As long as I live I'm going to have a lime kiln in my head for the word "Germans."

> Dear Sir: Such a filthy mind as Ben Hecht's has nothing but a bad influence on teenagers. In spite of what he says, there is still real love, faithfulness and marital contentment for the majority. —*Miss E.P., Woodside.*

The teenagers? I'd forgotten all about teenagers in my notions about love and fidelity and all those wondrous romantic things. I've been propagandized against teenagers. One remembers them now as people with switchblades and barbed wire belts. If there's one set of Romeo and Juliets, perhaps the world isn't as bad as I think it is.

November 25th

> My dear Mr. Hecht, at the Schiffly Lace and Embroidery Institute, [one of *The Ben Hecht Show*'s only sponsors] employers and employees represent practically every race, creed, and religion. Tolerance is exemplified nowhere to a greater extent than in our industry. Under the circumstances we are deeply concerned by your references to the German people. We have carefully gone over the scripts of your telecasts and feel that your castigation of the German people is all inclusive and is not restricted to people who may have committed atrocities in the past, or to those who are members of or who are in sympathy with the Nazi party. This letter is not written as a defense of the German people because no people as a whole need defending. What we're concerned with is the fact that your remarks smack of intolerance and might tend to ferment hatred and prejudice. Our position is crystal clear, we are against intolerance in any form. Signed, Schiffly.

I have two answers. The first answer is that my hatred of Germans has been too inclusive is an accurate charge. This is due to perhaps a blind spot or a little misthinking on my part because I've never considered German Americans as Germans. German Americans have always been to me Americans. When I've written, as I have frequently about Germany and Germans, I've never included in the pages anything about Germans who live in this country. German Americans are human beings like myself and the rest of American citizenry, and if German Americans are Germans then I can say some of my best friends are Germans. The other answer is that I am intolerant. To this I plead rather proudly, guilty. My intolerance will continue to be directed, as it has been directed towards the German nation that called itself the Third Reich. That acquiesced or participated in the murder of six million Jews, men, women and children. That called them garbage and disposed of them as garbage and I shall continue to hate these garbage makers of Europe as long as I live.

November 26th

> Mr. Hecht: Everybody knows your contempt for Hollywood, but what I'm curious about is, what does Hollywood think of you? Why do the movie bosses keep hiring you as a writer, have they no pride? — *Mr. J.P., Brooklyn.*

They don't keep hiring me as a writer. I haven't had a job for almost eight months. And the reason that they do hire me occasionally is that the movie bosses and I think exactly alike, the good ones that is. Most moviemakers feel that they're turning out sort of a sausage factory entertainment and they kind of like somebody to express their own secret feelings. I've been barred twice by the motion picture producers association, but they take me back if I keep scolding enough. They like that.

December 3rd

> Dear Ben: Last week, Mike Wallace mentioned the fact that your program was running at a deficit, the inference being that it wouldn't live long. I'm sending a small check for ten dollars to attest to my desire to see you remain on television and as a token attempt to reduce the deficit. Whereas I do not agree with you often, I wish I had your courage. — *Dr. D.S., Grand Concourse.*

I'll hang on to it and in case we're thrown off the air, I'll visit the doctor and give him two days of conversation he can't agree with.

December 17th

> Dear Mr. Hecht: I have been watching your show for several weeks now and I find that the proper adjective to describe your talents would be an irritant. I disagree with you thoroughly on most subjects. On a recent broadcast, you spoke at length about your theories of school, discipline, and juvenile delinquency. Why tolerate the thugs in school? I believe we should go back to slapping these miscreants. Teach them discipline. The kids are crying for it. — *Mr. C.S., Lexington Avenue.*

Sounds like a lovely, lovely parent. There are people who have such a deep anger towards kids. Not only people who don't have children but parents. We don't seem to be able to hit any theory that would explain it.

The theory I have about men like that is they have a rage, a sort of guilt. They feel a child points an accusative figure at them that says, look what you've become, look what I am, look what I promised to be and look what I grew up into, you. A foolish, stupid almost insensate human being without a single feather in his hair and no bounce in his feet. The sense of having betrayed their own childhood promises makes people angry at kids because they're portraying it more and more. The kid is that shining little light that says you should have been like me. You should have developed into something I am going to develop into.

This fellow is a little bit over the edge I think. I think anybody who theoretically wants to beat a kid is really an oddball. I can imagine wanting to beat a kid when the kid is around. Kids hit you on the head, step on you, scream in your ear, do all sorts of things. But a man who has a theory about beating children, when children aren't even harassing him, he's a little odd. Maybe he needs the beating.

January 28th

> Mr. Hecht: How do you mentally picture your fans and what kind of people do you think they are? And as a newborn performer, do you have a high regard and concern for your audience or do you just ignore them? — *Mr. C.L., the Bronx.*

I never think of who's listening. I just hope to end a sentence with a correct period.

I have never yet been aware of an audience. If there is an audience, and you can't see it through this microphone, I have never had an interest in the audience. I just hope that they continue to listen and that my job continues. I have neither regard or disregard for an audience.

> Dear Ben: I have several celebrity idols and I'd like your opinion of them. Marlon Brando, Rock Hudson, Kim Novak, Frank Sinatra and William Holden. —*Miss R.H., Bayonne.*

Two of them I don't understand at all. Kim Novak and Mr. Rock Hudson. I don't see why they ever got more than fifty bucks a week doing anything. Mr. Holden is a nice actor. I like Sinatra, he's very Americana.

I'm deeply fond of Mr. Brando. I remember I did a show once called *A Flag Is Born*, in which Mr. Brando appeared. It was a Jewish show that had to do with snatching Palestine from the British. Mr. Brando is no more a Jew than he is a Martian but he electrified the town. He was about twenty-one and terribly poor. We had to loan him twenty-five cents every day for lunch. Had to give a him sweater to wear as a costume. He had nothing. He overwhelmed the town with his performance and when the show was over, he vanished.

I remember Edie Van Klie who was the casting department at MCA asked me one day if I could locate Mr. Brando. She had five or six leads for him in new plays that were coming to town. Everybody wanted him. Nobody could find Marlon. One day I was going to a rehearsal hall on Ninth Avenue where Bill Ziff, one of the Irgun leaders, the rebellious Jews who were fighting Britain and making propaganda, was talking to a group of young men. He was indoctrinating them on speechifyng, how to overwhelm the British and knock them out.

In the group I saw Mr. Brando sitting with Sidney Lumet. It was a very hot June day and I told Brando that Edie Van Klie wanted to see him. He said he didn't have time. He was going off on a lecture tour. And he did. On this hot June and July he went off speaking for the Irgun in St. Louis and Kansas City. He had four dollars a day for expenses. He worked for three months, and scorned all the leads he was offered.

And now when the camera turns on Brando, it doesn't see a preening mountebank looking for applause. It sees a soul of a man looking for answers. I always admire Brando.

> Dear Mr. Hecht; How do you feel about this recent boon in Evangelism, especially on television with people like Mr. Billy Graham and Oral Roberts? Do you think this is a good thing? Do you think it's good for religion in general? —*J.S., Rego Park.*

Evangelism is a horrid thing. It's a mockery of religion. It substitutes hysteria for faith. Faith is a very difficult thing to achieve. You've got to have myths in order to have faith and myths are disappearing. Christian myths and Jewish myths are no more believable today than the Greek and Egyptian myths, so people are a little bit vague. They're full of God, but the steps to reach him have been taken away.

Evangelists are stepping in and they're very fine American go-getter clean-up moneymaking fools. They hurt religion no end by cheapening it, reducing it to voodoo business. They're a caterwauling nonsense that shouldn't be tolerated by a semi-civilized human being.

The best way to express religion? I think ritual and devotional exercises are helpful, but the only way I know that might express religion sanely is through character. A person who has a good heart, a kindly feeling, has a bit of tolerance, sensitivity and understanding. He's about as religious as a human being can be.

Any religious thoughts I have ever had have never led me into a synagogue. I find it more interesting to try to figure out about God myself than to go listen to his press agents in a church.

I used to think atheism was a sickness, a sort of a deep amnesia. The French skeptic, Anatole France wrote of atheism, that it was "the final infirmity of the human mind." I agree. A man protesting loudly that there is no God is like a man standing in front of a locked room yelling, "there's no one inside." If the room is empty, at whom is he yelling?

My not going to church, not being a church-goer isn't atheism or even irreligiousness. A man can be uninterested in real estate and still love his country.

The Lost Type

September 17, 1958: On the first program where he answered mail, Ben told a story from his days as occasional press agent in Chicago to illustrate his feelings concerning letter writers.

My story has to do with letter writers.

In Chicago some years ago I ran a weekly newspaper called the *Chicago Literary Times*. As part of my duties, I went to review the opening of the Moscow Art Players, Mr. Stanislavky's troupe at the Auditorium Theatre. They performed *The Brothers Karamazov* in Russian. Thirty-eight hundred people listened to some thirty Russians sitting in kitchen chairs on the stage talking incomprehensibly in Russian. At the end of the four hours, there was one of the biggest ovations I've ever heard in a theater. It irritated me because I was quite sure hardly twenty people out of the thirty-eight hundred had understood a word of what they were hearing.

I went to the paper and decided to have the review of the Moscow Art Players written in Russian. Fortunately my wife Rose Caylor knew how to write in Russian. She'd been with me and she wrote the review. We rushed it out to a West-side printer, Mr. Renshaw, who had Russian type. He set it up and we brought it back to our little office.

Usually we put it in the form. And putting it in the form, our printer Mr. Renshaw was a little bit liquored and he dropped half of the type on the floor, unable to figure out what the Russian words were. We put the type back willy-nilly in pied form in the tin and dropped the type into the form and closed it and printed the paper.

I usually received about ten or fifteen letters for an outstanding article in this paper. Three days later the mail started pouring in. There were some sixty letters arrived, all adulatory. All telling me that this was the finest thing that the *Chicago Literary Times* had ever printed. And since that hour I've always wondered about the sincerity of letter writers.

My Epitaph

Mankind, Today and Tomorrow

December 30, 1958: On a broadcast devoted to his own life, Ben discussed the present and the future.

I've always been rather idealistic towards my fellow man. I believe he's a very fine invention, a creature of genius, valor and full of wonders. I believe with Job in the Bible that there is a spirit in man that is part of some incomprehensible divinity. I have other notions about his institutions. This is what I'm a bit cynical towards. His institutions, meaning his banks, his churches, his government, and his parliaments are usually clownish, pompous or vicious. In fact, institutions function chiefly as pedestals on which pygmy-minded little politicians can pose for a moment as heroes.

As for his future, I have a theory that's haunted me for quite a while. And don't be too surprised. I have a theory that the space age is part of an evolutionary movement that's designed to get the human race off the earth. The earth is not going to be able to support the human race for more than another five hundred or a thousand years. Either through some divine or natural planning, we have a sudden burst of mental activity in the direction of power and speed due to the fact that people have to disembark. All evolution has been tending towards that. I think this planet was meant as sort of a proving grounds. A place for people to get training as human beings and then we're destined to go off to some other planet and all live there, a little more happily.

As for the state of the world today, as far as I know it consists of the fact that I am healthy and happy, with a modicum of vigor left and able still to enjoy myself. That's the state of the world. I've listened since the advent of television to these doom prophets, these

Cassandras who come tell us each time the year is fading that we've just spent a year working on a tightrope over an abyss and that next the year the chances are eight to five we fall off the tightrope.

I haven't got the faintest idea if it's all true. I don't care because what's true tomorrow doesn't bother me today. But I have an idea why they pedal it. The more doom a reporter can peddle, the more important he sounds for the moment. Our reporters are bright fellows, but lacking in words. They have to whirl fire pots of events around their heads to attract much attention. Also, the public loves to hear about disaster because when they hear they've just weathered a very bitter, violent year full of potential disasters, they get a sense of heroism in themselves. When they hear they've got another year ahead of them of worse disasters, they feel even nobler. They feel they're going to rise to great heights.

And at the end of a year, all I can think of is first the word grateful. One should feel terribly grateful one has lasted another year. Secondly, one should take an inventory. See how much stock is left, how much love is left, how much hope, how much kindness, how much anger, how much steam, if any, is on the shelves, and if there's enough left to last another year. And one should again feel grateful for the coming year. As for the stock of the world, this is an utter waste of time. It's like trying to read Sanskrit to try and figure out tomorrow.

My Attitude Towards Life

December 30, 1958: An erudite iconoclast like Hecht had no problem detailing his roots, and his perspective on life itself.

I never had to define it. It came along with my hair, fingernails and teeth. I've never measured myself or lived in the eyes of others. I've never measured myself with other people's opinions. Not when I was a baby, not when I was a boy and not since then until now. And this not letting other people measure you, but giving yourself your own report card marks has been a little road I've been following.

I was born this way, hatched out of family who were peasants, who for four hundred years were barefoot on a farm in south Russia. I arrived in the world as if I'd come to a carnival. I found nothing but wonders around me. I've insisted on enjoying them.

When I die, if I go anywhere where there's somebody around to ask me for an apology for the way I've spent my life, I'll apologize only for one thing. For having been a human being. Nothing else.

Is there a moral to this life? Well, the philosophers all said "It all ends in nothing." They were a little more sickly than I. I think there is no station, but there's a wondrous ride called life. I enjoy the ride without thinking of where I'm going.

The Only Way to Apologize

December 30, 1958: After an evening of "Ben on Ben," Mr. Hecht told a Bedtime Story concerning an influential member of his family.

With a happy grin, I remember a very important event in my life that may have marked me. Among the people in my family who adored me in addition to my parents, was a group of aunts. Very tall, Amazonian and childless. The head aunt of this group was my Tante Chasha. She used to steal me from my mother when I was eight and whisk me off to the Yiddish theater, where she was a great patron and fan.

One day she took me to a matinee where Thomashevsky, the great Yiddish actor, was playing. We sat in the first row of the balcony. I was watching the show and I saw something horrible happen. I saw a character arrested by a policeman for stealing a diamond bracelet that I had seen stolen by another character. I was outraged and jumped up and began to scream that they'd arrested the wrong man, that injustice was being done. The ushers came down to quiet me, but I wouldn't be quieted. Now my aunt was carrying an umbrella and she began to swing at the ushers. I began to yell and created a panic by demanding the arrest of the guilty actor, instead of the wrong one. Finally, we were thrown out of the balcony.

My aunt pulled herself together, preened her feathers, and we entered the lobby of the theater where the manager of the theater came up to my aunt. She knew the manager, knew him socially because she played poker with him all the time. He said, "Mrs. Swernofsky, I think you've done something pretty awful and I think you owe me an apology for the way you and your little nephew have behaved." "Yes," said my Tante Chasha, "I owe you an apology and here it is." She then socked him over the head with the umbrella.

He was floored and as he laid there in the foyer, my aunt turned to me and said, "Remember when you grow up, that's the only way to apologize."

Index

Actors and Sin 3, 141
Algren, Nelson 8
Anders, Sherwood 3, 17, 61, 143, 148, 154, 174
Anderson, Jack 87
Angels Over Broadway 3

Barrymore, Ethel 128
Barrymore, John 128-32, 189, 200
Barrymore, Lionel 128
Baruch, Bernard 167-68
Bathhouse John 83-85
Bean, Orson 42
Begin, Menachem 101, 169, 170
Ben-Gurion 17, 170, 171
Ben Hur 128
Benchley, Robert 157
Bennett, Constance 122
Bergson, Peter 162-63, 166, 169, 170
Bodenheim, Maxwell 3, 4, 17, 54, 74-76, 201
Brando, Marlon 4, 8, 169, 209-10
Briscoe, Robert 101, 169
Broun, Heywood 157
Burrows, Abe 138

Capone, Al 52, 53
Capote, Truman 63
Chaplin, Charles 117, 128, 132-36, 200-1
Charlie 4, 8, 196
Chicago American 24
Chicago Daily News 2, 71, 72, 73, 101, 108
Chicago Examiner 42, 66
Chicago Journal 23, 81
Chicago Literary Times 3, 75
Child of the Century 1, 4, 6, 7, 116, 146, 195
Churchill, Winston 10, 168
Clark, Thomas 97
Cohen, Mickey 6, 8, 35, 48, 49, 53, 57

Cohn, Harry 119-20
Como, Perry 157
Crime Without Passion 3, 149
Crosby, John 7, 10

Dalí, Salvador 4, 15, 106
Daly, John Charles 6, 7
Darrow, Clarence 2
DeMille, C.B. 140-41
Diamond, Jack "Legs" 53
Dickens, Charles 145
Dietrich, Marlene 33
DiMaggio, Joe 119
Duffy, Sherman 24, 25, 27, 31
Dulles, John Foster 91, 92, 203
Durante, Jimmy 4, 185-86

Eastman, John 23
Eisenhower, Dwight 10, 11, 86, 89, 92, 118, 197
Emery, Stephen 105
Erik Dorn 111

A Face in the Crowd 147, 149
Fairbanks, Douglas 112
A Farewell to Arms 8, 154
Fields, W.C. 184
Finnegan, Richard 24
A Flag Is Born 4, 169, 209
Fowler, Gene 17, 29, 122-25, 130, 132, 159-60
France, Anatole 144, 156, 191, 210
Frankfurther, Felix 97
The Front Page 3

Gabor, Zsa Zsa 38
Gaily, Gaily 4, 17
Gargoyles 111

217

Goldman, Natham 170
Goldwyn, Samuel 125–27, 136, 140–41, 187
Graham, Billy 210
Grauman, Sid 133
Great Magoo 124, 159–60
Guide for the Bedeviled 161

Haggerty, Christian Dane 30, 31
Harding, Warren 92
Hearst, William Randolph 28, 29
Hecht, Rose 60, 76
Hemingway, Ernest 143, 153–55, 188
Henie, Sonja 137
Herald Examiner 3, 28
Hinky Dink 83–85
His Girl Friday 125
Hiss, Alger 11, 12
Holden, William 209
Holliday, Billie 42
Humpty Dumpty 111
Huston, John 8

The Informer 149
Irgun Zvai Leumi 4, 101, 170, 171

Jessel, George 119, 138–40, 187
Johnny Got His Gun 150
Jones, John Paul 98–99
Journal American 16, 32

Kazan, Elia 151
Keaton, Buster 117
Kerouac, Jack 4, 14, 74, 202
Khrushchev, Nikita 118, 127
King, Alexander 75, 83
Kismet 125
Koretz, Leo 65–66

Langdon, Harry 117
Lasky, Jesse 140–41
Lederer, Charles 8, 122–23, 125–28, 135–36, 138–39, 161
Letter to the Terrorists of Palestine 4, 169
Letters from Bohemia 17
Little, Richard Henry 108
Lloyd, Harold 117
Lumet, Sidney 4, 209
Lyons, Leonard 33

MacArthur, Charles 3, 16, 17, 21, 30, 43, 122–23, 128, 130-31, 162, 195
McCarthy, Joseph 151
Mailer, Norman 14, 150
Makarios, Archbishop 15
Man with the Golden Arm 8, 191
Mansfield, Jayne 198
Marx, Groucho 50, 51, 116
Marx, Harpo 136–37
Marx Brothers 113
Masquerade Party 9
Mayer, Louis B. 118, 123, 141
Mencken, H.L. 2, 17, 71, 150, 174–76, 185
Merrill, Lynn 9
Miller, Arthur 152
Mitchell, Thomas 130
Molnar, Ferenc 70
Monkey Business (1931) 113
Monkey Business (1952) 113
Monroe, Marilyn 6, 119
The Moon Is Blue 141
Morgan, Henry 15, 76, 136
Morgan, J.P. 178
Muni, Paul 169
Mutiny on the Bounty 8

The Nation 10
New York Mirror 29
New York Post 11
Nietzsche, Friedrich 155, 191
Nixon, Richard 11, 86, 89, 197, 203, 204
Nothing Sacred 130, 148

O'Brian, Jack 32
On the Waterfront 147, 149
Ort, Charlie 78–80

Parson, Louella 10
Pearson, Drew 2, 4, 11, 85, 87–92, 203
Pegler, Westbrook 93–98
Perelman, S.J. 2, 4, 113–18, 122
Perfidy 17
PM 3
Preminger, Otto 4, 8, 141

Quill, Mike 104

Racket Squad 9
Ramrus, Al 5, 7, 9, 11, 12, 16
Ratoff, Gregory 137–40
Ride the Pink Horse 125

Index

Roberts, Oral 210
Roosevelt, Franklin 4, 10, 90, 163, 167–69
Roosevelt, Teddy 81–82, 84, 190
Rose, Billy 4, 159–60, 163–64, 190

Salisbury, Harrison 39
Sandberg, Carl 3, 61, 70–73, 148
Schulberg, B.P. 111–12, 148
Schulberg, Budd 2, 111, 147–53
Schultz, Dutch 52, 53
The Scoundrel 3, 149
Selznick, David 8, 16, 124, 127, 130, 148
The Sensualists 17
Shaw, George Bernard 123
Shock Theater 9
Sinatra, Frank 209
Son of Dracula 13
Specter of the Rose 3, 149
S.S. Ben Hecht 4, 169
Stalin, Joseph 10, 167–68
Stevens, Ashton 3
Stevenson, Adlai 86
Storm, Tempest 37
Studio One 9
Sullivan, Ed 33
The Sun Also Rises 154
Susann, Jacqueline 9, 13
Suspicion 9
Sutton, Willie 52
Swanson, Gloria 118

Tannen, Julius 121–22
The Thing 125
Thompson, William Hale 84
Thus Spake Zarathustra 155
Tierney, Gene 198
Time 10
Trumbo, Dalton 150
Turpin, Ben 117
TV Guide 10
Twain, Mark 154
Twentieth Century 128

Underworld 3, 111–12

van Vooren, Monique 69, 174
von Stroheim, Erich 50

Walk on the Wild Side 8
Wallace, Mike 4, 5, 6, 7, 8, 9, 12, 16, 103, 207
Washington, George 98–99
Watts, Richard 156, 158
We Will Never Die 4, 163–65, 170
Weegee 2, 11, 23, 51–58, 199
Weil, Kurt 162–63
Weitzman, Chaim 171
Welles, Orson 138–39
Wellman, William 148
Werfel, Franz 70
West, Mae 198
What Makes Sammy Run 149
Where the Sidewalk Ends 141
Whirlpool 141
Whitman, Walt 14
Winchell, Walter 33
Winkelberg 4, 5, 74
Wise, Rabbi Stephen 162, 170
Wollcott, Alexander 136–37, 160
Wright, Frank Lloyd 6
Wynn, Ed 59
Wynn, Keenan 59

Yates, Ted 4, 5, 7, 9, 11, 12, 13, 14, 16, 17, 30, 41, 49, 180
Young, Roland 130

Zacherle 9
Zanuck, Darryl F. 137–38
Zimbalist, Sam 128
Zukor, Adolph 112–13
Zweig, Stefan 70